CCNA GUIDE TO
Cisco Routing

Kurt Hudson, CCNA
Kelly Caudle, CCNA

COURSE
TECHNOLOGY

Thomson Learning™

ONE MAIN STREET, CAMBRIDGE, MA 02142

Australia • Canada • Denmark • Japan • Mexico • New Zealand • Philippines
Puerto Rico • Singapore • South Africa • Spain • United Kingdom • United States

CCNA Guide to Cisco Routing is published by Course Technology.

Associate Publisher	Kristen Duerr
Senior Acquisitions Editor	Stephen Solomon
Product Manager	David George
Production Editor	Ellina Beletsky
Developmental Editor	Jill Batistick
Technical Editor	Kelly Cannon, CCNA, CCAI
Associate Product Manager	Laura Hildebrand
Marketing Manager	Susan Ogar
Text Designer	GEX, Inc.
Composition House	GEX, Inc.
Cover Designer	Efrat Reis

Disclaimer

Course Technology reserves the right to revise this publication and make changes from time to time in its content without notice.

The Web addresses in this book are subject to change from time to time as necessary without notice.

For more information, contact Course Technology, One Main Street, Cambridge, MA 02142; or find us on the World Wide Web at *www.course.com*.

For permission to use material from this text or product, contact us by
- Web: www.thomsonrights.com
- Phone: 1-800-730-2214
- Fax: 1-800-730-2215

ISBN 0-619-00092-9

Printed in Canada

1 2 3 4 5 6 7 8 9 WC 04 03 02 01 00

BRIEF CONTENTS

TABLE OF CONTENTS

CHAPTER THREE
Access Lists   63

Introduction

If you haven't heard of Cisco Systems, you soon will. Cisco is the undisputed world-wide leader in networking equipment for the Internet. Cisco manufactures routers, switches, access servers, and network management software designed to interconnect LANs and WANs around the globe.

Currently, there is a worldwide shortage of IT professionals, especially those with the skills to configure the high tech equipment designed by Cisco Systems. Recognizing this problem, Cisco partnered with educational institutions around the world to help prepare students to become qualified to build and maintain complex networks. The Cisco Networking Academies Program was launched in October of 1997, and its graduates are the IT professionals who will design, configure, and operate the LANs and WANs of tomorrow.

At the time of this writing, there are more than 2600 Cisco Networking Academies worldwide, and that number continues to increase. The program is designed as a complete, four-semester curriculum that can be taught at the high school or college level. The curriculum includes instruction on installing, configuring, and operating simple-routed LAN, routed WAN, and switched LAN networks. After completion of the program, students are prepared and encouraged to sit for the Cisco Certified Network Associate (CCNA) exam. This certification is the first step in the path in attaining the networking industry's highest and most respected status, the Cisco Certified Internetwork Expert (CCIE) certification.

Some institutions, especially at the college level, have chosen to implement the Cisco Networking Academies' four-semester program in two semesters. This text parallels and complements semesters three and four of the Cisco Networking Academies' on-line curriculum. As such, it is appropriate for part two of a two-part course structure, or for the last two courses of the traditional four-semester program. *CCNA Guide to Cisco Networking Fundamentals*, by Hudson and Cannon, Course Technology, 1999, is available for use with the first part of the Networking Academies' curriculum.

FEATURES

To aid you in fully understanding Cisco networking concepts, there are many features in this book designed to improve its pedagogical value:

♦ **Chapter Objectives.** Each chapter in this book begins with a detailed list of the concepts to be mastered within that chapter. This list provides you with a quick reference to the contents of that chapter and serves as a useful study aid.

♦ **Illustrations and Tables.** Numerous illustrations of server screens and components aid you in the visualization of common setup steps, theories, and concepts. In addition, many tables provide details and comparisons of both practical and theoretical information.

♦ **Chapter Summaries.** Each chapter's text is followed by a summary of the concepts it has introduced. These summaries provide a helpful way to recap and revisit the ideas covered in each chapter.

♦ **Review Questions.** End-of-chapter assessment begins with a set of review questions that reinforce the ideas introduced in each chapter. These questions are written to ensure that you have mastered the concepts.

♦ **Case Projects.** Located at the end of each chapter are several case projects. In these extensive case examples, you implement the skills and knowledge gained in the chapter through real-design and implementation scenarios.

TEXT AND GRAPHIC CONVENTIONS

Wherever appropriate, additional information and exercises have been added to this book to help you better understand what is being discussed in each chapter. Icons appear throughout the text to alert you to additional materials. They are described below.

Tips are included based on the author's experience, and provide extra information on how to attack a given problem, or what to do to in certain real-world situations.

Cautions are included to help you anticipate potential mistakes or problems, so you can prevent them from happening.

Case Project icons mark the running case project. These are more involved, scenario-based assignments. In these extensive case examples, you are asked to implement independently what you have learned.

INSTRUCTOR'S MATERIALS

The following supplemental materials are available when this book is used in a classroom setting. All the supplements available with this book are provided to the instructor on a single CD-ROM.

Electronic Instructor's Manual. The Instructor's Manual that accompanies this textbook includes:

- ◆ Additional instructional material to assist in class preparation, including suggestions for lecture topics, suggested lab activities, tips on setting up a lab for the hands-on projects, and alternate lab setup ideas in situations where lab resources are limited.

- ◆ Solutions to all end-of-chapter materials, including the Project and Case assignments.

Course Test Manager 1.3. Accompanying this book is a powerful assessment tool known as the Course Test Manager. Designed by Course Technology, this cutting-edge Windows-based testing software helps instructors design and administer tests and pre-tests. In addition to enabling the instructor to generate tests that can be printed and administered, this full-featured program also has an online testing component that allows students to take tests at the computer, and have their exams automatically graded.

PowerPoint presentations. This book comes with Microsoft PowerPoint slides for each chapter. These are included as a teaching aid for classroom presentation, to make available to students on the network for chapter review, or to be printed for classroom distribution. Instructors, please feel at liberty to add your own slides for additional topics you introduce to the class.

LAB MANUAL

The Lab Manual that was written to accompany this book provides hands-on instruction on topics that are part of the Cisco Networking Academies curriculum, and skills that every networking professional should possess. To order a copy, consult your sales representative, or point your browser to *www.course.com*.

ACKNOWLEDGMENTS

I would like to thank Dave George and Stephen Solomon for their continued support throughout this project. I would also like to thank Kelly Cannon, Jill Batistick, and Kelly Caudle for their help. A special thanks goes to Rob, Mitch, and Sarah Pinion for allowing me to mess with, and take pictures of, The Logical Choice's Frame Relay and T1 connections. Also, I would like to thank the Smit family (Sharon, Theo, and Kristeen), and the Marcinkiewicz family (Carmen, Lori, Daniel, and Frank) for their support during this project. -**Kurt Hudson**

First and foremost, I must thank the Lord for giving me the opportunity to write this book. I also need to thank Stephen Solomon, acquisitions editor at Course Technology, for taking a chance on a first-time author. Along the same lines, I must thank Jill Batistick for putting up with me. In light of my ranting and raving early in the review process, she could easily have given up on me. Instead, she patiently persisted and in the end truly helped me strengthen my writing. Thanks Jill. Also, without Dave George at Course Technology, this project would never have succeeded. Thank you Dave for all the help you gave me as a first-time author (in other words, thanks for extending some of those deadlines!). Kurt Hudson, my co-author, helped me by laying the groundwork with the first book and with overall design considerations for this book. Thank you Kurt.

I would be remiss if I failed to mention a very special group that participated in the writing of this book. I must thank all of my coworkers in the Information Systems Department at Stanly Community College for putting up with me during this very stressful time. Many of them covered classes for me when a deadline approached, or simply offered words of encouragement. Thanks gang; you are the best. I also want to thank Max Boylen for encouraging me to accept the challenge of writing a book. Without your insights Max, I might have let this wonderful opportunity pass me by.

Finally, I must thank my beautiful and loving wife Susan for putting up with me over the many months of this project. Susan, of all the gifts I have been given in my life, you are the greatest. –**Kelly Caudle**

NETWORK ROUTING AND REVIEW

After reading this chapter and completing the exercises you will be able to:

- ♦ Describe the functions of the seven layers of the OSI model
- ♦ Identify network segmentation using repeaters, bridges, and routers
- ♦ Define IP address classes and create subnet masks
- ♦ Understand basic router components and configurations on a Cisco router
- ♦ Troubleshoot router connectivity problems using ping, trace, and debug commands

In the introduction you learned that this book is a continuation and expansion of the concepts contained in Course Technology's *CCNA Guide to Networking Fundamentals*. Before continuing your CCNA studies in this text, you must have a solid understanding of several key networking and routing concepts. Therefore, in this chapter, you will review the Open Systems Interconnection model, network segmentation, Internet Protocol addressing, basic router components and configuration, and router connectivity troubleshooting.

THE OSI MODEL

The first concept you must review before continuing in the CCNA Guide to Cisco Routing is the **Open Systems Interconnection (OSI) model**. This model of network communication, created in 1984 by the International Organization for Standardization, provides a seven-layer conceptual model for how two devices communicate on a network. The OSI model solves many problems associated with conceptualizing how two devices "talk" to one another and provides the following benefits:

- Compatibility and standardization among vendors
- Interoperability among vendors
- A simplified networking model that eases understanding of the communication process
- A modular model of networking components that allows one layer to change without affecting other layers

The seven layers of the OSI model, from layer seven to layer one, are the Application layer, Presentation layer, Session layer, Transport layer, Network layer, Data Link layer and Physical layer.

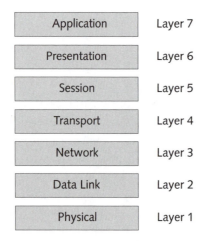

Application	Layer 7
Presentation	Layer 6
Session	Layer 5
Transport	Layer 4
Network	Layer 3
Data Link	Layer 2
Physical	Layer 1

Figure 1-1   Seven layers of the OSI model

> **TIP** If you need an easy way to remember the seven layers, from layer seven to layer one, use the following saying: All People Seem To Need Data Processing or Application, Presentation, Session, Transport, Network Data Link, Physical. To remember layer one to layer seven use: Please Do Not Throw Sausage Pizza Away or Physical, Data Link, Network, Transport, Session, Presentation, Application.

Peer-to-Peer OSI Communication

The seven layers of the OSI reference model communicate with one another via peer-to-peer communication. In other words, each layer will only talk to its peer on the opposite side of the communications process. Figure 1-2 shows peer-to-peer communication, where the layers on the source node only talk with the opposite and equivalent layers on the destination node.

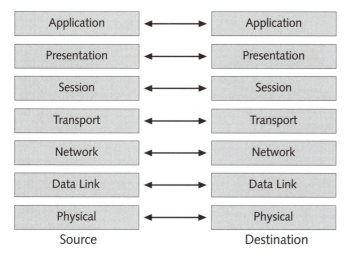

Figure 1-2   Peer-to-peer communication

The OSI layers are unaware of the processing occurring at the layers above or below them. As a result, each layer is unaware of the activities of all other layers of the model, and each layer will only communicate with its opposite equivalent. Figure 1-2 shows how this occurs between a source node and a destination node. Peer-to-peer communication allows error checking to occur on two separate layers simultaneously. Even if the Transport layer is already providing reliable transmission of data, the Data Link layer is unaware of what goes on above it and will provide Data Link error control in the form of the cyclical redundancy check (**CRC**).

Each layer does provide services to the layer above it and receives services from the layer below it, but, these services are not acknowledged by any layer in any way. Instead, each layer concentrates just on its function in the overall communications process. As a result, each layer of the OSI model takes information from the layer above, encapsulates that information into specific formats, and passes that information to the layer below.

The Seven Layers of the OSI Model

In order to understand the OSI model, you must have a clear understanding of what each layer does. You must also realize that each layer can seemingly perform the same function (i.e., error checking). Starting with layer 1, the seven layers and functions are:

- **Physical layer** (layer 1): This is the bit-pusher of the OSI model. The Physical layer is responsible for actually putting bits onto the physical media (coax, fiber, UTP cable) or a wireless medium (infrared, microwave). The Physical layer also deals with encoding the bits (0s and 1s) into voltage or light patterns. The most common encoding scheme is Manchester Encoding. Cables, connectors, **repeaters**, and hubs are common networking devices that function at the Physical layer.

- **Data Link layer** (layer 2): This layer is concerned with physical addressing (MAC addresses), media access, network topology, packaging data into frames, and flow control. The Cyclical redundancy check is added as a trailer at this layer. The Data Link layer is further divided into the Logical Link Control and Media Access Control sublayers. Bridges, switches, and network interface cards are common networking devices that function at the Data Link layer.

- **Network layer** (layer 3): This layer is responsible for routing packets along the best path between multiple networks. Routing decisions are based upon logical addresses such as TCP/IP addresses and IPX/SPX addresses assigned by the network administrator. Routers function at the Network layer. IP and IPX are examples of protocols that function at this layer.

- **Transport layer** (layer 4): This layer ensures that packets arrive intact, in sequence without duplication. The Transport layer can provide connection-oriented services via TCP or other connection-oriented protocols. Connectionless services may also be provided via UDP or other connectionless protocols. TCP, UDP, and SPX are examples of protocols that function at this layer.

- **Session layer** (layer 5): This layer creates, maintains, and terminates sessions between applications. Sessions are dialogs between two applications. A good example is a SQL request to retrieve information from a database. SQL and RPC are examples of protocols that function at this layer.

- **Presentation layer** (layer 6): This layer translates data into an intermediary form that can be passed down the OSI stack. If encryption and compression are used, they occur at the Presentation layer. JPEG, GIF, BMP, WAV, MPEG, MIDI, EBCDIC, and ASCII are examples of standards at this layer.

- **Application layer** (layer 7): This layer interacts directly with network applications and network-aware applications, applications that can make use of network resources such as file sharing, networking printing, etc. FTP, telnet, and SMTP are examples of protocols that function at this layer.

> **TIP** Although the OSI model specifies seven layers to the communication process, most real-world implementations of protocol stacks do not use seven distinct layers. For example, TCP/IP uses a four-layer approach, while IPX/SPX loosely maps to the OSI model. Still, as mentioned earlier, the model is useful to help conceptualize the network communication process.

NETWORK SEGMENTATION

Network **segmentation** is the second essential concept you must understand and review in order to complete the CCNA and understand the contents of this book. In particular, you must understand network segmentation using **bridges** and **routers**. You must also understand

1

the function that a repeater performs in a network. As a result, they are included in this section even though they do not perform network segmentation.

Ethernet networks based on the IEEE 802.3 standards define the use of a **Carrier Sense Multiple Access with Collision Detection** (**CSMA/CD**) access method. CSMA/CD specifies that each node (before placing packets onto the networking media) must first listen to the network media to determine if the media is currently free of packets. Then, if no other node currently has packets on the media, the node can place packets on the media. Obviously, it is possible for two nodes to listen, find the wire empty, and send packets at the same exact time. The end result is a collision in which both packets are destroyed. The CSMA/CD access method specifies that a node, that determines that a collision has taken place must perform the **backoff algorithm**, waiting a random amount of time before making an attempt to retransmit data.

Problems occur when network administrators place too many nodes on the same network segment. As the number of nodes increases, the amount of traffic on a segment increases, as does the chance that two nodes will transmit data at exactly the same time. This causes the number of collisions to increase. The result is a large amount of network bandwidth being used to retransmit packets that have been destroyed by collisions. Segmentation is the answer to this problem.

Segmentation is the breaking down of a single heavily populated network segment into smaller segments populated by fewer nodes. Figure 1–3 shows an example of network segmentation.

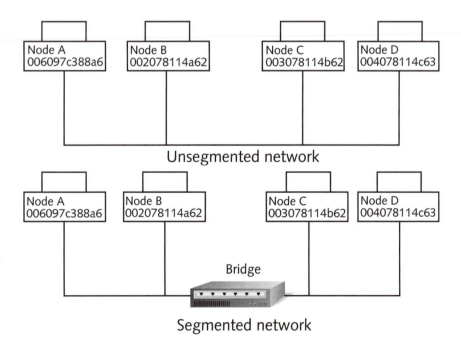

Figure 1-3 Network segmentation

In Figure 1-3, the first graphic depicts a network consisting of four nodes using a single segment. In this unsegmented network, all computers would be affected by the traffic of other nodes. The second segmented network shows the same network segmented to have only two computers per segment. This segmentation reduces the number of computers that must contend for use of the network. As a result, network collisions and retransmissions are reduced.

Repeaters

Repeaters are networking devices that do not actually segment networks, but are included in this discussion because of the important role they do play. Repeaters function at the physical layer of the OSI model and are responsible for amplifying signals that lose strength due to attenuation or electromagnetic interference while travelling along the networking media. They do not **filter** traffic according to physical or logical addresses. Also, they in no way decrease the number of collisions that occur on a network segment.

You can use repeaters to increase the length of a cable run beyond what would normally be the cable length limit that is set as a result of **attenuation** problems. For example, unshielded twisted-pair cable has a total maximum specified cable length of 100 meters. If you need to run cable further than 100 meters between nodes or networking devices, you can add a repeater to your network to boost the signal strength and allow another 100 meters before attenuation becomes a problem.

Bridges

Bridges are networking devices that function at the Data Link layer of the OSI model and are used to segment networks, using routing tables of media access control addresses (physical addresses). As nodes communicate, bridges can dynamically learn the **MAC address** of every node attached to their ports. They build routing tables of these MAC addresses so packets can be filtered based on network segments. For example, in Figure 1-4, the bridge between segments 1 and 2 has a routing table of MAC addresses listing which nodes reside on each segment.

If node A sends a message to node B, the bridge will not pass the packet over to segment 2 because its routing table states that node A and B are on segment 1. Likewise, any packets passed between MAC addresses on segment 2 will not be passed to segment 1. As a result of this MAC address filtering, collisions are reduced. Also, the size of **collision domains** is reduced.

Although bridges do perform some filtering, they do not stop broadcasts. If a node sends out a packet to the destination MAC address FFFFFFFFFFFF, the **broadcast** MAC address, a bridge forwards the packet to all connected segments. Bridges, therefore, cannot stop broadcasts or limit broadcast storms.

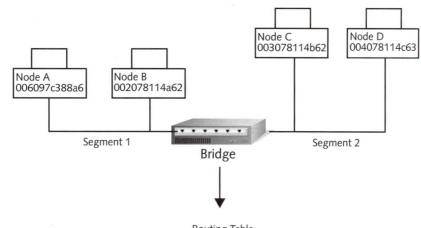

Segment 1		Segment 2
MAC ID 006097c388a6		MAC ID 003078114b62
MAC ID 002078114a62		MAC ID 004078114c63

Routing Table

Figure 1-4 Routing Table

Switches, another common internetworking device, are really just multiport bridges.

Routers

Another internetworking device you can use to segment networks is a router. Routers are networking devices that function at the Network layer of the OSI model. They route packets from one network or subnet to another by the best available path. Routers build routing tables of logical network addresses.

Logical network addresses could be TCP/IP addresses or IPX/SPX addresses.

Routers only forward packets based upon source and destination network addresses. They will not pass broadcasts. Routers are used to create separate broadcast domains in order to limit broadcasts.

IP ADDRESSING AND SUBNET MASKS

IP addressing and subnet masking are the third, and possibly most important, concept you must understand to explore the contents of this book. Without a solid understanding of these two concepts, the ideas concerning access lists in Chapter 3 and routing in Chapter 4 will be nearly impossible to grasp.

IP addresses are 32-bit logical Network layer addresses that represent a network ID, an optional subnet ID, and a host ID; an example is the IP address 192.168.2.3. Although you normally interact with IP addresses as dotted decimals such as 192.168.2.3, you must remember that each address is actually a binary number consisting of four octets of 8 bits each. The number 192.168.2.3 can be written as 11000000.10101000.00000010.00000011. In fact, networking devices use the binary number in calculating information about IP addresses.

IP addresses are grouped into five classes based on starting decimal values in the first octet and the bit boundaries, also present in the first octet. Table 1-1 shows the properties of each class of address.

Table 1-1   Classes of IP addresses

Class	Decimal Value of First Octet	Binary Value(s) of Leading Bits in First Octet	Network/Node Octet Arrangement
Class A	1-127	0	network.node.node.node
Class B	128-191	10	network.network.node.node
Class C	192-223	110	Network.network.network.node
Class D	224-239	1110	Reserved for multicast
Class E	240-254	1111	Reserved for experimentation

Network administrators interact mostly with Class A, B, and C addresses. Once a network is assigned to an organization, the local administrator is responsible for ensuring that an IP scheme is put in place that will give each node on the network a unique IP address, a subnet mask, and, if necessary, a default gateway.

 A **default gateway** is not required on a node if the network does not have any paths to external networks. Therefore, a small LAN without a router will not need a default gateway set at each individual client.

Subnet Masks

As mentioned above, each IP address consists of a network address and a node address. In order to distinguish between each portion, all devices on an IP network require a **subnet mask**. Subnet masks (32-bit addresses that appear normally in dotted decimal format) mask, or hide, the portion of the address that is the network or subnetwork (a term covered in the next section) from the node address.

Networking devices use a subnetwork mask to determine what portion of the address is the network ID or node ID, and if a node is local or remote. For class A, B, and C addresses, default subnet masks that place all ones in the network portion of the IP address are already defined. For example the default subnet mask for a Class A address is 255.0.0.0. All ones are placed in the octet representing the network ID. Table 1–2 shows the default subnet masks for the major IP classes.

Table 1-2   Default subnet masks

Address Class	Default Subnet Mask
A	255.0.0.0
B	255.255.0.0
C	255.255.255.0

Subnetting

Because of the network and node formats (refer back to Table 1-1) of IP addresses, Class A, B, and C addresses have limits on the number of networks or hosts they can support. Table 1-3 shows the number of hosts and networks that each class can support.

Table 1-3   Networks and host support

Address Class	Usable Networks in Entire Address Range	Usable Hosts per Network
A	126	16,776,214
B	16,384	65,534
C	2,097,152	254

On occasion, you may encounter a LAN that requires more networks than the default number of networks provided by each class of address. By default, as shown in Table 1-3, Class A addresses allow for 126 networks, Class B addresses allow for 16,384 networks, and Class C addresses allow for 2,097,152 networks. The network configuration in Figure 1-5 needs more than a single network.

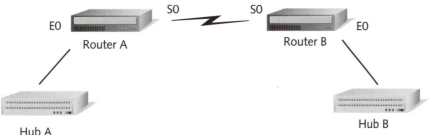

Figure 1-5   Sample network

This network configuration requires three networks, one for the shared serial connection between Router A and Router B and one each for the Ethernet ports connected via E0. If you have a Class C address of 192.168.2.0 assigned to your organization, you have one network of 254 hosts that you can use. However, you do not have enough networks to fit the **physical topology** of your network. In order to obtain the three networks you need, you must create subnetworks of the network 192.168.2.0. You accomplish subnetting by borrowing from the available host bits to increase the number of network bits.

In a normal Class C address, as shown in Table 1-4, the first three octets represent the network ID, and the last octet represents the node ID. Twenty-four bits are reserved for the network ID, and eight bits are reserved for the node ID. To create subnets, you need to borrow host bits. The resulting subnetting mask is added to the default subnet mask to create a mask that specifies the network and subnet ID and then the node ID.

In a network that uses the default subnet mask on the network 192.168.2.0, you have one network of 254 usable node IP addresses. Since you need three for the network in Figure 1-5, the default subnet mask will not work, because you cannot apply this Class C license to the network in Figure 1-5. You must subnet the network.

Table 1-4   Class C address with no subnetting

Network	192.168.2.0
Subnet Mask	255.255.255.0
Number of Networks	1
Number of Nodes	254

The first step in subnetting is determining how many subnets you need. In Figure 1-5, three networks at a minimum are needed. Leaving room for some growth in subnetworks is recommended, but for every extra subnet you create you lose bits dedicated to your host. More subnets equal fewer hosts per subnet. The formula for determining the number of subnets created is 2 raised to the power of the number of bits you borrow from the host portion of the address minus two:

Number of Subnets = 2^number of borrowed bits - 2

To obtain three subnets, you must borrow three bits: $2^3 = 8$. Then, $8 - 2 = 6$ usable subnets. You will have three subnets remaining for future use. Because you borrow three bits, the subnet mask will change from 255.255.255.0 to 255.255.255.224. When you look at the network number and subnet mask numbers in binary, you can see how the borrowed bits determine the new subnet mask. Figure 1-6 illustrates these concepts.

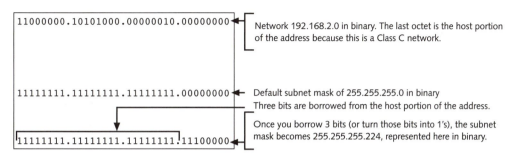

Figure 1-6   Borrowed bits determining subnet mask for Class C address

You must then find the range of addresses within each subnet. You can determine the subnet increment number by looking at the lowest bit turned on in the octet from which you borrowed bits for subnetting. In the above example, the last bit borrowed (or turned on) is the bit representing the 32 value in the octet. Therefore, 32 is your subnet increment. The subnet number will increase by this increment. The range of subnets is shown in Table 1-5.

Table 1-5   Subnet ranges for network 192.168.2.0 with a subnet mask
of 255.255.255.224

Subnet ID	Subnetwork #	Host Range of Addresses	Subnetwork Broadcast Addresses
0	192.168.2.0	192.168.2.1 to 192.168.2.30	192.168.2.31
1	192.168.2.32	192.168.2.33 to 192.168.2.62	192.168.2.63
2	192.168.2.64	192.168.2.65 to 192.168.2.94	192.168.2.95
3	192.168.2.96	192.168.2.97 to 192.168.2.126	192.168.2.127
4	192.168.2.128	192.168.2.129 to 192.168.2.158	192.168.2.159
5	192.168.2.160	192.168.2.161 to 192.168.2.190	192.168.2.191
6	192.168.2.192	192.168.2.193 to 192.168.2.222	192.168.2.223
7	192.168.2.224	192.168.2.225 to 192.168.2.254	192.168.2.255

> **TIP**
> At this point, you may ask why the chart in Table 1-5 lists eight subnets and the text states that you only have six available. The first and last subnetworks are designated as the network number and network broadcast address, respectively and are, for the purpose of the CCNA exam, unusable. In implementing subnetting in the real world, some organizations might make use of the subnet zero.

The result of subnetting the Class C address above is six usable subnets of 30 hosts each (you calculate the number of hosts by raising 2 to the power of the number of host bits left after borrowing for subnetting, and then subtracting two from that value).

If you look at the same sample network, but start with a Class B network you get similar results. For the Class B network, Figure 1-7 shows how the addresses look in decimal and binary.

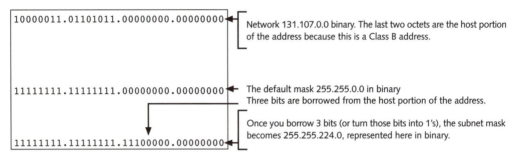

Figure 1-7   Borrowed bits determining subnet mask for Class B address

The ranges for the Class B addresses are calculated in exactly the same way as the Class C ones. You must remember, however, that in a class B address the fourth octet is not affected by borrowing from the third octet. The result is a range of usable addresses between 1 and 254 for the last octet.

Table 1-6   Subnet ranges for network 131.107.0.0 with a subnet mask of 255.255.224.0

Subnet ID	Range of Address
Subnet 0	131.107.0-31.1-254
Subnet 1	131.107.32-63.1-254
Subnet 2	131.107.64-95.1-254
Subnet 3	131.107.96-127.1-254
Subnet 4	131.107.128-159.1-254
Subnet 5	131.107.160-191.1-254
Subnet 6	131.107.192-223.1-254
Subnet 7	131.107.224-255.1-254

The result of subnetting the Class B network 131.107.0.0 with a 19-bit subnet mask (Cisco will reference masks by the total number of bits, including default bits, in the subnet mask) is six usable subnets with 8190 nodes. You get these numbers by using the formulas for subnet numbers and host numbers. In this example, the number of subnets equals $2^3 = 8. 8 - 2 = 6$ usable subnets. The number of hosts equals 2 raised to the power of the number of host bits left after borrowing. In this example, it would be $2^{13} = 8192. 8192 - 2 = 8190$ hosts per subnet.

ROUTER COMPONENTS AND CONFIGURATION

As you learned earlier, routers are internetworking devices that function at layer 3, or the Network layer, of the OSI model. Routers are responsible for routing packets across the best path among multiple paths. They do not pass broadcasts and are used in many organizations to limit broadcast domains. Routers are specialized hardware configured with specialized software to perform the task of routing packets.

Router Components

Cisco routers are powered by the Cisco **Internetwork Operating System (IOS)**. The IOS allows Cisco routers to be configured to perform certain tasks. Since each IOS version may implement a feature in a slightly different way (or may not have a feature set at all), you must be aware of which IOS is in use on your routers. You can establish this with the show version command. When you type the show version command, you will receive output similar to that displayed in Figure 1-8.

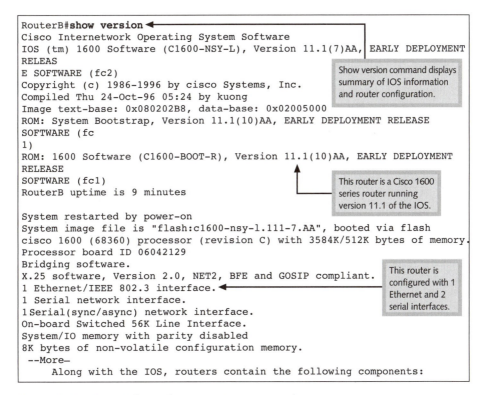

```
RouterB#show version
Cisco Internetwork Operating System Software
IOS (tm) 1600 Software (C1600-NSY-L), Version 11.1(7)AA, EARLY DEPLOYMENT
RELEAS
E SOFTWARE (fc2)
Copyright (c) 1986-1996 by cisco Systems, Inc.
Compiled Thu 24-Oct-96 05:24 by kuong
Image text-base: 0x080202B8, data-base: 0x02005000
ROM: System Bootstrap, Version 11.1(10)AA, EARLY DEPLOYMENT RELEASE
SOFTWARE (fc
1)
ROM: 1600 Software (C1600-BOOT-R), Version 11.1(10)AA, EARLY DEPLOYMENT
RELEASE
SOFTWARE (fc1)
RouterB uptime is 9 minutes

System restarted by power-on
System image file is "flash:c1600-nsy-1.111-7.AA", booted via flash
cisco 1600 (68360) processor (revision C) with 3584K/512K bytes of memory.
Processor board ID 06042129
Bridging software.
X.25 software, Version 2.0, NET2, BFE and GOSIP compliant.
1 Ethernet/IEEE 802.3 interface.
1 Serial network interface.
1 Serial(sync/async) network interface.
On-board Switched 56K Line Interface.
System/IO memory with parity disabled
8K bytes of non-volatile configuration memory.
 --More—
     Along with the IOS, routers contain the following components:
```

Show version command displays summary of IOS information and router configuration.

This router is a Cisco 1600 series router running version 11.1 of the IOS.

This router is configured with 1 Ethernet and 2 serial interfaces.

Figure 1-8 Output from show version command

Along with the IOS software, routers normally consist of the following five items:

- **Random access memory (RAM):** RAM that holds the router's running configuration, routing tables, and buffers. Contents of RAM are lost when the router is powered down.

- **Nonvolatile random access memory:** Special RAM used to hold the router's startup configuration file. NVRAM does not lose its contents if a router is turned off.

- **Flash memory:** Rewritable memory used to hold the IOS image (the version of the software in use) for the router. Contents of flash memory are not lost if the router is powered down.

- **Read-only memory (ROM):** Also known as the bootstrap; usually it contains a minimal version of the IOS that can be used to boot the router if the flash memory is erased or becomes corrupt. On some newer routers, the ROM contains an entire version of the IOS.

- **Interfaces:** These are the hardware connectivity points to the router such as Serial0 or the console port.

The IOS contains commands to view each of the router's components. To view the contents of RAM, you can issue one of several commands (because several components reside in RAM). One of the most common commands is the show running-config command. With this command, you can view the current configuration that is running in RAM. Figure 1-9 shows the results of typing the show running-config command. Two other common commands that can show the contents of RAM are show memory and show buffers. Because they produce long, detailed output, their output has not been included in this text.

```
RouterB#show running-config
Building configuration...

Current configuration:
!
version 11.1
service udp-small-servers
service tcp-small-servers
!
hostname RouterB
!
enable secret 5 $1$RHhg$ngXce3OBeC7GprpPjtqsP1
!
ipx routing 0060.474f.6506
!
interface Ethernet0
 ip address 172.22.2.1 255.255.255.0
 ipx access-group 800 out
 ipx network 300
!
interface Serial0
 no ip address
!
interface Serial1
 ip address 172.22.3.2 255.255.255.0
!
router rip
 network 172.22.0.0
!
no ip classless
access-list 800 deny 300 500
access-list 800 permit FFFFFFFF FFFFFFFF
!
!
!
!
line con 0
line vty 0 4
 password password
 login
!
end

RouterB#
```

Show running-config command shows the configuration currently running in RAM on a router.

This router is configured to route both IPX and IP traffic. IPX is discussed in detail in Chapter 2.

This router is using the RIP routing protocol. RIP is discussed further in Chapter 4.

Figure 1-9   Output from show running-config command

Another very useful command is the show startup-configuration command. With this command you can display the current startup configuration file on the router, which is stored in NVRAM. It is also possible to view the status and types of interfaces on the router with the show interfaces command. When you type the show interfaces command, you should receive output similar to that found in Figure 1-10.

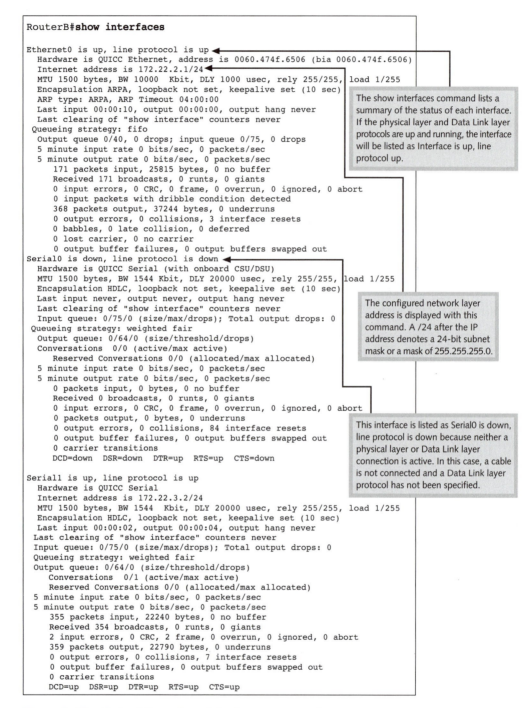

```
RouterB#show interfaces

Ethernet0 is up, line protocol is up
  Hardware is QUICC Ethernet, address is 0060.474f.6506 (bia 0060.474f.6506)
  Internet address is 172.22.2.1/24
  MTU 1500 bytes, BW 10000 Kbit, DLY 1000 usec, rely 255/255, load 1/255
  Encapsulation ARPA, loopback not set, keepalive set (10 sec)
  ARP type: ARPA, ARP Timeout 04:00:00
  Last input 00:00:10, output 00:00:00, output hang never
  Last clearing of "show interface" counters never
  Queueing strategy: fifo
  Output queue 0/40, 0 drops; input queue 0/75, 0 drops
  5 minute input rate 0 bits/sec, 0 packets/sec
  5 minute output rate 0 bits/sec, 0 packets/sec
    171 packets input, 25815 bytes, 0 no buffer
    Received 171 broadcasts, 0 runts, 0 giants
    0 input errors, 0 CRC, 0 frame, 0 overrun, 0 ignored, 0 abort
    0 input packets with dribble condition detected
    368 packets output, 37244 bytes, 0 underruns
    0 output errors, 0 collisions, 3 interface resets
    0 babbles, 0 late collision, 0 deferred
    0 lost carrier, 0 no carrier
    0 output buffer failures, 0 output buffers swapped out
Serial0 is down, line protocol is down
  Hardware is QUICC Serial (with onboard CSU/DSU)
  MTU 1500 bytes, BW 1544 Kbit, DLY 20000 usec, rely 255/255, load 1/255
  Encapsulation HDLC, loopback not set, keepalive set (10 sec)
  Last input never, output never, output hang never
  Last clearing of "show interface" counters never
  Input queue: 0/75/0 (size/max/drops); Total output drops: 0
  Queueing strategy: weighted fair
  Output queue: 0/64/0 (size/threshold/drops)
  Conversations  0/0 (active/max active)
    Reserved Conversations 0/0 (allocated/max allocated)
  5 minute input rate 0 bits/sec, 0 packets/sec
  5 minute output rate 0 bits/sec, 0 packets/sec
    0 packets input, 0 bytes, 0 no buffer
    Received 0 broadcasts, 0 runts, 0 giants
    0 input errors, 0 CRC, 0 frame, 0 overrun, 0 ignored, 0 abort
    0 packets output, 0 bytes, 0 underruns
    0 output errors, 0 collisions, 84 interface resets
    0 output buffer failures, 0 output buffers swapped out
    0 carrier transitions
    DCD=down  DSR=down  DTR=up  RTS=up  CTS=down

Serial1 is up, line protocol is up
  Hardware is QUICC Serial
  Internet address is 172.22.3.2/24
  MTU 1500 bytes, BW 1544 Kbit, DLY 20000 usec, rely 255/255, load 1/255
  Encapsulation HDLC, loopback not set, keepalive set (10 sec)
  Last input 00:00:02, output 00:00:04, output hang never
  Last clearing of "show interface" counters never
  Input queue: 0/75/0 (size/max/drops); Total output drops: 0
  Queueing strategy: weighted fair
  Output queue: 0/64/0 (size/threshold/drops)
    Conversations  0/1 (active/max active)
    Reserved Conversations 0/0 (allocated/max allocated)
  5 minute input rate 0 bits/sec, 0 packets/sec
  5 minute output rate 0 bits/sec, 0 packets/sec
    355 packets input, 22240 bytes, 0 no buffer
    Received 354 broadcasts, 0 runts, 0 giants
    2 input errors, 0 CRC, 2 frame, 0 overrun, 0 ignored, 0 abort
    359 packets output, 22790 bytes, 0 underruns
    0 output errors, 0 collisions, 7 interface resets
    0 output buffer failures, 0 output buffers swapped out
    0 carrier transitions
    DCD=up  DSR=up  DTR=up  RTS=up  CTS=up
```

The show interfaces command lists a summary of the status of each interface. If the physical layer and Data Link layer protocols are up and running, the interface will be listed as Interface is up, line protocol up.

The configured network layer address is displayed with this command. A /24 after the IP address denotes a 24-bit subnet mask or a mask of 255.255.255.0.

This interface is listed as Serial0 is down, line protocol is down because neither a physical layer or Data Link layer connection is active. In this case, a cable is not connected and a Data Link layer protocol has not been specified.

Figure 1-10   Output from show interfaces command

Eventually, instead of only looking at the router's configuration, you will want to actually configure parameters on a router. The next section examines router configuration.

Router Configuration

Before you start configuration of a Cisco router, you must understand the two EXEC modes available on a router: **user EXEC mode** and **privileged EXEC mode**. User mode allows you to perform basic troubleshooting tests, telnet to remote hosts, and list router system information. You know that the router is in this mode if the prompt is the router name followed by the greater than sign. "RouterB>" is an example of the user mode prompt. Privileged mode, sometimes called "enable mode," allows for full router configuration and advanced troubleshooting. "RouterB#" is an example of the privileged mode prompt.

If you log into a router via a console, telnet or auxiliary port connection, you enter user mode. Privileged mode requires that you issue the enable command. Figure 1-11 is an example of logging into the router via the console port and then changing into privileged mode by typing the enable command.

```
RouterB con0 is now available
Press RETURN to get started.
RouterB>enable ◄──────────────  Typing enable at the user mode prompt will place you into privileged mode.
Password:
RouterB#
```

Figure 1-11   Entering privileged mode with the enable command

In the above example, a password was required to enter privileged mode. Since you can create, erase, or modify all settings on the router in privileged mode, it is highly recommended that you set an enable mode password. Greater security can be accomplished with the use of several other passwords used in conjunction with the enable password. Cisco's IOS provides a myriad of passwords for securing routers. The most commonly used are console passwords, virtual terminal line passwords, and the enable or enable secret passwords.

Although most routers are locked in a telecommunications closet for security, you should still secure the console port with a console password. You accomplish console password configuration by placing the router in interface configuration mode and applying the commands shown in Figure 1-12.

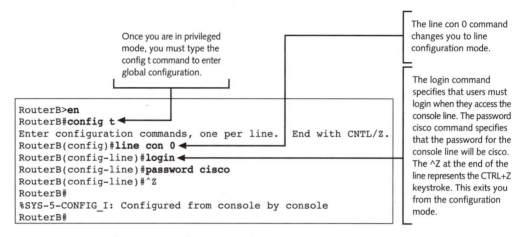

Figure 1-12   Applying a console password

Issuing the commands in Figure 1-10 requires that all users trying to access the router via the console port know the console password. You should avoid easily guessed passwords. On production routers, use a combination of letters and numbers, while avoiding common, easy-to-guess items such as the company name, your name, or your spouse's name. Users see the output in Figure 1-13 when they try to access the router via the console port.

```
RouterB con0 is now available

Press RETURN to get started.
User Access Verification
Password:
```

You will see this prompt once the console session has been properly established. If the console password has been correctly set up, you will be prompted for the console password.

Figure 1-13   Console password example

You can also configure passwords on the virtual terminal lines (five virtual terminal lines exist on every router) in much the same way as on the console port. You must go into the interface configuration mode on the router for the vty lines and add the login and password commands. Figure 1-14 shows the process of applying a vty password.

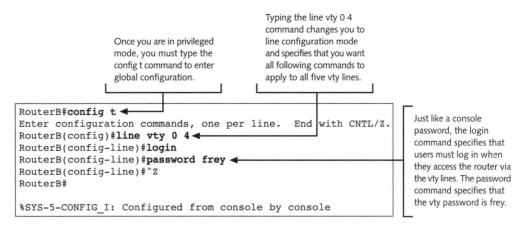

Once you are in privileged mode, you must type the config t command to enter global configuration.

Typing the line vty 0 4 command changes you to line configuration mode and specifies that you want all following commands to apply to all five vty lines.

```
RouterB#config t
Enter configuration commands, one per line.   End with CNTL/Z.
RouterB(config)#line vty 0 4
RouterB(config-line)#login
RouterB(config-line)#password frey
RouterB(config-line)#^Z
RouterB#

%SYS-5-CONFIG_I: Configured from console by console
```

Just like a console password, the login command specifies that users must log in when they access the router via the vty lines. The password command specifies that the vty password is frey.

Figure 1-14   Applying a vty password

Passwords can be placed on auxiliary ports in the same way they are placed on console or vty ports. Using all three of these passwords will at least slow down someone trying to enter your routers. If they happen to get through these passwords, the single most important password, the enable mode password, can stop them from actually modifying the router's configuration.

The enable mode password is confusing because there are actually two enable passwords. The enable password *[password]* command, issued in global configuration mode creates an enable mode password that is stored in the startup-configuration file in plaintext. This produces a significant security risk. As a result, you should always configure the enable secret password with the enable secret *[password]* command. The enable secret password overrides the enable password and is stored in encrypted form in the configuration files. Figure 1-15 shows the enable password and enable secret password as they appear in the router configuration files.

Proper configuration of passwords can ensure that your router is safe from attack from inside and outside your organization. You should always configure console, vty, and enable secret passwords on your router.

```
RouterB#show run
Building configuration...
Current configuration:
!
version 11.1
service udp-small-servers
service tcp-small-servers
!
hostname RouterB
!
enable secret 5 $1$RHhg$ngXce3OBeC7GprpPjtqsP1

enable password stuff

!
ipx routing 0060.474f.6506
!
interface Ethernet0
 ip address 172.22.2.1 255.255.255.0
 ipx access-group 800 out
 ipx network 300
!
interface Serial0
 no ip address
!
interface Serial1
 ip address 172.22.3.2 255.255.255.0
!
router rip
 network 172.22.0.0
!
no ip classless
access-list 800 deny 300 500
access-list 800 permit FFFFFFFF FFFFFFFF
!
!
!
!
line con 0
 password cisco
 login
line vty 0 4
 password password
 login
!
end

RouterB#
```

The enable secret password is stored in an encrypted form for increased security.

The enable password is stored as plaintext and can pose a security risk.

Figure 1-15   The enable password and enable secret password

Global Configuration Mode and Interface Configuration Mode

Before you actually configure a Cisco router, you must understand the two main configuration modes: global configuration mode and interface configuration mode. You use global configuration mode to configure router settings that affect overall router operation. For example, turning on IPX routing is accomplished via global configuration mode. To enter global configuration mode, you type the configure command from privileged EXEC mode. Figure 1-16 shows the output from the configure command.

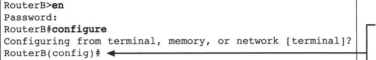

```
RouterB>en
Password:
RouterB#configure
Configuring from terminal, memory, or network [terminal]?
RouterB(config)# ◄
```

This prompt signifies that you are in global configuration mode.

Figure 1-16   Output from the configure command

By default (the item in brackets is the default), configuration occurs from the terminal. To avoid having to choose the options, many administrators use the configure t or config t commands. Both of these commands place the router in global configuration mode, using the terminal screen as the source of commands. Once you place the router in global configuration mode, the router prompt is displayed as RouterB(config)#.

At this point, you can type a ? to view all available global configuration commands. Figure 1-17 shows the output from typing a ? at the global configuration prompt.

```
RouterB(config)#?
Configure commands:
aaa                       Authentication, Authorization and Accounting.
access-list               Add an access list entry
alias                     Create command alias
arp                       Set a static ARP entry
async-bootp               Modify system bootp parameters
banner                    Define a login banner
boot                      Modify system boot parameters
bridge                    Bridging Group.
buffers                   Adjust system buffer pool parameters
busy-message              Display message when connection to host fails
cdp                       Global CDP configuration subcommands
chat-script               Define a modem chat script
clock                     Configure time-of-day clock
config-register           Define the configuration register
default-value             Default character-bits values
dialer-list               Create a dialer list entry
dnsix-dmdp                Provide DMDP service for DNSIX
dnsix-nat                 Provide DNSIX service for audit trails
downward-compatible-config Generate a configuration compatible with older
                          software
enable                    Modify enable password parameters
end                       Exit from configure mode
exit                      Exit from configure mode
frame-relay               global frame relay configuration commands
help                      Description of the interactive help system
hostname                  Set system's network name
interface                 Select an interface to configure
ip                        Global IP configuration subcommands
ipx                       Novell/IPX global configuration commands
key                       Key management
line                      Configure a terminal line
logging                   Modify message logging facilities
login-string              Define a host-specific login string
map-class                 Configure static map class
map-list                  Configure static map list
menu                      Define a user-interface menu
modemcap                  Modem Capabilities database
netbios                   NETBIOS access control filtering
no                        Negate a command or set its defaults
ntp                       Configure NTP
partition                 Partition device
priority-list             Build a priority list
privilege                 Command privilege parameters
prompt                    Set system's prompt
queue-list                Build a custom queue list
resume-string             Define a host-specific resume string
rlogin                    Rlogin configuration commands
rmon                      Remote Monitoring
route-map                 Create route-map or enter route-map command mode
router                    Enable a routing process
scheduler                 Scheduler parameters
service                   Modify use of network based services
snmp-server               Modify SNMP parameters
state-machine             Define a TCP dispatch state machine
tacacs-server             Modify TACACS query parameters
terminal-queue            Terminal queue commands
tftp-server               Provide TFTP service for netload requests
username                  Establish User Name Authentication
x25                       X.25 Level 3
x29                        X29 commands

RouterB(config)#
```

> Typing a ? invokes the help system of the IOS. In this case, all commands available in global configuration mode are displayed.

Figure 1-17   Output from the ? command

If you wish to configure a particular interface, you must use interface configuration mode. To enter this mode you must first be in global configuration mode. You then enter the interface

1

command followed by the name and number of the interface you wish to enter. For example, to enter the Ethernet0 interface, you type the commands found in Figure 1-18 (the use of the help command is provided to show what options are available).

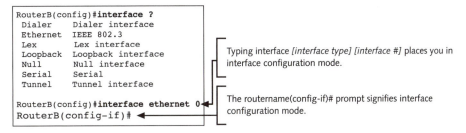

```
RouterB(config)#interface ?
  Dialer    Dialer interface
  Ethernet  IEEE 802.3
  Lex       Lex interface
  Loopback  Loopback interface
  Null      Null interface
  Serial    Serial
  Tunnel    Tunnel interface

RouterB(config)#interface ethernet 0
RouterB(config-if)#
```

Typing interface *[interface type] [interface #]* places you in interface configuration mode.

The routername(config-if)# prompt signifies interface configuration mode.

Figure 1-18 Interface configuration mode commands

To save time, you can shorten the name of most types of interfaces to just the first letter of the interface name. The command int e0 is the same as typing interface ethernet 0. To access interface configuration mode for a serial interface such as serial 0, you can use the command int s0 instead of interface serial 0. Both commands accomplish the same task. You save time by using these shortened commands.

Distinguishing between global configuration mode and interface configuration mode is very simple. If the router is in global configuration mode the router prompt is displayed as routername(config)#. Interface configuration mode is designated by the router prompt routername(config-if)#. You will use both of these modes extensively throughout this book.

PING, TRACE, AND DEBUG

Troubleshooting connectivity problems does not have to be an impossible task. The final area you need to review before beginning this book is the use of the ping, trace, and debug commands. These commands will allow you to methodically and efficiently troubleshoot your network.

You use the **Packet Internet Groper (Ping)** command to verify that a remote host is up and running. When you issue the ping command, the source node sends out **Internet Control Message Protocol (ICMP)** echo request packets to the specified destination node. The destination node, if it is up and running correctly, replies with ICMP echo reply packets. A simple ping request can be issued by typing the ping *[ip #]* command. Figure 1-19 shows the output of the ping command.

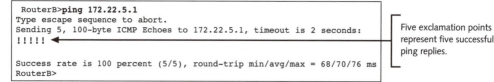

```
RouterB>ping 172.22.5.1
Type escape sequence to abort.
Sending 5, 100-byte ICMP Echoes to 172.22.5.1, timeout is 2 seconds:
!!!!!

Success rate is 100 percent (5/5), round-trip min/avg/max = 68/70/76 ms
RouterB>
```

Five exclamation points represent five successful ping replies.

Figure 1-19   Output from the ping command

The reply of five exclamation points means that all five echo request packets were responded to with echo reply packets. The following table shows a list of possible replies:

Table 1-7   Ping responses

Ping Response	Result
!	Echo request successfully replied to with echo reply
.	Timeout (no response from destination)
U	Destination unreachable
?	Unknown packet type
&	Time-to-live exceeded
C	Packet experienced congestion

Cisco routers include two ping commands: standard ping and extended ping. You run the standard ping shown from user EXEC mode. Extended ping requires that the router is in privileged EXEC mode. Figure 1-20 shows the proper syntax for the extended ping command.

The extended ping allows you to specify more echo request packets and larger packets. You can also use this command to ping IPX nodes with the IPX protocol. Overall, the standard and extended ping commands give you an excellent tool for determining the status of remote hosts on your network.

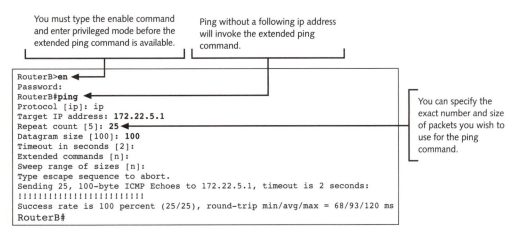

You must type the enable command and enter privileged mode before the extended ping command is available.

Ping without a following ip address will invoke the extended ping command.

You can specify the exact number and size of packets you wish to use for the ping command.

```
RouterB>en
Password:
RouterB#ping
Protocol [ip]: ip
Target IP address: 172.22.5.1
Repeat count [5]: 25
Datagram size [100]: 100
Timeout in seconds [2]:
Extended commands [n]:
Sweep range of sizes [n]:
Type escape sequence to abort.
Sending 25, 100-byte ICMP Echoes to 172.22.5.1, timeout is 2 seconds:
!!!!!!!!!!!!!!!!!!!!!!!!!
Success rate is 100 percent (25/25), round-trip min/avg/max = 68/93/120 ms
RouterB#
```

Figure 1-20   Extended ping example

Another useful troubleshooting command is the **trace** command. The trace command shows the exact path a packet takes from the source to the destination. This is accomplished through the use of the **time-to-live (TTL)** counter. The packet is sent out first with a time-to-live of one. Once it finds the first hop on the path to the destination, the packet is returned with a destination unreachable message. The TTL is incremented to two and the packet is resent. This process continues until the packet reaches the destination or times out. Figure 1-21 shows a trace to a router port with IP address 172.22.5.1.

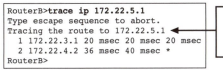

```
RouterB>trace ip 172.22.5.1
Type escape sequence to abort.
Tracing the route to 172.22.5.1
  1 172.22.3.1 20 msec 20 msec 20 msec
  2 172.22.4.2 36 msec 40 msec *
RouterB>
```

The trace command shows you the exact route packets take to reach a destination. You can use this information to pinpoint where network problems are occurring.

Figure 1-21   Trace command output

The final, and probably most powerful, troubleshooting tool you need to understand is the debug command. This extremely powerful command is only available from privileged EXEC mode. Debug has numerous subcommands that allow you to troubleshoot particular protocols. It also has a debug all mode, which will display all debugging counters at the cost of severe router performance degradation. Figure 1-22 shows normal output that can occur from the debug all command.

```
RouterB#debug all
This may severely impact network performance. Continue? [confirm]

All possible debugging has been turned on
RouterB#
IP: s=172.22.3.1 (Serial1), d=255.255.255.255, len 76, rcvd 2
UDP: rcvd src=172.22.3.1(520), dst=255.255.255.255(520), length=52
RIP: received v1 update from 172.22.3.1 on Serial1
     172.22.4.0 in 1 hops
     172.22.5.0 in 2 hops
RIP: Update contains 2 routes
SERVICE_MODULE(0): lxt441 interrupt 1 status A7 loop 0
SERVICE_MODULE(0): lxt441 interrupt 1 status 87 loop 0
SERVICE_MODULE(0): lxt441 interrupt 1 status A7 loop 0
SERVICE_MODULE(0): lxt441 interrupt 1 status 87 loop 0
Serial1: HDLC myseq 6631, mineseen 6631, yourseen 6580, line up
SERVICE_MODULE(0): lxt441 interrupt 1 status A7 loop 0
SERVICE_MODULE(0): lxt441 interrupt 1 status 87 loop 0
SERVICE_MODULE(0): lxt441 interrupt 1 status A7 loop 0
SERVICE_MODULE(0): lxt441 interrupt 1 status 87 loop 0
RIP: sending v1 update to 255.255.255.255 via Ethernet0 (172.22.2.1)
     subnet  172.22.3.0, metric 1
     subnet  172.22.4.0, metric 2
     subnet  172.22.5.0, metric 3
RIP: Update contains 3 routes
IP: s=172.22.2.1 (local), d=255.255.255.255 (Ethernet0), len 55, sending broad/m
ulticast
RIP: sending v1 update to 255.255.255.255 via Serial1 (172.22.3.2)
     subnet  172.22.2.0, metric 1
RIP: Update contains 1 routes
IP: s=172.22.3.2 (local), d=255.255.255.255 (Serial1), len 67, sending broad/mul
ticast
SERVICE_MODULE(0): lxt441 interrupt 1 status A7 loop 0
SERVICE_MODULE(0): lxt441 interrupt 1 status 87 loop 0
Serial0: attempting to restart
Serial1: HDLC myseq 6632, mineseen 6632, yourseen 6581, line up
IP: s=172.22.5.1 (Ethernet0), d=255.255.255.255, len 106, rcvd 2
UDP: rcvd src=172.22.5.1(520), dst=255.255.255.255(520), length=72
RIP: ignored v1 update from bad source 172.22.5.1 on Ethernet0
SERVICE_MODULE(0): lxt441 interrupt 1 status A7 loop 0
SERVICE_MODULE(0): lxt441 interrupt 1 status 87 loop 0
SERVICE_MODULE(0): lxt441 interrupt 1 status A7 loop 0
SERVICE_MODULE(0): lxt441 interrupt 1 status 87 loop 0
SERVICE_MODULE(0): lxt441 interrupt 1 status A7 loop 0
SERVICE_MODULE(0): lxt441 interrupt 1 status 87 loop 0
Serial1: HDLC myseq 6633, mineseen 6633, yourseen 6582, line up
All possible debugging has been turned off
RouterB#
```

> The debug all command warns you that issuing this command could cause severe network congestion. This command should only be used for a short period of time as a troubleshooting tool.

Figure 1-22 Debug all command output

You can also issue the debug command for particular protocols. Figure 1-23 shows the debug ip rip command, which can be used to troubleshoot RIP issues.

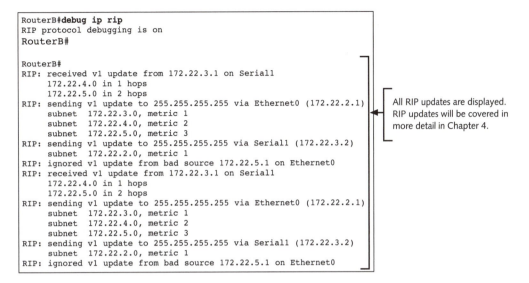

```
RouterB#debug ip rip
RIP protocol debugging is on
RouterB#

RouterB#
RIP: received v1 update from 172.22.3.1 on Serial1
     172.22.4.0 in 1 hops
     172.22.5.0 in 2 hops
RIP: sending v1 update to 255.255.255.255 via Ethernet0 (172.22.2.1)
     subnet  172.22.3.0, metric 1
     subnet  172.22.4.0, metric 2
     subnet  172.22.5.0, metric 3
RIP: sending v1 update to 255.255.255.255 via Serial1 (172.22.3.2)
     subnet  172.22.2.0, metric 1
RIP: ignored v1 update from bad source 172.22.5.1 on Ethernet0
RIP: received v1 update from 172.22.3.1 on Serial1
     172.22.4.0 in 1 hops
     172.22.5.0 in 2 hops
RIP: sending v1 update to 255.255.255.255 via Ethernet0 (172.22.2.1)
     subnet  172.22.3.0, metric 1
     subnet  172.22.4.0, metric 2
     subnet  172.22.5.0, metric 3
RIP: sending v1 update to 255.255.255.255 via Serial1 (172.22.3.2)
     subnet  172.22.2.0, metric 1
RIP: ignored v1 update from bad source 172.22.5.1 on Ethernet0
```

All RIP updates are displayed. RIP updates will be covered in more detail in Chapter 4.

Figure 1-23   Debug ip rip command output

As you can see all RIP updates are displayed so an administrator can quickly spot potential problems. The debug tool is extremely powerful, but also very resource-intensive. It should not be used for extended periods of time or it will have a detrimental effect on router performance.

CHAPTER SUMMARY

The OSI reference model is a seven-layer conceptual model of network communication. The model provides the following benefits: compatibility and standardization among vendors, interoperability among vendors, simplified modeling of the communication process to ease understanding, and a modular model that allows for easy upgrade of individual layers. The seven layers from layer seven to layer one are: Application, Presentation, Session, Transport, Network, Data Link and Physical. Each layer performs very specific functions and will only talk to its peer via peer-to-peer communication.

Network segmentation is the process of breaking heavily populated segments down into smaller collision domains. You use routers and bridges to segment networks, while repeaters can only be used to increase the distance of cable runs. Routers and bridges create smaller collision domains. Routers create smaller broadcast domains.

IP addresses are 32-bit logical network addresses that are usually displayed in dotted decimal format. Each IP address consists of a network ID and a node ID. An optional subnet ID may be included if needed. Class A addresses use the network.node.node.node format and provide for 126 different networks of 16,776,214 hosts each. Class B addresses use the network.network.node.node format and provide for 16,384 networks of 65,534 hosts each. Class C addresses use the network.network.network.node format and provide for 2,097,152 networks of 254 hosts each. Subnet masks are 32-bit addresses, in which all ones are placed in the network portion of an IP address. The default subnet masks are as follows:

- Class A   255.0.0.0
- Class B   255.255.0.0
- Class C   255.255.255.0

The process of subnetting is the process of borrowing bits from the host address to increase the number of network bits. The new subnet mask is added to the default mask to provide for the masking of the subnetwork number.

Routers have many different configuration modes. You use global configuration mode to set parameters that affect overall router operation. Interface configuration mode allows you to configure individual interface parameters.

The ping command checks for the status of a remote host. The trace command allows an administrator to follow the path a packet takes from source to destination. For more advanced router troubleshooting, you use the debug command to display router status updates.

KEY TERMS

Application layer — Layer seven of the OSI model; provides services directly to network applications; FTP, telnet, and SMTP are protocols that function at this layer.

attenuation — The natural degradation of a transmitted signal over distance.

backoff algorithm — Mathematical calculation performed by computers after a collision occurs on a CSMA/CD network; forces machines to wait a random amount of time before resending the destroyed packet.

bridges — Internetworking devices that build routing tables of MAC address; used to segment networks into smaller collision domains; will not stop broadcasts or broadcast storms; operate at the Data Link layer of the OSI model.

broadcasts — Any packet sent to all devices on a network.

Carrier Sense Multiple Access with Collision Detection (CSMA/CD) — Access method specified by the IEEE Ethernet 802.3 standard. In this method, a node will listen to see if the line is clear and then, if the line is clear, send. Two nodes may send at the same time and cause a collision. Two nodes will then perform the backoff algorithm.

collision domain — A portion of a network within which collisions are propagated.

Data Link layer — Layer two of the OSI model; broken into two sublayers: Logical Link Control and Media Access Control. Media access, topology, flow control, and packaging data into frames are all responsibilities of this layer. Bridges and switches (layer 2 switches) function at this layer.

debug — Tool and command that display real-time information concerning a router's status.

default gateway — IP address of the router port directly connected to a network; used as the default path from one network or subnet to other networks.

filter — Process of blocking or manipulating network data traffic. Normally, filtering a particular type of data traffic means you are blocking that traffic.

flash memory — Rewritable memory used to store the IOS image in use by a router.

interface — Physical port connections on a router such as Serial0, Ethernet1, or the console port.

Internet Control Message Protocol (ICMP) — A layer 3 protocol in the TCP/IP protocol stack that provides messaging for applications such as ping and trace, which use the IP protocol.

Internetworking Operating System (IOS) — The operating system loaded on a router, which controls all router functions.

MAC address — Also known as the physical address; 48-bit addresses "burned" in to the ROM on every network interface card.

Network layer — Layer three of the OSI model that handles routing packets between multiple networks; routers and the protocols IP and IPX function at this layer.

Nonvolatile random access memory — RAM that does not lose its contents when a router is powered off; contains the startup configuration file.

Open Systems Interconnection Model — Conceptual model of network communications created by the International Organization for Standardization in 1984; consists of the following seven layers: Application, Presentation, Session, Transport, Network, Data Link, and Physical.

Packet Internet Groper (Ping) — Troubleshooting utility that verifies that a remote host is currently running and accessible.

Physical layer — Layer one of the OSI model; deals with actually putting packets onto the wire; cables, connectors, and repeaters function at this layer.

physical topology — The physical layout of your network; normally created via the cabling type you use and the number of internetworking devices in the network.

Presentation layer — Layer six of the OSI model; converts data into an intermediate format that lower layers can understand; encryption and compression are functions of this layer, and JPEG, GIF, and EBCDIC are all examples of formats at this layer.

privileged EXEC mode — Also known as enable mode; allows for advanced router configuration and troubleshooting.

Random access memory (RAM) — Temporary storage space used by routers to hold buffers, routing tables, and the running configuration.

read-only memory (ROM) — Contains the bootstrap, which performs the POST for a router; on most routers, ROM also holds a minimal version of the IOS, which can boot the router if configuration information is missing or corrupt.

repeaters — Networking devices that regenerate the electrical signals that carry data; they function at the Physical layer of the OSI model.

routers — Internetworking devices that build routing tables of network addresses; they limit both collisions and broadcasts; they function at the Network layer of the OSI model.

segmentation — The process of breaking a network into smaller broadcast or collision domains.

Session layer — Layer five of the OSI model. This layer is responsible for creating, maintaining, and terminating a session between two applications. Provides services to presentation layer applications. SQL and RPC function at this layer.

subnet mask — 32-bit address used to distinguish between the network or subnet ID and the node ID in an IP address.

switch — A networking device that acts as a multiport bridge; layer 2 devices for the purpose of the CCNA.

time-to-live (TTL) — The amount of time that a packet is considered valid.

trace — Troubleshooting tool (and command) that shows the exact path a packet takes through the internetwork from the source to a destination.

Transport layer — Layer four of the OSI model; ensures that packets arrive intact, in sequence, and unduplicated. TCP, UDP, and SPX function at this layer.

user EXEC mode — Configuration mode that only allows you to view basic information about the router, telnet to remote hosts, and perform basic troubleshooting.

REVIEW QUESTIONS

1. Which of the following addresses is a Class A address?
   a. 131.107.2.5
   b. 205.116.12.5
   c. 128.0.0.1
   d. 27.15.42..1

2. Which of the following are layers of the OSI model? (Choose all that apply)
   a. OSI
   b. physical
   c. IEEE
   d. Data Link

3. Which layer of the OSI model is responsible for media access and packaging data into frames?
   a. network layer
   b. physical layer

   c. Data Link layer

   d. transport layer

4. At which layer of the OSI model will encryption and compression occur?

   a. presentation

   b. session

   c. application

   d. network

5. Flash memory stores _____ . (Choose all that apply)

   a. startup–configuration file

   b. running–configuration file

   c. bootstrap program

   d. IOS image

6. Using the network 140.25.0.0, what will be the default subnet mask?

   a. 255.255.255.0

   b. 255.255.0.0

   c. 0.255.255.255

   d. 255.0.0.0

7. What would the subnet mask be if you borrowed 4 bits from the network 140.25.0.0?

   a. 255.255.0.0

   b. 255.255.224.0

   c. 255.255.192.0

   d. 225.255.240.0

8. At which layer of the OSI model does a bridge function?

   a. physical

   b. network

   c. transport

   d. Data Link

9. Which of the following shows the privileged mode router prompt?

   a. Router(config)#

   b. Router#

   c. Router>

   d. Router-A

10. The _____ layer is responsible for finding the best path to route packets within an internetwork.

    a. transport

    b. network

    c. session

    d. Data Link

11. What Ping response signifies that a successful echo reply has been received?

    a. ?

    b. U

    c. !

    d. .

12. The range of starting decimal values for Class C addresses is _____.

    a. 110

    b. 192–223

    c. 128–191

    d. 255.255.0.0

13. Which of the following can be used to segment networks and limit broadcast domains?

    a. repeaters

    b. bridges

    c. switches

    d. routers

14. Which of the following lists the layers of the OSI model from layer 7 to layer 1?

    a. Application, Session, Transport, Network, Presentation, Data Link, Physical

    b. Physical, Data Link, Network, Transport, Session, Presentation, Application

    c. Application, Presentation, Session, Transport, Network, Data Link, Physical

    d. Presentation, Application, Session, Network, Transport, Data Link, Physical

15. Which layer of the OSI model deals with delivering data intact, in sequence, and unduplicated?

    a. transport

    b. presentation

    c. Data Link

    d. application

16. Class B addresses can be identified by which of the following attributes? (Choose all that apply)

    a. starting binary value of 10

    b. starting decimal range of 1–126

    c. network.network.node.node format

    d. starting decimal range of 128–192

17. Which of the following commands shows the exact route a packet travels through an internetwork?

    a. Ping

    b. trace

    c. debug

    d. show trace

18. ROM contains _____. (Choose all that apply)

    a. startup-config

    b. bootstrap

    c. backup copy of the IOS

    d. routing tables

19. The format for a Class C address is _____.

    a. network.node.node.node

    b. network.network.network.network

    c. network.network.node.node

    d. network.network.network.node

20. The enable command will place the router in _____.

    a. privileged EXEC mode

    b. global configuration mode

    c. interface configuration mode

    d. user EXEC mode

CASE PROJECTS

1. Hillier and Parmer Inc. has hired you to design a subnetting scheme for their new worldwide organization. They have been assigned the Class B network 156.80.0.0 by the Internet Assigned Numbers Authority. Company executives inform you that due to the physical topology of the network, they will require a minimum of 900 subnets. Design a subnetting scheme, complete with charts of the first 10 usable subnets and the required subnet mask.

2. Your colleague, Susan Hager, is preparing a presentation for new clients. She asks you to prepare a short part of that report, in which you describe the differences between segmentation with repeaters, routers, and bridges. Prepare this short report.

3. This afternoon, you will be explaining the OSI model to senior management. They are interested in it. Design a flow chart showing how the OSI model facilitates the transferring of data from a source to a destination node.

IPX/SPX

After reading this chapter and completing the exercises you will be able to:

- ♦ Describe the IPX/SPX protocol stack and map its major protocols to the OSI model
- ♦ Identify the parts of an IPX/SPX network address
- ♦ Define the Data Link layer frame formats supported by NetWare and the Cisco IOS
- ♦ Describe the function of Service Advertisement Protocol advertisements and the processes Cisco routers use when dealing with SAP advertisements
- ♦ Configure IPX/SPX on a router
- ♦ Monitor IPX/SPX on a router

In a perfect world, network administrators would run a single protocol stack that worked flawlessly with network operating systems from all vendors. In the real world (right now anyway), you must normally run at least two protocol stacks to get the functionality that your network needs. For instance, many networks using Novell's NetWare products run both the IPX/SPX and TCP/IP protocol stacks. Up until this point, you have focused on TCP/IP as the protocol stack of choice for use on all internetworks. In this chapter, you will learn about IPX/SPX as an internetworking protocol stack.

IPX/SPX PROTOCOL STACK

Internetwork Packet Exchange/Sequenced Packet Exchange (IPX/SPX) was originally derived by Novell from the Xerox Network Systems protocol stack, and its role as a networking protocol stack expanded quickly as Novell's NetWare became the standard network operating system in many organizations during the late 1980s and early 1990s. Then, in the mid-1990s, the Internet took hold and TCP/IP became the protocol of choice among networking professionals. Still, in order for some NetWare-aware applications to run correctly, many organizations must continue to run IPX/SPX. Therefore, even though NetWare has been able to use TCP/IP for some time now (and will run it natively under NetWare 5), network administrators find themselves dealing with many multiprotocol networks using TCP/IP and IPX/SPX.

As is evident in Figure 2-1, the IPX/SPX protocol stack does not follow the seven-layer OSI model exactly. Instead, like most modern protocol stacks, it maps loosely to the model.

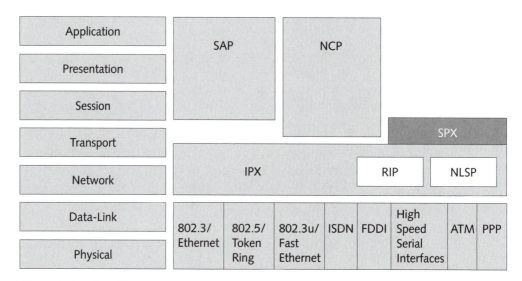

Figure 2-1 IPX/SPX protocol stack

Internetwork Packet Exchange (IPX), **Sequenced Packet Exchange (SPX)**, **Service Advertisement Protocol (SAP)**, **NetWare Core Protocol (NCP)**, **Routing Information Protocol (RIP)**, and **NetWare Link State Protocol (NLSP)** are several of the main protocols in the IPX/SPX protocol stack. They perform the following functions:

- IPX is a connectionless, predominantly layer 3 protocol, although, as you can see in Figure 2-1, it does spill over into some layer 4 functions. It is responsible for finding the best path through a mulitpath IPX network. IPX is similar in function to the IP protocol found in the TCP/IP protocol stack. It can use RIP and NLSP to determine the best path among multiple paths through the internetwork.

- SPX, a connection-oriented layer 4 protocol, provides guaranteed delivery services for the connectionless IPX protocol. SPX is similar in function to TCP in the TCP/IP protocol stack.

- SAP, which operates at layers 5, 6, and 7, advertises services running on IPX/SPX servers and helps clients locate network services.

- NCP facilitates client/server interaction on a NetWare network. NCP handles basic file and print sharing, authentication services, and directory services. NCP functions at layers 4, 5, 6, and 7 of the OSI model.

- RIP is an integrated distance vector routing protocol (see Chapter 4 for details on distance vector routing protocols). It uses **ticks** (1/18 of a second time counts used to determine the desirability of a particular route) and hop count as **metrics** (factors used to determine the best path among multiple paths). These metrics determine the best path within an IPX/SPX internetwork. The RIP used in IPX/SPX sends out routing table updates every 60 seconds and uses ticks as its main metric (hop count is used to break ties). RIP functions at layer 3 of the OSI model.

- NLSP is a link state routing protocol designed by Novell as the successor to RIP. Like RIP, NLSP functions at layer 3 of the OSI model.

IPX/SPX ADDRESSING

IPX/SPX addressing, when compared with TCP/IP addressing, is actually quite simple. **IPX/SPX addresses** are 80-bit addresses that use a network.node format. The network portion of the address consists of up to 32 bits displayed as eight hexadecimal digits. The network administrator assigns the network portion of the address. The node portion on the address is the 48-bit physical MAC address of a node. It is displayed as 12 hexadecimal digits. The following example shows an IPX/SPX address:

200.0020.7811.4a62

The assigned network address is 200, while 0020.7811.4a62 represents the node portion of the address (and therefore the MAC address of the node). The MAC address starts with the rightmost bits and goes for 48 bits, or 12 hexadecimal digits. The network number will always start with the leftmost bits and can be 32 bits in length.

The above example shows an important concept relating to IPX/SPX addressing. The network portion of the address can be up to 32 bits, but it is not required to fill the entire 32-bit space to be valid. Our example shows a node with the MAC address of 0020.7811.4a62 on the IPX/SPX network 200.

The arbitrary manner of assigning IPX/SPX network numbers makes determining the network number on an IPX/SPX segment a daunting task. Asking the network administrator for the segment's network number is the easiest and, therefore, the recommended method for finding out the network number. If you have physical access to a router that has an interface port on the segment on which you want to determine the network number, you can use the IOS command show ipx interface to find the network number. Lastly, you can use the show cdp neighbors command from an adjacent router to determine the network numbers of neighboring routers.

IPX/SPX DATA LINK LAYER FRAME TYPES

In order for all nodes on an IPX/SPX network to communicate, they must share a common Data Link layer frame **encapsulation**, which is the process of wrapping Protocol Data units from upper layers with headers and, at the Data Link layer, with trailer information. If two computers do not share this encapsulation, they cannot communicate because their data packets use a different form of Data Link layer header. Also, in order for Cisco routers to participate in IPX/SPX networks, their interfaces must use the same encapsulation type as the networks to which they are attached. The most common Data Link layer frame formats and their characteristics are listed in Table 2-1.

Table 2-1   Data Link Layer Encapsulations

Novell Frame Format Designation	Used by Networks Running:
802.3	NetWare 3.11 or lower
802.2	NetWare 3.12 or higher
Ethernet_II	Both IPX/SPX and TCP/IP
Ethernet_snap	IPX/SPX, TCP/IP, and AppleTalk

Although the above formats and designations are easy enough to comprehend and use, confusion arises due to the terminology the Cisco IOS uses for frame formats. Table 2-2 shows the Novell Ethernet frame format designations and the associated Cisco encapsulation terminology. Later in this chapter, you use the Cisco encapsulation terms to set frame encapsulation on a router's interface ports.

Table 2-2   Cisco Encapsulation Terminology

Novell Ethernet Frame Format Designation	Cisco Encapsulation Terminology
802.3	novell-ether (default setting on Ethernet)
802.2	sap
Ethernet_II	arpa
Ethernet_snap	snap

IPX/SPX networks running in a wide-area network environment often cross serial interfaces. When it crosses the interfaces, it is encapsulated in the Cisco default serial encapsulation of HDLC. This is because Novell doesn't specify a default serial Data Link format. Because of this default, the category "serial" can not live in either Table 2-1 or 2-2.

Other frame formats supported by IPX/SPX and the Cisco IOS are displayed in Table 2-3.

All nodes on an IPX/SPX network (including all router ports) must be configured with the same Data Link layer frame encapsulation. Otherwise, the nodes cannot communicate with one another. In essence, two nodes using different frame formats speak two different and totally incompatible languages. You can fix this problem by ensuring that all nodes on your IPX/SPX network use the same Data Link layer frame type.

Table 2-3   Other Supported Frame Types

Other Novell Frame Formats	Cisco Encapsulation Terminology
Token_ring	sap
Token_ring_snap	snap
FDDI_snap	snap
FDDI_802.2	sap
FDDI_raw	novell-fddi

SAP ADVERTISEMENTS

SAP advertisements on an IPX/SPX network allow servers to "advertise" running services such as print services, directory services, and file sharing services to network clients. Clients also use SAP advertisements to request a list of services from a server's SAP table. SAP tables contain a list of all services available on a network segment. For example, in Figure 2-2, the SAP table for NetWare Server A includes all services that it currently provides, plus all services provided by NetWare Server B.

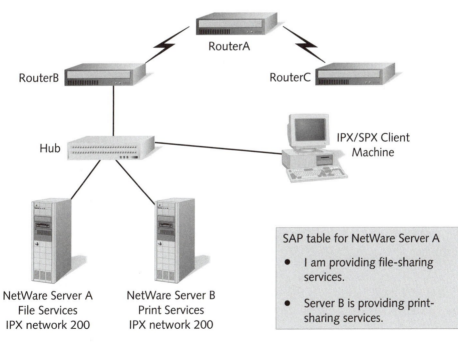

Figure 2-2   SAP example

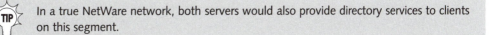

In a true NetWare network, both servers would also provide directory services to clients on this segment.

Servers take SAP broadcasts, which occur every 60 seconds by default, and build SAP tables. Therefore, all servers on a segment learn about all services provided by their peers on that segment. Clients can request SAP information from any server, and that server, if SAP broadcasts are working correctly, should be able to provide the client with a list of all services on the local segment.

The **Get Nearest Server (GNS)** request used by clients at startup allows them to find the nearest running NetWare server. The GNS request takes the form of a SAP broadcast. As a result, if the segment has a local NetWare server, the nearest server responds with its location and available services. Again, using Figure 2-2 as an example, if the IPX/SPX client issues a GNS request, either NetWare Server A or NetWare Server B responds to the request (the closest server to the client would respond first). SAP advertisements become slightly complicated when routers get involved.

Since SAP broadcasts occur every 60 seconds by default, they would quickly overwhelm most WAN links if all SAP broadcasts by all servers were forwarded through routers. However, SAP broadcasts are such an integral part of IPX/SPX communications that a method is needed to pass the information contained in SAP broadcasts without passing the broadcasts themselves. Routers—which by default block broadcasts in order to reduce unnecessary traffic—accomplish this task by building and using SAP tables. Thus, routers can respond to SAP requests if no NetWare server is available on a local segment.

Figure 2-3 shows a network where the IPX/SPX client on network 200 has no access to a local NetWare server. If the client sends out a GNS request, RouterB will respond to the request with the information in its SAP table.

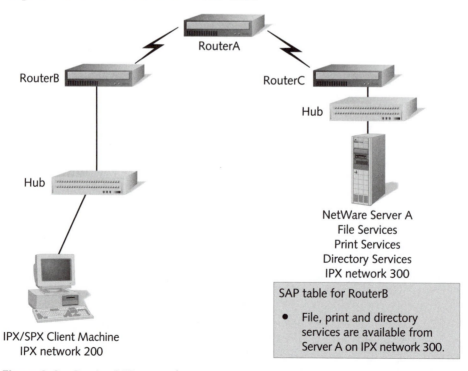

RouterA

RouterB

RouterC

Hub

Hub

NetWare Server A
File Services
Print Services
Directory Services
IPX network 300

SAP table for RouterB

• File, print and directory services are available from Server A on IPX network 300.

IPX/SPX Client Machine
IPX network 200

Figure 2-3 Router SAP example

In Figure 2-4, RouterB informs the client that the nearest NetWare server is Server A on network 300.

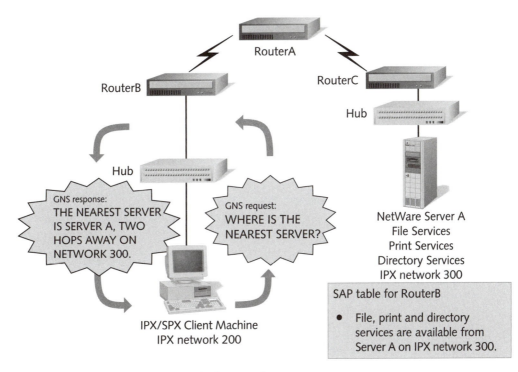

RouterA

RouterC

RouterB

Hub

Hub

GNS response:
THE NEAREST SERVER
IS SERVER A, TWO
HOPS AWAY ON
NETWORK 300.

GNS request:
WHERE IS THE
NEAREST SERVER?

NetWare Server A
File Services
Print Services
Directory Services
IPX network 300

IPX/SPX Client Machine
IPX network 200

SAP table for RouterB

• File, print and directory
  services are available from
  Server A on IPX network 300.

Figure 2-4   Router response to SAP requests

All SAP requests by IPX/SPX clients on network 200 initiate a response by RouterB. RouterB also informs all other routers of its SAP table via a directed message sent every 60 seconds. Router SAP tables eliminate the need for large numbers of SAP broadcasts to traverse the internetwork. The number and type of SAP entries in a router's table and the types of entries propagated to other routers can be controlled via access lists known as SAP filters. SAP filters are discussed in Chapter 3 of this text.

CONFIGURING IPX/SPX

Configuring IPX/SPX on Cisco routers is a multistep process. First, you must enter global configuration mode and enable IPX routing. Then, if your network has multiple paths, you should enable multiple paths for IPX routing with the ipx maximum-paths *[# of paths]* command. You would replace the # of paths variable with the number of possible paths in your IPX network (up to a total of 512 paths). This command is a **load-balancing** command. If you enable maximum-paths with a value greater than one, the router will load balance between the two paths or between the number of paths designated. Finally, you must configure IPX network numbers and encapsulation types on each interface.

The default value for maximum-paths is one. In other words, load balancing is disabled by default.

The first step in configuring IPX requires that you log in to your router and enter global configuration mode. The process is detailed in Figure 2-5.

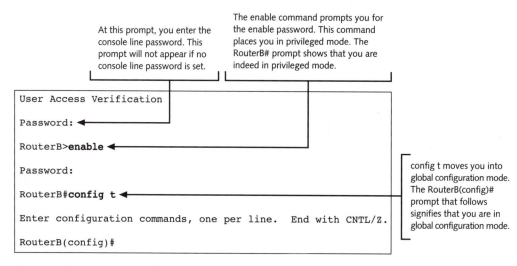

Figure 2-5 Entering global configuration mode

Once you see the routername(config)# prompt, you are in global configuration mode. The config t (short for configure terminal) command places you in this mode. To configure IPX routing, you enter the ipx routing command. Figure 2-6 shows the commands necessary to enable IPX routing.

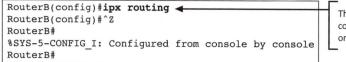

Figure 2-6 Enabling IPX routing

You can verify that ipx routing has been added to the configuration by trying the show run command. This command produces the output found in Figure 2-7.

```
RouterB#show run
    Building configuration...

    Current configuration:
    !
    version 11.1
    service udp-small-servers
    service tcp-small-servers
    !
    hostname RouterB
    !
    enable secret 5 $1$RHhg$ngXce3OBeC7GprpPjtqsP1
    !
    ipx routing 0060.474f.6506
    !
    interface Ethernet0
    ip address 172.22.2.1 255.255.255.0
    !
    interface Serial0
    no ip address
    !
    interface Serial1
    ip address 172.22.3.2 255.255.255.0
    !
    router rip
    network 172.22.0.0
    !
    no ip classless
    !
    !
    !
    !
    line con 0
    password password
    login
    line vty 0 4
    password password
    login
    !
    end
RouterB#
```

The ipx routing entry in the running configuration shows that IPX routing is on. The hexadecimal number following the ipx routing entry is the MAC address of the configured interface.

Figure 2-7   Verifying IPX routing

If you properly add ipx routing, the ipx routing entry will be added to the running configuration. The configuration in Figure 2-7 also contains a TCP/IP address because this is a multiprotocol network. To save the configuration changes, you should issue the copy run start command. This ensures that the running configuration is copied into the startup configuration.

TIP   IP routing is enabled by default on all Cisco routers. If for some reason IP routing is ever turned off on a router, you can enable it with the ip routing command.

If you have a network consisting of multiple paths, you should use the ipx maximum-paths command to enable load balancing. Figure 2-8 shows a network where the ipx maximum-paths value for RouterB should be set to 2 because the router has two equal distance and cost paths that are usable.

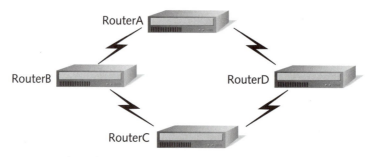

Figure 2-8   Multipath IPX network

Figure 2-9 shows the commands necessary to complete this task on the router.

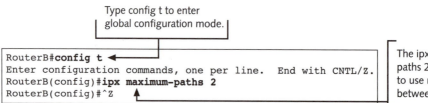

Figure 2-9   Configuring ipx maximum-paths

If you enter the show run command after enabling multiple paths, the ipx maximum-paths statement is visible. Figure 2-10 shows the output from typing the show run command.

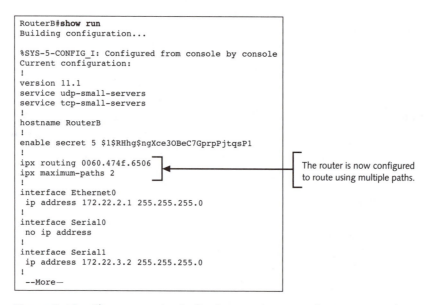

Figure 2-10   Show run output after ipx maximum-paths 2 command

The More statement at the end of this output in Figure 2-10 denotes that you need to hit the Spacebar to display additional lines. For the sake of brevity, the extra output is not displayed in this example. You will notice, however, that the show run output now has the ipx maximum-paths 2 statement added. The paths statement is changed to 2 because in the example network, the router has two equal cost and distance paths available for it to use. To make this change permanent, you must issue the copy run start command. It is important to note that the only required command to enable IPX routing on a router is the ipx routing command; the ipx maximum-paths command is optional.

Once you configure IPX routing globally on a router, you must enable IPX/SPX on each individual interface. Configuring IPX on an interface is a two-step process:

1. First, you must assign an IPX network number to an interface.

2. Then, you configure an encapsulation on an interface.

Configuring encapsulation becomes necessary only if you wish to use an encapsulation type that is different from the default. The default for all Ethernet interfaces is novell-ether (which translates to frame type 802.3). The default for all serial interfaces is **High-level Data Link Control (HDLC)**. Since many modern NetWare networks consist of 4.11 servers with a default frame type of 802.2, you will likely need to change the encapsulation on most of the Ethernet ports on a router.

We now begin the actual configuration of interfaces. Throughout the following example, all command inputs and router outputs use Figure 2-11 as a reference; all commands occur on RouterB.

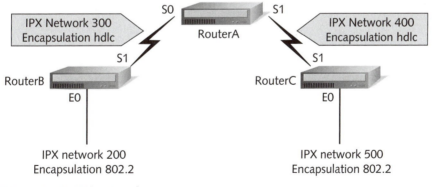

Figure 2-11 IPX network

In order to begin interface configuration, you must log in to the router, enter privileged mode, and then enter global configuration mode. Figure 2-12 shows how you enter global configuration mode.

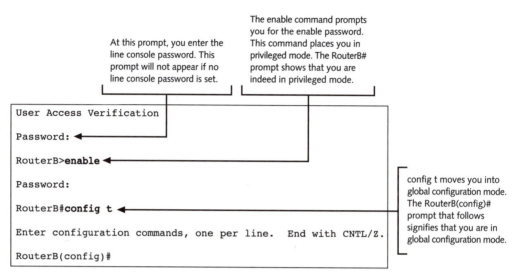

At this prompt, you enter the line console password. This prompt will not appear if no line console password is set.

The enable command prompts you for the enable password. This command places you in privileged mode. The RouterB# prompt shows that you are indeed in privileged mode.

```
User Access Verification
Password:
RouterB>enable
Password:
RouterB#config t
Enter configuration commands, one per line.  End with CNTL/Z.
RouterB(config)#
```

config t moves you into global configuration mode. The RouterB(config)# prompt that follows signifies that you are in global configuration mode.

Figure 2-12   Entering global configuration mode

To configure an interface, you need to switch to interface configuration mode. The interface command can be used to switch to a particular interface. In this example, referring back to Figure 2-6, you wish to configure IPX/SPX on the Ethernet0 interface of RouterB. Figure 2-13 shows how you enter configuration mode for interface Ethernet0.

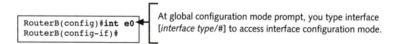

```
RouterB(config)#int e0
RouterB(config-if)#
```

At global configuration mode prompt, you type interface [interface type/#] to access interface configuration mode.

Figure 2-13   Entering interface configuration mode

The int e0 (short for interface ethernet0) command moves you into the interface configuration mode. The RouterB(config-if)# prompt allows you to distinguish that you are currently in interface configuration mode. At this point, you configure the IPX network number and type of encapsulation. Figure 2-14 shows the commands necessary to accomplish this task.

2

```
RouterB(config)#int e0
RouterB(config-if)#ipx ?
access-group             Enable IPX accounting on this interface
accounting
advertise-default-route-only  Only advertise the IPX/RIP default route out onto this network
bandwidth-percent        Set EIGRP bandwidth limit
compression              Select IPX compression commands
delay                    Set a Novell delay on the interface, in 'ticks'
down                     Bring an IPX network administratively down
encapsulation            Novell encapsulation
gns-reply-disable        Disable Get Nearest Server replies on this interface
gns-response-delay       Delay in answering GNS on this interface
hello-interval           Configures IPX EIGRP hello interval
helper-address           Forward broadcasts to a specific address
helper-list                  Filter helpered IPX packets on input
hold-down                Configures IPX EIGRP routes hold down time
hold-time                Configures IPX EIGRP hold time
input-network-filter     Filter incoming routing updates
input-sap-filter         Filter services learned from the Service Advertising Protocol
ipxwan                       Configure IPXWAN on this interface
link-delay               Set an IPX link delay on the interface, in microseconds
netbios                      Setup IPX NetBIOS filters and caching on this interface
network                  Assign an IPX network & enable IPX routing
nlsp                         Select NLSP commands
output-gns-filter        Filter services reported in response to Get Nearest Server
output-network-filter    Filter outgoing routing updates
output-rip-delay         Interpacket delay for RIP updates
output-sap-delay         Interpacket delay for SAP updates
output-sap-filter        Filter services reported via SAP
pad-process-switched-packets  Pad odd-length packets on output (process-switched only)
ppp-client               Configure interface for PPP client mode
rip-max-packetsize       Maximum size of RIP packets being sent on interface
rip-multiplier           Multiple of RIP update interval for aging of RIP routes
route-cache              Enable fast switching
router-filter                Filter sources of routing updates
router-sap-filter        Select source router and service type of SAP updates
sap-incremental          Send incremental SAP updates - for IPX EIGRP networks only
sap-interval             Set SAP update period
sap-max-packetsize           Maximum size of SAP packets being sent on interface
sap-multiplier           Multiple of SAP update interval for aging of SAP routes
split-horizon            Perform split horizon
spx-idle-time            Set an SPX idle time on the interface, in seconds
spx-spoof                Spoof SPX keepalives packets
throughput               Set IPX link throughput in bit per second
triggered-rip-delay      Interpacket delay for triggered RIP updates
                             (override output-rip-delay for triggered updates only)
triggered-sap-delay      Interpacket delay for triggered SAP updates
                             (override output-rip-delay for triggered updates only)
type-20-propagation      Forward IPX type 20 propagation packets
update-time              Set IPX routing update timer
watchdog-spoof           Answer Server Watchdog packets for Client machines
```

Once in interface configuration mode, the ipx command followed by the ? results in a Help screen that lists all available commands.

The network command is the command used to configure an IPX network number on an interface.

Figure 2-14 Configuring an IPX network number

You enter the network portion of the command next and specify the IPX network number assigned by the network administrator to this segment. Figure 2-15 shows the commands necessary to add 200, which is the IPX network number, to an interface.

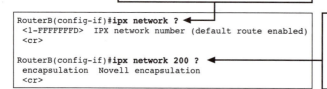

You can use the ? to access the Help functions
of the IOS. In this example, the Help system
shows that a network number is required. This
interface resides on network 200.

```
RouterB(config-if)#ipx network ?
<1-FFFFFFFD>  IPX network number (default route enabled)
<cr>

RouterB(config-if)#ipx network 200 ?
 encapsulation  Novell encapsulation
 <cr>
```

After a network number has beed added to the
configuration, you must set an encapsulation.
If you do not specify an encapsulation, the
default encapsulation for the type of interface
being configured is used.

Figure 2-15   Configuring an interface for IPX

The next major item that must be configured is the encapsulation type. You enter the
encapsulation portion of the command followed by the encapsulation type. If you forget
the Cisco IOS terminology for each Novell frame encapsulation type, you can use the
context-sensitive ? command to display all possible options. Figure 2-16 shows output
that lists the encapsulation types supported by the IOS.

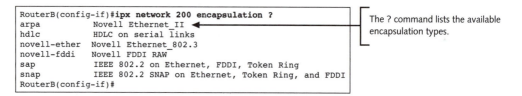

```
RouterB(config-if)#ipx network 200 encapsulation ?
arpa          Novell Ethernet_II
hdlc          HDLC on serial links
novell-ether  Novell Ethernet_802.3
novell-fddi   Novell FDDI RAW
sap           IEEE 802.2 on Ethernet, FDDI, Token Ring
snap          IEEE 802.2 SNAP on Ethernet, Token Ring, and FDDI
RouterB(config-if)#
```

The ? command lists the available
encapsulation types.

Figure 2-16   Identifying available encapsulation types

In Figure 2-11, port E0 resides on a segment using the 802.2 frame type. Therefore, it must
be configured with sap encapsulation. Figure 2-17 displays the commands necessary to perform this task.

If you are unsure if a command is
complete, placing the ? command at the
end of a line will list all command options
still available. In this example, you see
that a command called secondary is
available. Secondary interfaces will be
discussed later in this chapter.

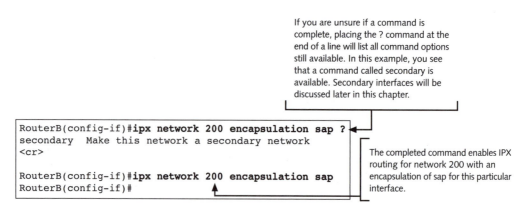

```
RouterB(config-if)#ipx network 200 encapsulation sap ?
secondary  Make this network a secondary network
<cr>

RouterB(config-if)#ipx network 200 encapsulation sap
RouterB(config-if)#
```

The completed command enables IPX
routing for network 200 with an
encapsulation of sap for this particular
interface.

Figure 2-17   Configuring encapsulation on an IPX interface

Your final command, ipx network 200 encapsulation sap, configures Ethernet0 to reside on IPX network 200 using 802.2 encapsulation. If all the routers in Figure 2-11 were configured as indicated in this chapter, IPX/SPX communications would now be possible across the internetwork.

The Secondary Command

On occasion, you may need to configure multiple networks using multiple frame types on a single interface. For instance, in Figure 2-18, E0 on RouterB must support IPX network 200 using 802.2 encapsulation and IPX network 2f using Ethernet_II encapsulation.

You can accomplish this support by using the secondary command. (In future releases of the IOS, the secondary command will no longer be available. Instead, you will have to add multiple networks and encapsulations through subinterfaces. Subinterfaces are discussed in the next section.) Using the secondary command, you can add IPX network 2f as a secondary network on the interface Ethernet0. The router output in Figure 2-19 displays proper use of this command.

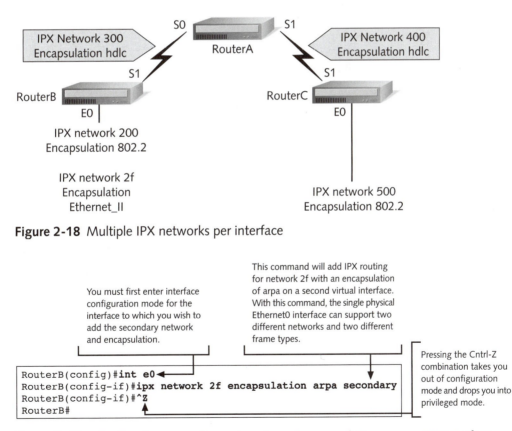

Figure 2-18 Multiple IPX networks per interface

Figure 2-19 Configuring secondary networks and encapsulations on an IPX interface

Typing the show run command allows you to see that a secondary network and encapsulation type have been added to port Ethernet0. Figure 2-20 shows the output from typing the show run command after configuring the secondary network and encapsulation.

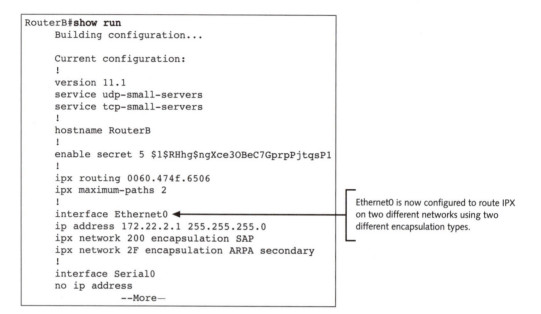

```
RouterB#show run
    Building configuration...

    Current configuration:
    !
    version 11.1
    service udp-small-servers
    service tcp-small-servers
    !
    hostname RouterB
    !
    enable secret 5 $1$RHhg$ngXce3OBeC7GprpPjtqsP1
    !
    ipx routing 0060.474f.6506
    ipx maximum-paths 2
    !
    interface Ethernet0
    ip address 172.22.2.1 255.255.255.0
    ipx network 200 encapsulation SAP
    ipx network 2F encapsulation ARPA secondary
    !
    interface Serial0
    no ip address
              --More--
```

Ethernet0 is now configured to route IPX on two different networks using two different encapsulation types.

Figure 2-20   Show run output displaying secondary network and encapsulation

Subinterfaces

The secondary command does have two problems associated with it. First, you can only add one secondary network and encapsulation per interface. If you need more, the secondary command will not work for you. In addition, the secondary command may not be included in future versions of the Cisco IOS. Thus, Cisco recommends the use of subinterfaces. **Subinterfaces**, which are virtual interfaces associated with a physical interface, provide a means to add a practically unlimited number of networks and encapsulations. (The actual number of subinterfaces that can be configured on a physical interface numbers in the billions.) Figure 2-21 displays the commands necessary to enter subinterface configuration mode.

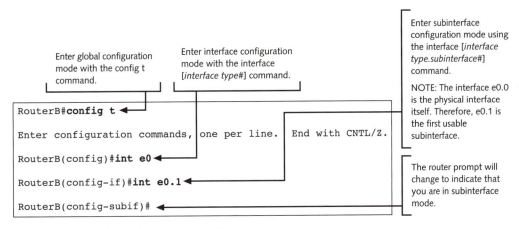

Figure 2-21 Subinterface configuration

> 💡 TIP The router output in Figure 2-22 shows the addition of the IPX network 2f using Ethernet_II encapsulation via the use of a subinterface.

```
RouterB#config t
Enter configuration commands, one per line.  End with CNTL/Z.
RouterB(config)#int e0.1
RouterB(config-subif)#ipx network 2f encap arpa
RouterB(config-subif)#^Z
RouterB#
%SYS-5-CONFIG_I: Configured from console by console
RouterB#
```

The int e0.1 command switches you to subinterface configuration mode. This mode is denoted by the RouterB(config-subif)# prompt.

Figure 2-22 Subinterface configuration with the subinterface method

You can verify that the subinterface has been added with the show run command. Figure 2-23 shows the output from the show run command.

Directly below the Ethernet0 configuration information, the Ethernet0.1 subinterface information shows that IPX network 2f with Ethernet_II encapsulation has been added. If you needed another network and encapsulation, you would add it to subinterface Ethernet0.2.

Configuration of interfaces constitutes the second in a series of steps necessary for configuration of IPX/SPX on a router. Each interface should be assigned a network number and encapsulation type to ensure that IPX/SPX communication can occur.

```
RouterB#show run
Building configuration...

Current configuration:
!
version 11.1
service udp-small-servers
service tcp-small-servers
!
hostname RouterB
!
enable secret 5 $1$RHhg$ngXce3OBeC7GprpPjtqsP1
!
ipx routing 0060.474f.6506
ipx maximum-paths 2
!
interface Ethernet0
ip address 172.22.2.1 255.255.255.0
ipx network 200 encapsulation SAP
!
interface Ethernet0.1
ipx network 2F encapsulation ARPA
!
interface Serial0
no ip address
--More—
```

A virtual interface Ethernet0.1 has been added to the running configuration.

Figure 2-23   Show run command output after adding a subinterface

Monitoring IPX/SPX

A variety of IOS commands allow you to monitor the performance of IPX/SPX on your routers. Useful commands include show ipx route, show ipx interface, show ipx servers, debug ipx (various subcommands exist for this command), and the extended ping command.

The first monitoring command, show ipx route, displays the current IPX routing tables contained on a router. Using Figure 2-24 as the sample network, Figure 2-25 details how RouterA learns of IPX network 200 and 2f via RIP updates from RouterB. Remember that the RIP used by IPX/SPX is not the same as RIP configured for TCP/IP.

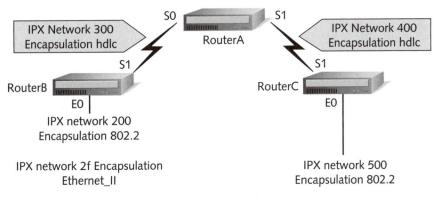

Figure 2-24 Multiple IPX networks per interface

The R at the beginning of each route entry signifies that the router learned the route via a RIP update. The C signifies that network 300 is directly connected via the Serial0 interface.

This route table shows that RouterA learned of a route to networks 2f and 200 that has an administrative distance of 7 and is 1 hop away (the 07 equals administrative distance, and the 01 represents the number of hops, or routers, a packet must pass through to get to the destination network).

```
RouterA#show ipx route
Codes: C - Connected primary network,    c - Connected secondary network
   S - Static, F - Floating static, L - Local (internal), W - IPXWAN
   R - RIP, E - EIGRP, N - NLSP, X - External, A - Aggregate
   s - seconds, u - uses

3 Total IPX routes. Up to 1 parallel paths and 16 hops allowed.

No default route known.

C       300 (HDLC),         Se0
R        2F [07/01] via     300.0060.474f.6506,    49s, Se0
R       200 [07/01] via     300.0060.474f.6506,    49s, Se0
RouterA#
```

Figure 2-25   Output from show ipx route command

You can use the show ipx traffic command to display the amount of IPX traffic a router has sent and received. Figure 2-26 contains typical router output you may receive from the show ipx traffic command.

```
RouterB>show ipx traffic
System Traffic for 0.0000.0000.0001 System-Name: RouterB
Rcvd:    2 total, 2 format errors, 0 checksum errors, 0 bad hop count,
         2 packets pitched, 0 local destination, 0 multicast
Bcast:   0 received, 625 sent
Sent:    625 generated, 0 forwarded
         0 encapsulation failed, 0 no route
SAP:     0 SAP requests, 0 SAP replies, 0 servers
         0 SAP advertisements received, 0 sent
         0 SAP flash updates sent, 0 SAP format errors
RIP:     0 RIP requests, 0 RIP replies, 3 routes
         0 RIP advertisements received, 604 sent
         9 RIP flash updates sent, 0 RIP format errors
Echo:    Rcvd 0 requests, 0 replies
         Sent 0 requests, 0 replies
         0 unknown: 0 no socket, 0 filtered, 0 no helper
         0 SAPs throttled, freed NDB len 0
Watchdog:
         0 packets received, 0 replies spoofed
Queue lengths:
         IPX input: 0, SAP 0, RIP 0, GNS 0
         SAP throttling length: 0/(no limit), 0 nets pending lost route reply
         Delayed process creation: 0
EIGRP:   Total received 0, sent 0
         Updates received 0, sent 0
         Queries received 0, sent 0
         Replies received 0, sent 0
         SAPs received 0, sent 0
NLSP:    Level-1 Hellos received 0, sent 0
        PTP Hello received 0, sent 0
         Level-1 LSPs received 0, sent 0
         LSP Retransmissions: 0
         LSP checksum errors received: 0
         LSP HT=0 checksum errors received: 0
         Level-1 CSNPs received 0, sent 0
         Level-1 PSNPs received 0, sent 0
         Level-1 DR Elections: 0
         Level-1 SPF Calculations: 0
         Level-1 Partial Route Calculations: 0
RouterB>
```

> RouterB has sent 625 broadcasts and 9 RIP updates. No broadcast or RIP updates have been received. On a production network, this may indicate a problem with a neighbor router. In this case, RouterA, the closest neighbor to RouterB, had its DCE/DTE cable to RouterC removed.

Figure 2-26   Show IPX traffic command output

Another useful monitoring command is the show ipx interface command. When issuing this command, you can use the show ipx interface command to display all IPX interfaces and their configurations, or you can specify a single interface. For example, if you want to monitor IPX on Ethernet0, you use the show ipx interface e0 command. Figure 2-27 shows the result of this command on RouterB.

```
RouterB>show ipx interface e0 ◄─────────────────────────────────┐
    Ethernet0 is up, line protocol is up                         │
    IPX address is 200.0060.474f.6506, SAP [up] line-up, RIPPQ: 0, SAPPQ:│ 0
    Delay of this IPX network, in ticks is 1 throughput 0 link delay 0   │
    IPXWAN processing not enabled on this interface.             │
    IPX SAP update interval is 1 minute(s)            ┌──────────────────┐
    IPX type 20 propagation packet forwarding is disabled│This command will │
    Incoming access list is not set                  │display all IPX   │
    Outgoing access list is not set                  │parameters associated│
    IPX helper access list is not set                │with this interface.│
    SAP GNS processing enabled, delay 0 ms, output filter list is not set
    SAP Input filter list is not set
    SAP Output filter list is not set
    SAP Router filter list is not set
    Input filter list is not set
    Output filter list is not set
    Router filter list is not set
    Netbios Input host access list is not set
    Netbios Input bytes access list is not set
    Netbios Output host access list is not set
    Netbios Output bytes access list is not set
    Updates each 60 seconds, aging multiples RIP: 3 SAP: 3
    SAP interpacket delay is 55 ms, maximum size is 480 bytes
    RIP interpacket delay is 55 ms, maximum size is 432 bytes
    IPX accounting is disabled
    IPX fast switching is configured (enabled)
    RIP packets received 0, RIP packets sent 548
    SAP packets received 0, SAP packets sent 4
RouterB>
```

Figure 2-27   Output from the show ipx interface e0 command

The final show command—show ipx servers—allows you to view all IPX servers on a network. It takes entries from a router's SAP tables and builds a list of all available services. Network administrators use this command to verify that their NetWare servers are advertising the services that have been configured for clients to access.

The debug ipx command gives network administrators the ability to do real-time monitoring of IPX traffic across a router. Like the debug ip command, the debug ipx command can produce an enormous amount of router overhead. Debug ipx is so powerful that it is only accessible in privileged mode. You should only use this command for troubleshooting; do not leave it on continuously. If the debug ipx command is on continuously, it is possible that your router may not be able to handle the normal routing of packets. The result is dropped packets and inconsistent network performance.

The router output that follows uses the context-sensitive Help features to display all possible options for the debug ipx command. The final subcommand, debug ipx routing activity, turns on debugging for RIP routing updates and NLSP routing updates. Figure 2-28 shows how to correctly type this command on a router.

```
RouterB>en ◄──────────────────────────────────────────────────────────┐
     Password:                                                          │
RouterB#debug ipx ?◄───────────────────────────────┐    ┌──────────────────────────┐
     compression     IPX compression                │    │ Debug commands are only  │
     eigrp           IPX EIGRP packets              │    │ available in privileged  │
     ipxwan          Novell IPXWAN events           │    │ mode. The en, short for  │
     nlsp            IPX NLSP activity              │    │ enable, command allows you│
     packet          IPX activity                   │    │ to enter privileged mode.│
     redistribution  IPX route redistribution       │    └──────────────────────────┘
     routing         IPX RIP routing information     │
     sap             IPX Service Advertisement information
     spoof           IPX and SPX Spoofing activity
                                                          ┌──────────────────────────┐
     RouterB#debug ipx routing ? ◄──────────────┐        │ You can use the help      │
     activity   IPX RIP routing activity         │        │ command ? to find the exact│
     events     IPX RIP routing events           │        │ syntax of a debug command.│
                                                          └──────────────────────────┘
     RouterB#debug ipx routing activity◄─────┐
     IPX routing debugging is on ◄───────────┤   ┌──────────────────────────┐
     RouterB#                                 └───│ The result of the debug ipx│
     RouterB#                                     │ routing activity command is│
     IPXRIP: positing full update to 200.ffff.ffff.ffff via Ethernet0 (broadcast)
     IPXRIP: positing full update to 2F.ffff.ffff.ffff via Ethernet0.1 (broadcast)
     IPXRIP: positing full update to 300.ffff.ffff.ffff via Serial1 (broadcast)
     IPXRIP: sending update to 200.ffff.ffff.ffff via Ethernet0
     IPXRIP: sending update to 2F.ffff.ffff.ffff via Ethernet0.1
     IPXRIP: src=200.0060.474f.6506, dst=200.ffff.ffff.ffff, packet sent
         network 2F, hops 1,  delay 2
         network 300, hops 1,  delay 2
     IPXRIP: sending update to 300.ffff.ffff.ffff via Serial1
     IPXRIP: src=2F.0060.474f.6506, dst=2F.ffff.ffff.ffff, packet sent
         network 200, hops 1,  delay 2
         network 300, hops 1,  delay 2
     IPXRIP: src=300.0060.474f.6506, dst=300.ffff.ffff.ffff, packet sent
         network 2F, hops 1,  delay 7
         network 200, hops 1,  delay 7
RouterB#
```

Figure 2-28   Using the debug ipx routing activity command

Debugging helps you determine what routes are being sent to neighboring routers. To turn off IPX debugging, you issue the no debug ipx routing activity command.

The extended ping command, available only in privileged mode, allows users to ping IPX addresses across the network. To determine the IPX address of a destination router port, you can use the show ipx interface command at the destination router. The show cdp neighbor detail command also lists the IPX address of neighbor routers. Figure 2-29 shows the use of the extended ping command. Note that an exclamation point signifies a success response to the ping request.

2

```
RouterB#ping ◄──────────────────────┐        ┌──────────────────────────────┐
Protocol [ip]: ipx                   │        │ The extended ping command,   │
Target IPX address:300.0000.0c8d.e633│        │ available only in privileged mode,│
Repeat count [5]:                    │        │ can be used to ping IPX addresses.│
Datagram size [100]:                 │        └──────────────────────────────┘
Timeout in seconds [2]:              │        ┌──────────────────────────────┐
Verbose [n]:                         │        │ The exclamation points (!) indicate│
Novell Standard Echo [n]:            │        │ five successful replies from the│
Type escape sequence to abort.       │        │ destination host.            │
Sending 5, 100-byte IPX cisco Echoes to 300.0000.0c8d.e633, timeout is 2
seconds

!!!!!◄───────────────────────────────┘
Success rate is 100 percent (5/5), round-trip min/avg/max = 36/36/36 ms
RouterB#
```

Figure 2-29 Extended ping command

Just like a typical ping, the extended ipx ping verifies that IPX address 300.0000.0c8d.e633 exists and is functional.

CHAPTER SUMMARY

This chapter introduces you to the IPX/SPX protocol stack. The IPX/SPX protocol stack, like TCP/IP, contains many separate protocols that work together to accomplish the task of network communication. Layer 3 protocols in the IPX/SPX protocol stack include IPX, RIP, and NLSP. Layer 4 protocols such as SPX provide connection-oriented services for the connectionless IPX. Also, as with most protocol stacks, upper-layer protocols such as NCP and SAP exist in IPX/SPX to support particular client/server functions. In particular, SAP allows servers to broadcast available services and clients to request services. The GNS request is an example of a SAP request.

This chapter also describes IPX/SPX addressing. IPX/SPX addresses are 80-bit addresses in a network.node format. Thirty-two bits of the address are reserved for the network portion of the address. Network administrators assign this portion of the address. The MAC address becomes the node portion, consisting of 48 bits. IPX/SPX addresses usually appear in hexadecimal.

Another important concept this chapter covers is Data Link layer frame formats. Novell specifies four Data Link layer formats: 802.3, 802.2, and Ethernet_II, and Ethernet_snap. The Cisco IOS refers to these formats as novell-ether, sap, arpa, and snap.

Servers and routers use SAP advertisements to build SAP tables of all IPX/SPX services on the network. SAP broadcasts occur every 60 seconds by default. Routers do not by default pass SAP broadcasts. Instead, each router builds a SAP table from all SAP advertisements it sees and passes that table to its IPX/SPX-enabled neighbor routers every 60 seconds. This process reduces the number of broadcasts that would otherwise have to be passed over slow WAN links.

Network administrators use two steps to configuring IPX/SPX on a router: (1) enable IPX routing with the ipx routing command, and (2) enable IPX on each interface with the ipx network [*network #*] encapsulation [*encapsulation keyword*] command. If necessary, the ipx maximum-paths command can be used to enable load balancing on an IPX network. By default, load balancing is not configured.

The final area this chapter covers is IPX monitoring. Common monitoring commands include show ipx route, show ipx interface, show ipx servers, debug ipx (various subcommands exist for this command), and the extended ping command.

KEY TERMS

encapsulation — The process of wrapping Protocol Data Units from upper-layer protocols into a Data Link layer format; common frame types are 802.3, 802.2, and Ethernet_II.

Get Nearest Server (GNS) — A SAP request sent by clients; attempts to locate the nearest NetWare server.

High-level Data Link Control (HDLC) — The default Data Link layer encapsulation for all Cisco serial interfaces.

Internetwork Packet Exchange (IPX) — Predominantly a layer 3 protocol used by the IPX/SPX protocol stack for routing packets along the shortest path in an IPX internetwork.

Internetwork Packet Exchange/Sequenced Packet Exchange (IPX/SPX) — Protocol stack developed by Novell from the Xerox Network System protocol stack.

IPX/SPX addresses — Eighty-bit addresses consisting of a 32-bit network portion and a 48-bit node portion; the network administrator arbitrarily assigns the network portion; the MAC address of the node makes up the node portion of the address; addresses normally appear in hexadecimal format.

load balancing — The ability of a router to distribute packets among multiple same cost paths.

metrics — Measurements used by routing protocols to determine the best path between multiple networks; examples include hop count, ticks, load, and reliability.

NetWare Core Protocol (NCP) — Upper-layer protocol that handles most of the client/server interaction on a Novell NetWare network.

NetWare Link State Protocol (NLSP) — Layer 3, link state routing protocol built into the IPX/SPX protocol stack.

Routing Information Protocol (RIP) — Layer 3, distance vector routing protocol built into the IPX/SPX protocol stack; not the same RIP found in TCP/IP; sends out routing table updates every 60 seconds.

Sequenced Packet Exchange (SPX) — Layer 4, connection-oriented protocol used to provide guaranteed delivery services to IPX.

Service Advertisement Protocol (SAP) — Upper-layer protocol used by IPX/SPX servers to advertise available services; also used by clients to discover what services are available on the local segment.

subinterfaces — Logical interfaces used to add multiple networks and multiple frame types to a single physical interface; a replacement for the older secondary command.

ticks —1/18-second time counts used to determine the desirability of a particular route.

REVIEW QUESTIONS

1. If you are running the 802.2 frame type on your network, which Cisco encapsulation type would you define on your router ports?

   a. arpa

   b. snap

   c. sap

   d. novell-ether

2. Which layer 3 protocol in the IPX/SPX protocol stack is connectionless and finds the best path to route packets throughout an internetwork?

   a. IPX

   b. SPX

   c. NCP

   d. SAP

3. Which command would you enter in global configuration mode to turn on IPX routing?

   a. route ipx

   b. show ipx route

   c. routing ipx

   d. ipx routing

4. How often are SAP advertisements broadcast by default?

   a. every 30 seconds

   b. every 60 seconds

   c. never

   d. one per client GNS request

5. Which monitoring command displays IPX routing tables for a router?

    a. extended ping

    b. show ipx traffic

    c. show ipx intefaces

    d. show ipx route

6. If you are running IPX over a serial interface, what is the default encapsulation setting?

    a. hdlc

    b. novell-ether

    c. serial

    d. snap

7. Which of the following shows the correct command sequence for adding the network 3f with Ethernet_II encapsulation to a subinterface of Ethernet0?

    a. int e0.1, ipx network 3f encap arpa sec snap

    b. int e0, ipx network 3f encap arpa

    c. int e0.1, ipx network 3f encap arpa

    d. int e0.1, encap arpa

8. Which of the following monitoring commands displays information concerning the number and types of IPX packets sent and received?

    a. show ipx route

    b. show ipx traffic

    c. debug ipx routing activity

    d. show ipx interface

9. The RIP protocol found in IPX/SPX broadcasts routing table information every _____.

    a. 60 seconds

    b. 35 seconds

    c. 2 minutes

    d. 30 seconds

10. In the address 2bc4.0020.7811.4a62, which portion is the network and which portion is the node address? (Choose all correct answers.)

    a. network 2bc4.0020

    b. node 0020.7811.4a62

    c. network 0020.7811.4a62

    d. network 2bc4

2

11. What is the default frame encapsulation type on Ethernet interfaces? (Choose all correct answers.)

   a. 802.3

   b. arpa

   c. novell–ether

   d. snap

12. What command would you use to enable load balancing between three possible routes on an IPX/SPX network?

   a. ipx routing

   b. ipx maximum-paths 3

   c. ipx maximum 3

   d. route ipx maximum-paths 3

13. Which of the following correctly shows the sequence of commands to add IPX network 300 with 802.2 encapsulation to interface Ethernet0?

   a. int e0, encap arpa, ipx network 300

   b. int e0, ipx network 300 encap arpa

   c. int e0.1, ipx network 300 encap sap

   d. int e0, ipx network 300, encap sap

14. You can add a second IPX network and encapsulation to a physical interface with the secondary command. True or False?

15. The routing protocols built into IPX/SPX are _____. (Choose all correct answers.)

   a. OSPF

   b. NLSP

   c. RIP

   d. IGRP

16. Cisco routers cannot respond to GNS requests from IPX/SPX clients. True or False?

17. Which of the following router prompts signifies subinterface configuration mode?

   a. RouterB(config-subif)#

   b. RouterB(config-if)#

   c. Router(config)#

   d. Router#

18. Servers and routers use which of the following protocols to send out tables of available IPX/SPX services?

   a. RIP

   b. NLSP

   c. SAP

   d. SNAP

19. What is the Cisco IOS terminology for Ethernet_snap encapsulation?

   a. novell-ether

   b. sap

   c. arpa

   d. snap

20. From which of the following router prompts can you issue the extended ping command for ipx?

   a. RouterB>

   b. RouterB(config)#

   c. RouterB#

   d. RouterB(ping)#

CASE PROJECTS

1. Parmer and Smith Inc. have hired you to configure their new network infrastructure. They are currently running both Netware 3.12 servers and Netware 4.11 servers. After the upgrade of their routers, no one can access resources on the Netware 3.12 servers. What could be causing this problem?

2. Drake and Associates needs someone to troubleshoot problems within their predominantly IPX network. What commands could you use to monitor and troubleshoot their network? Also, briefly describe what each monitoring and troubleshooting command tells you about the network.

3. A customer is considering upgrading his network to Cisco routers and equipment. Before he does this, he wants to learn how Cisco routers deal with SAP tables and SAP updates. Create a short memo that details how Cisco routers deal with SAP tables and SAP updates.

3

ACCESS LISTS

After reading this chapter and completing the exercises you will be able to:

- ◆ Describe the usage and rules of access lists
- ◆ Establish standard IP access lists
- ◆ Produce extended IP access lists
- ◆ Develop standard IPX access lists
- ◆ Create extended IPX access lists
- ◆ Define IPX SAP filters
- ◆ Apply access lists to interfaces
- ◆ Monitor and verify access lists

In this chapter, you will learn how to create and apply access lists to control both traffic flow and network security. In the process, you will review the use and rules of access lists. Then, you will be introduced to the creation of standard and extended IP access lists. In addition, you will read about how to create IPX standard access lists, extended IPX access lists, and SAP filters. After learning the proper techniques for creating access lists, you will review how to apply such lists to router interfaces. Finally, you will learn how to monitor and verify access lists.

ACCESS LISTS: USAGE AND RULES

Network traffic flow and security influence the design and management of computer networks. Fortunately, access lists, which are built into the Cisco IOS, solve many of the problems associated with these two tasks. **Access lists** are permit or deny statements that filter traffic based on the source address, destination address, and protocol type of a packet. They are available for IP, IPX, AppleTalk, and many other protocols.

Access List Usage

You can create a standard access list that examines a packet for the packet's source header information. For instance, RouterA can use an access list to deny access from Network 4 to Network 1; both networks are shown in Figure 3-1. If a packet from Network 4 arrives at the interface where you placed the access list, the router examines the packet and uses the access list to determine if it needs to discard the packet.

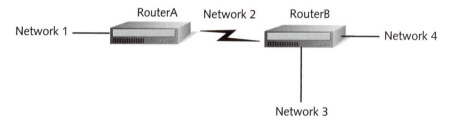

Figure 3-1   Sample network

With the following conceptual syntax, you create the standard access list to block access from Network 4 to Network 1:

    access-list 1 deny Network 4

    access-list 1 permit any

The access list ends with an **implicit deny any**, which blocks all packets that do not meet the requirements of the access list. Access-list 1, if applied to the interface of RouterA connected to Network 1, blocks only the traffic coming from Network 4 to Network 1. If you wanted to deny traffic from Network 3 and Network 4, the conceptual access list syntax would then become the following:

    access-list 1 deny Network 3

    access-list 1 deny Network 4

    access-list 1 permit any

The above access-list statements are not the exact Cisco IOS syntax for the access list command. Actual IOS syntax will be covered later in the chapter.

3

The final permit any statement is necessary because all access lists in the Cisco IOS end with an implicit deny any. If you apply the access list to the interface of RouterA that is connected to Network 1, it blocks traffic from Networks 3 and 4, while allowing all other network traffic to access Network 1.

With careful planning, you can create access lists that control which traffic crosses particular links, and which segments of your network will have access to others. In other words, you can control traffic flow and security. Security is enhanced because you can permit or deny particular networks access to parts of your network. In the example above, Network 4 may be a student network, and Network 1 may be an administrative network. The first list stops students from Network 4 from accessing any resources in Network 1, the administrative network.

 Although access lists can help with network security, they do not take the place of more advanced security measures, such as firewalls. Access lists, combined with dedicated firewalls at the edge of your network, provide the greatest security.

Problems with Access Lists

One of the most common problems associated with access lists is a lack of planning. Before you even begin the process of creating access lists on your router, you must plan exactly what needs to be filtered and where it needs to be filtered. Careful planning prior to the creation of lists can cut down on simple logic mistakes, which commonly occur when you do not think through the effects of your actions.

Another troublesome area is the sequential nature in which you must enter the list into the router. You cannot move individual statements once they are entered. When making changes, you must remove the list, using the no access-list command, and then retype the commands. Many network administrators simplify this time-consuming process by creating their access lists in a simple word processor, such as Notepad, and then copying and pasting the access list into the router configuration. Using this method, an administrator can create a perfect access list (free of typos) and then apply the list to any single router or a group of routers. This allows a type-once, use-many scenario that reduces errors and the time necessary to configure a router.

Finally, many new network administrators find themselves in trouble when they Telnet into a router and begin applying an access list. Access lists begin working the second they are applied to an interface. It is very possible that many new administrators will find themselves inadvertently blocked from the very router on which they are applying an access list. While this is not a serious problem when the router is in the same building as the administrator, it is a serious problem when the router is in another city and thus physically inaccessible.

Fortunately, the reload command can save you from a long car ride or an embarrassing phone call to a local administrator to explain the problem. With the reload command, an administrator can schedule the router to reload in a certain number of minutes, hours, or even days. For access list configuration, you probably want to schedule the reload to the granularity of minutes or hours. The syntax for the reload command is reload in *[hh:]mm* (reloads in a certain number of hours or minutes) or reload at *hh:mm [month day | day month]* (reloads at a certain time on a certain date). For example, before modifying or adding access lists to a remote router, an administrator could type the following command:

RouterB#reload in 30

If an access list locks the administrator out, the router would reload in 30 minutes with a running-config that did not contain the access-list that blocked the administrator's access. Note, however, that in this case, the reload command will only work if you do not copy the running-config to the startup-config while working with the access lists. If you create and apply the lists and they have the intended results, you can cancel the scheduled reload with the reload cancel command.

Access List Rules

Regardless of the type of access list you create, standard or extended, you must follow certain rules. For instance, you must create and apply access lists sequentially. Also, as stated earlier, access lists always end with an implicit deny.

The following example shows the structure of a standard IP access list. The router applies each line in the order in which you type it into the access list:

RouterA(config)#access-list 1 deny 172.22.5.2 0.0.0.0

RouterA(config)#access-list 1 deny 172.22.5.3 0.0.0.0

RouterA(config)# access-list 1 permit any

The previous example is a standard IP access list that denies the hosts 172.22.5.2 and 172.22.5.3, while allowing all other traffic. The list is applied sequentially from the top down as the router checks the packets arriving at the interface where this access list is applied, in order to check if the packets match the permit and deny statements.

In the process of applying access lists, the router first checks an arriving packet to determine if it matches the deny 172.22.5.2 0.0.0.0 statement. If it does, the router discards the packet. If it does not, the router applies the second statement, deny 172.22.5.3 0.0.0.0. If the packet matches the second statement, the router discards the packet. Once again, if the packet does not meet the rules of the first two lines, the router applies the final permit any statement, and the packet is forwarded through the interface.

If you want to add another deny line to this list, you can go back into global configuration mode and do so. Because all new lines are added to the end of the list, adding this line

RouterA(config)# access-list 1 deny 172.22.5.5 0.0.0.0 will produce the following list:

access-list 1 deny 172.22.5.2 0.0.0.0

access-list 1 deny 172.22.5.3 0.0.0.0

access-list 1 permit any

access-list 1 deny 172.22.5.5 0.0.0.0

The new line is appended to the end of access list 1. The router checks the packet against the first three statements. Once the packet matches one of the statements, the router discards or forwards it based on that match. Since the third statement says that all packets are permitted and can be forwarded, the existence of the fourth line has no effect; a packet from 172.22.5.5 would be forwarded before it ever reached the deny 172.22.5.5 0.0.0.0 statement. To fix this problem, you must remove the access-list completely and recreate it using the correct sequence.

If you wish to remove an access-list, you use the no access-list *[list #]* command. For example, to remove the above list, you enter global configuration mode and type the no access-list command. Figure 3-2 shows the correct procedure for typing this command.

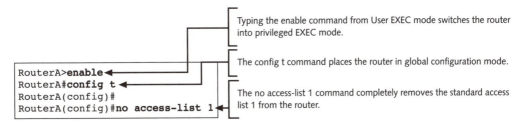

Figure 3-2   No access-list command

This command will remove the entire list. You cannot remove a particular line in an access list. As a general rule, you should place first in the list the lines with the most potential matches so that packets will not undergo unnecessary processing. You should also avoid unnecessarily long access lists. A very long access list will consume large sums of CPU processing time and could cause your router to act as a bottleneck on your network.

In order to ease the administrative load associated with access lists, Cisco recommends using a text editor to create them. You can then easily make changes to the list and apply it to the router configuration using copy and paste. You must place a no access-list *[list #]* command as the first line of the text file. This command allows you to completely remove an access list from a router. If you don't use this command, the lines of the access list in the text file will be appended to the end of the existing list when you paste it into the configuration.

After you create access lists, you must apply them to interfaces so they can begin filtering traffic. You apply a list as either an outgoing or an incoming filter. To determine how to apply the list, you have to look through the eyes of "The man in the router." Traffic coming in to the man in the router, through any of the interfaces, is considered inbound and needs to be filtered using incoming traffic filters, as shown in Figure 3-3.

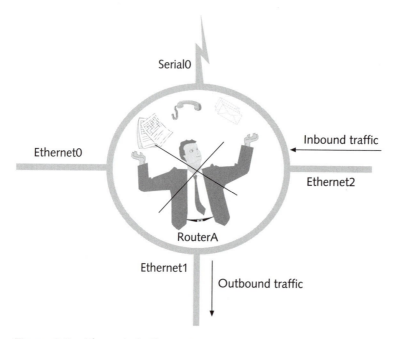

Figure 3-3   The man in the router

You would apply the access list to an interface with the following command:

ip access-group 1 in (the one in this example represents the access-list numbered 1)

Once traffic gets to the "The man in the router," he must push it out to one of the interfaces. Access lists to block his outward delivery must be applied as outbound filters. You would use this command to set an outbound access list filter:

ip access-group 1 out (again, the 1 specifies that you are applying access list 1 to the interface)

Outbound is the default, if the direction is not specified in the command. The final rule that access lists must follow states that an interface cannot have more than one inbound or outbound list, per protocol, assigned to it. This means that a router can have no more than one inbound Internet Protocol (IP) access list and one outbound applied at the same time. Multiple lists are allowed only if the lists are different protocols.

In summary, all access lists follow these rules:

- Routers apply lists sequentially in the order in which you type them into the router.

- Routers apply lists to packets sequentially, from the top down, one line at a time.

- Packets are processed only until a match is made and then they are acted upon based on the access list criteria contained in access list statements.

- Lists always end with an implicit deny. Routers discard any packets that do not match any of the access list statements.

- Access lists must be applied to an interface as either inbound our outbound traffic filters.

- Only one list, per protocol, per direction can be applied to an interface.

Now that you understand the basic rules of access lists, you need to understand specific types of access lists. The main types of access lists you will learn about are standard and extended IP and IPX lists.

3

STANDARD IP ACCESS LISTS

Standard IP access lists filter network traffic based on the source IP address. Using a standard IP access list, you can filter traffic by a host IP, subnet, or a network address. In order to configure standard IP access lists, you must create the list and then apply it to an interface using the syntax following this paragraph. A detailed explanation of each item is contained in the subsequent bulleted list. The brackets in each command syntax are not part of the command; they group items that are replaced within each specific entry.

access-list *[list #] [permit | deny] [source address] [source wildcard mask]*

- *[list #]*: Standard IP access lists are represented by a number in the range of 1–99 (in IOS versions 11.2 and greater, they can also be represented by text names).

- *[permit | deny]*: Used to specify the nature of the access list line. It is either a permit or a deny statement.

- *[source address]*: The IP address of the source

- *[source wildcard mask]*: A **wildcard mask**, or **inverse mask**, applied to determine which bits of the source address are significant

Wildcard masks are one of the most important concepts in IP access lists. Routers use them to determine which bits in an address will be significant. Unlike subnet masks, 0's are placed in bit positions deemed significant, and 1's are placed in positions that are not significant. Consider these addresses and wildcard masks:

Table 3-1 Wildcard mask examples

IP Address	Wildcard Mask	Result
172.22.5.2	0.0.0.0	All bit positions must match exactly. Therefore, the access list line will only be applied to host 172.22.5.2.
172.22.5.0	0.0.0.255	Bit positions in the first three octets must match exactly, but the last octet can be any valid number. The access list line will apply to all hosts in the 172.22.5.0 subnet.
172.22.1.0	0.0.254.255	The first two octets must match exactly, as must the least significant bit position in the third octet. The last octet can be any valid number. This mask would allow you to permit or deny odd subnets from the 172.22.0.0 major network. The example assumes a subnet mask of 255.255.255.0 for a Class B network.

To understand wildcard masking, you may find it helpful to examine the addresses in binary format. Consider the example in Figure 3-4, which shows a wildcard mask that forces the packet to match all four octets of the source address.

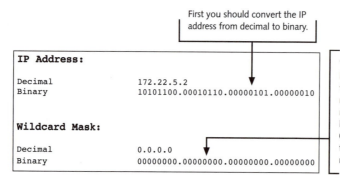

Figure 3-4   Wildcard masking example matching a single host

Since 0's represent significant bits, you can see that in Figure 3-4 a wildcard mask of 0.0.0.0 requires that the source address match exactly. The second example, in Figure 3-5, shows how you permit or deny an entire subnet.

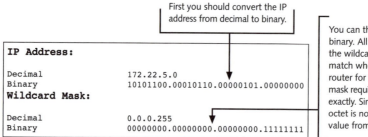

Figure 3-5   Wildcard masking example matching a complete subnet

Again, if you remember that 0's represent significant bits, you see that the first three octets must match. The final octet of the wildcard mask consists of 1s and signifies that the value of the fourth octet is not significant.

The final example of wildcard masking is a bit tougher and requires examining two IP addresses to fully understand it. Figure 3-6 illustrates the first address, an odd subnet.

3

This wildcard mask requires that the first two octets and the final bit position of the third octet match the IP address in the access list. The values in the last octet are not significant. Since the final bit positions in the third octet of the IP address in the access list are turned on (set to 1), all packets that the access list will permit or deny must have a 1 in the final bit position of the third octet.

```
IP Address:

IP address in access list in decimal    172.22.1.0
IP address in access list in binary     10101100.00010110.00000001.00000000


Wildcard Mask:

Decimal                                 0.0.254.255
Binary                                  00000000.00000000.11111110.11111111
```

Figure 3-6 Wildcard masking example

In this example, the first two octets must match exactly. Also, the final bit place in the third octet must match; it must be a 1! Therefore, an access list that states access-list 1 permit 172.22.1.0 0.0.254.255 will allow traffic from any odd-numbered subnet to pass. Even-numbered subnets are blocked because their last bit position in the third octet is a 0.

If you use a source of 172.22.1.0 and a wildcard mask of 0.0.254.255, any packet that the list will act upon must have a 1 in the least significant bit position of the third octet. If a packet with the IP address of 172.22.2.1 is examined by the access list in the previous paragraph, the router ignores it because the least significant bit of the third octet (see below) is a 0, not a 1. Figure 3-7 shows why this is true.

Since the least significant bit positions do not match, any address within the subnet 172.22.2.0 is out of the required range of the access list and is thus discarded (or ignored, depending on the function of the access list).

This wildcard mask requires that the first two octets and the final bit position of the third octet match the IP address in the access list. The values in the last octet are not significant. Since the final bit position in the third octet of the examined IP address and the IP address in the access list do not match (one is a 0 and the other is a 1), any line in an access list with a permit or deny 172.22.1.0 0.0.254.255 would not apply to the address 172.22.2.1. In fact, no even subnet could be affected because all even subnets would have a value of 0 in the last bit position of the third octet.

```
Decimal of examined IP address      172.22.2.1

Binary of examined IP address       10101100.00010110.00000010.00000001

IP address in access list:          10101100.00010110.00000001.00000000

Wildcard mask:                      00000000.00000000.11111110.11111111
```

Figure 3-7 Wildcard masking example without match

Standard IP Access List Examples

Standard IP access lists permit or deny packets based only upon the source address. These addresses can be a single host address, a subnet address, or a full network address. Consider the IP network in Figure 3-8:

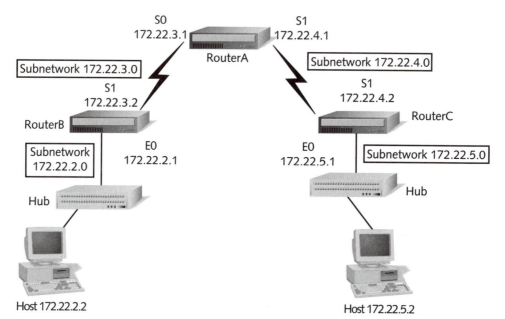

Figure 3-8   Sample IP Network

Using the sample network in Figure 3-8, you can create a standard IP access list that blocks host 172.22.5.2 from accessing subnet 172.22.2.0. Figure 3-9 shows the commands you would type to accomplish this task.

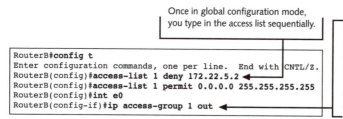

Once in global configuration mode, you type in the access list sequentially.

```
RouterB#config t
Enter configuration commands, one per line.  End with CNTL/Z.
RouterB(config)#access-list 1 deny 172.22.5.2
RouterB(config)#access-list 1 permit 0.0.0.0 255.255.255.255
RouterB(config)#int e0
RouterB(config-if)#ip access-group 1 out
```

To apply a list, the router must be in interface configuration mode. In this example, the access list will be applied to Ethernet0 on RouterB. The ip access-group 1 out command applies access-list 1 (created above) to the e0 interface as an outbound access-list.

Figure 3-9   Creating a standard IP access list

In global configuration mode, you add each line of the access list sequentially and then apply it to an interface in order to cause it to take affect. In this example, the deny statement does not include a source wildcard mask, because the default mask for standard IP access lists is 0.0.0.0, which is the exact mask needed in the example. It is also possible to replace the 0.0.0.0 255.255.255.255 entry, which represents all hosts and all networks, with the **any** keyword. Once the list is applied to RouterB's Ethernet0 interface, packets from 172.22.5.2 will be blocked from going out the interface.

Correct placement of a list is imperative. If the list were placed on RouterB's S1 interface as an inbound list, it would work with the sample network. However, if RouterB had another Ethernet interface, as shown in Figure 3-10, placing the access list on S1 would inadvertently block traffic to the second Ethernet interface, e1.

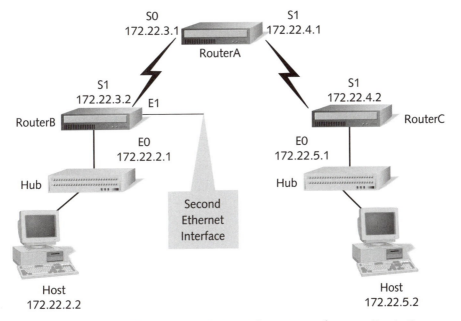

Figure 3-10 Sample IP network with two Ethernet interfaces on RouterB

Applying the previous list as an inbound access list on S1 blocks all traffic from host 172.22.5.2 to other ports on RouterB. Since you only want to block access to subnet 172.22.2.0, this is not the correct way to apply the list; you should apply the standard IP access list as close to the destination as possible. Otherwise, you will inadvertently block access to portions of your network.

To view the access lists defined on your router, use the show access-lists command. Since this is an IP access list, you could also use the show ip access-lists command. Figure 3-11 shows the correct procedures to type in both commands.

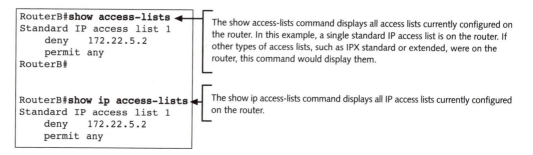

```
RouterB#show access-lists
Standard IP access list 1
    deny    172.22.5.2
    permit any
RouterB#
```
The show access-lists command displays all access lists currently configured on the router. In this example, a single standard IP access list is on the router. If other types of access lists, such as IPX standard or extended, were on the router, this command would display them.

```
RouterB#show ip access-lists
Standard IP access list 1
    deny    172.22.5.2
    permit any
```
The show ip access-lists command displays all IP access lists currently configured on the router.

Figure 3-11   Show access-lists and show ip access-lists commands

RouterB has one standard IP access list defined on it. To view which interfaces have IP access lists set, use the show ip interface command. Your router will return a list of all interfaces and details about which access lists are applied, inbound and outbound. For the sake of brevity, only Ethernet0 is displayed in Figure 3-12.

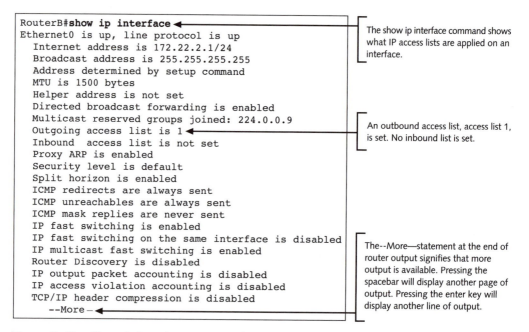

```
RouterB#show ip interface
Ethernet0 is up, line protocol is up
    Internet address is 172.22.2.1/24
    Broadcast address is 255.255.255.255
    Address determined by setup command
    MTU is 1500 bytes
    Helper address is not set
    Directed broadcast forwarding is enabled
    Multicast reserved groups joined: 224.0.0.9
    Outgoing access list is 1
    Inbound  access list is not set
    Proxy ARP is enabled
    Security level is default
    Split horizon is enabled
    ICMP redirects are always sent
    ICMP unreachables are always sent
    ICMP mask replies are never sent
    IP fast switching is enabled
    IP fast switching on the same interface is disabled
    IP multicast fast switching is enabled
    Router Discovery is disabled
    IP output packet accounting is disabled
    IP access violation accounting is disabled
    TCP/IP header compression is disabled
      --More--
```
The show ip interface command shows what IP access lists are applied on an interface.

An outbound access list, access list 1, is set. No inbound list is set.

The --More--statement at the end of router output signifies that more output is available. Pressing the spacebar will display another page of output. Pressing the enter key will display another line of output.

Figure 3-12   Show ip interface command

If, for some reason, you decide that an access list needs to be removed from an interface, you can remove it with the no ip access-group [*list #*] command, as shown in Figure 3-13.

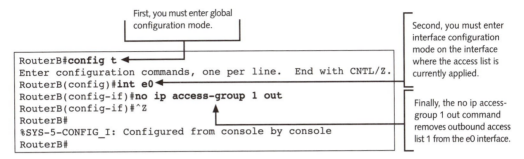

First, you must enter global configuration mode.

Second, you must enter interface configuration mode on the interface where the access list is currently applied.

Finally, the no ip access-group 1 out command removes outbound access list 1 from the e0 interface.

Figure 3-13   Removing an access list from an interface

If you type the show ip interface command, it will show that access list 1 is no longer an outbound access list. Figure 3-14 displays the results of the show ip interface command after you type the no ip access-group 1 out command.

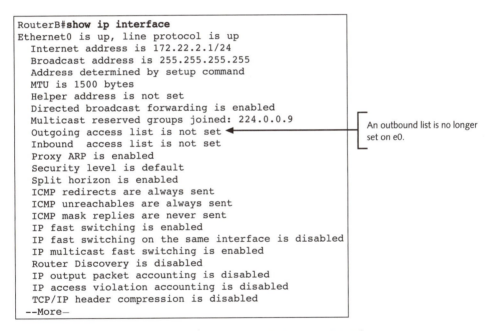

An outbound list is no longer set on e0.

Figure 3-14   Show ip interface after removal of access list 1 from e0

Now, assume that instead of blocking a single host from subnet 172.22.5.0, you want to block all traffic from this subnet to subnet 172.22.2.0, using a standard IP access list. To do this, you need to create the access list and apply the access list to an interface. In this example, you will apply the list as an outbound filter on RouterB's Ethernet0 interface. (Recall that Figure 3-8 shows the network that contains RouterB.) Both parts of the task can be accomplished at the same time; the router output in Figure 3-15 shows both the creation of the list and the application of the list as an outbound filter on Ethernet0.

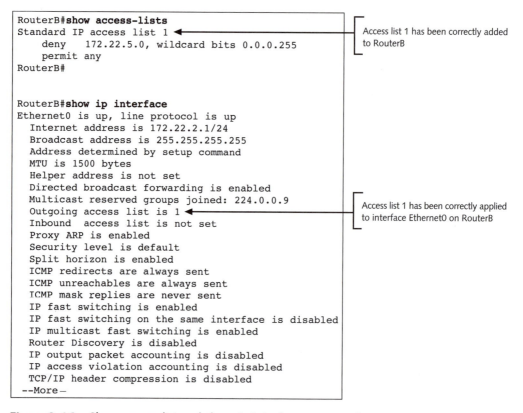

```
RouterB con0 is now available

Press RETURN to get started.

    RouterB>en
    Password:
    RouterB#config t
    Enter configuration commands, one per line.  End with CNTL/Z.
    RouterB(config)#access-list 1 deny 172.22.5.0 0.0.0.255
    RouterB(config)#access-list 1 permit any
    RouterB(config)#int e0
    RouterB(config-if)#ip access-group 1 out
    RouterB(config-if)#^Z
    RouterB#
    %SYS-5-CONFIG_I: Configured from console by console
    RouterB#
```

From global configuration mode, you enter the commands for the access list.

In interface configuration mode, you apply the access list to the e0 interface as an outbound list.

Figure 3-15   Creation and application of standard IP access list

You can use the show access-lists or show ip access-lists command and then the show ip interface command to verify that the list has been entered and applied correctly. Figure 3-16 shows the results of these two commands after the procedures in Figure 3-15 have been performed.

```
RouterB#show access-lists
Standard IP access list 1
    deny   172.22.5.0, wildcard bits 0.0.0.255
    permit any
RouterB#


RouterB#show ip interface
Ethernet0 is up, line protocol is up
  Internet address is 172.22.2.1/24
  Broadcast address is 255.255.255.255
  Address determined by setup command
  MTU is 1500 bytes
  Helper address is not set
  Directed broadcast forwarding is enabled
  Multicast reserved groups joined: 224.0.0.9
  Outgoing access list is 1
  Inbound  access list is not set
  Proxy ARP is enabled
  Security level is default
  Split horizon is enabled
  ICMP redirects are always sent
  ICMP unreachables are always sent
  ICMP mask replies are never sent
  IP fast switching is enabled
  IP fast switching on the same interface is disabled
  IP multicast fast switching is enabled
  Router Discovery is disabled
  IP output packet accounting is disabled
  IP access violation accounting is disabled
  TCP/IP header compression is disabled
--More-
```

Access list 1 has been correctly added to RouterB

Access list 1 has been correctly applied to interface Ethernet0 on RouterB

Figure 3-16   Show access-list and show ip interface commands

Finally, assume that you want to block access to the 172.22.2.0 subnet from all hosts on subnets 172.22.4.0 and 172.22.5.0. You can accomplish this task by entering the commands shown in Figure 3-17.

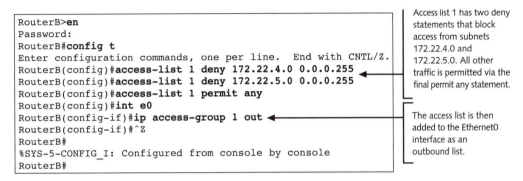

```
RouterB>en
Password:
RouterB#config t
Enter configuration commands, one per line.  End with CNTL/Z.
RouterB(config)#access-list 1 deny 172.22.4.0 0.0.0.255
RouterB(config)#access-list 1 deny 172.22.5.0 0.0.0.255
RouterB(config)#access-list 1 permit any
RouterB(config)#int e0
RouterB(config-if)#ip access-group 1 out
RouterB(config-if)#^Z
RouterB#
%SYS-5-CONFIG_I: Configured from console by console
RouterB#
```

Access list 1 has two deny statements that block access from subnets 172.22.4.0 and 172.22.5.0. All other traffic is permitted via the final permit any statement.

The access list is then added to the Ethernet0 interface as an outbound list.

Figure 3-17   Access list that blocks multiple subnets

Again, you can use the show ip access-list or show access-list commands to verify that the access list was entered correctly. The show ip interface command will show all IP interfaces. If you wish to view a specific interface, you can use show ip interface *[interface#]*. For example, throughout these examples, you could have used the show ip interface e0 command to view just the Ethernet0 interface.

Monitoring Standard IP Access Lists

Three main commands are available for monitoring access lists on your router. The first two, show access-lists and show ip access-lists, display the exact syntax of all access lists and IP access lists, respectively. The show interface or show ip interface command is used to verify that an access list has been successfully applied to an interface. It is a good idea to run each of these commands after creating and applying access lists, to visually inspect and verify that statements were typed in correctly and that the lists will function as entered.

EXTENDED IP ACCESS LISTS

Standard IP access lists are limited to filtering by source IP addresses only. **Extended IP access lists**, on the other hand, can filter by source IP address, destination IP address, protocol type, and application port number. This granularity allows you to design extended IP access lists that permit or deny a single type of IP protocol, such as TCP, and then filter by a particular port of a particular protocol, port 21 or FTP, for example.

In order to configure extended IP access lists, you must create the list and then apply it to an interface using the following syntax (a detailed explanation of each item is contained in the subsequent bulleted list):

access-list *[list #] [permit|deny] [protocol] [source IP address] [source wildcard mask] [destination IP address] [destination wildcard mask] [operator] [port] [log]*

- *[list #]*: Extended IP access lists are represented by a number in the range of 100–199 (in IOS versions 11.2 and greater, they can also be represented by text names).

- *[permit | deny]*: Used to specify the nature of the access list line. It is either a permit or a deny statement.

- *[protocol]*: The IP protocol to be filtered can be IP (which includes all protocols in the TCP/IP suite) TCP, UDP, ICMP, or others.

- *[source address]*: The IP address of the source

- *[source wildcard mask]*: A wildcard mask, or inverse mask, applied to determine which bits of the source address are significant

- *[destination address]*: The IP address of the destination

- *[destination wildcard mask]*: A wildcard mask, or inverse mask, applied to determine which bits of the destination address are significant

- *[operator]*: Can contain lt (less than), gt (greater than), eq (equal to), or neq (not equal to). It is used if an extended list filters by a specific port number.

- *[port]*: If necessary, the port number of the protocol to be filtered

- *[log]*: Turns on logging of access list activity

Extended IP Access List Examples

With extended IP access lists, you should determine what the list will filter before you create the list itself. Using Figure 3-18 as an example, this section discusses how to block host 172.22.5.2 from accessing Web and FTP services on server 172.22.2.2. The first extended IP access list example shows how to block WWW access using the context-sensitive, built-in help features in the Cisco IOS that display all available IOS options. The second example shows just the configuration information needed to create and apply a list that blocks both WWW and FTP access.

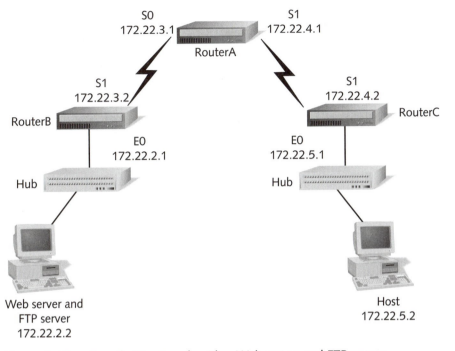

Figure 3-18   Sample IP network with a Web server and FTP server

The configuration begins when you type the enable command to enter global configuration mode on RouterC. Typing "?" at the privileged mode prompt shows all available commands. Figure 3-19 displays all the commands you must type to create the extended IP access list.

```
RouterC>enable
Password:
RouterC#config t
Enter configuration commands, one per line.   End with CNTL/Z.
RouterC(config)#?
Configure commands:
  aaa                         Authentication, Authorization and Accounting.
  access-list                 Add an access list entry
  alias                       Create command alias
  arp                         Set a static ARP entry
  async-bootp                 Modify system bootp parameters
  banner                      Define a login banner
  boot                        Modify system boot parameters
  bridge                      Bridging Group.
  buffers                     Adjust system buffer pool parameters
  busy-message                Display message when connection to host fails
  cdp                         Global CDP configuration subcommands
  chat-script                 Define a modem chat script
  clock                       Configure time-of-day clock
  config-register             Define the configuration register
  default-value               Default character-bits values
  dialer-list                 Create a dialer list entry
  dnsix-dmdp                  Provide DMDP service for DNSIX
  dnsix-nat                   Provide DNSIX service for audit trails
  downward-compatible-config  Generate a configuration compatible with older
                              software
  enable                      Modify enable password parameters
--More —
```

> Typing the ? command displays all commands available from this prompt. Notice that access-list is the second command on the list.

> You then enter the access-list command to begin typing the access list. Again, the ? command reveals correct syntax for the command and possible number ranges for different access lists.

```
RouterC(config)#access-list ?
  <1-99>        IP standard access list
  <100-199>     IP extended access list
  <1000-1099>   IPX SAP access list
  <1100-1199>   Extended 48-bit MAC address access list
  <1200-1299>   IPX summary address access list
  <200-299>     Protocol type-code access list
  <700-799>     48-bit MAC address access list
  <800-899>     IPX standard access list
  <900-999>     IPX extended access list


RouterC(config)#access-list 100 ?
```

> Since this list is an extended IP address, it will be designated with the number 100.

Figure 3-19   Extended IP access list example

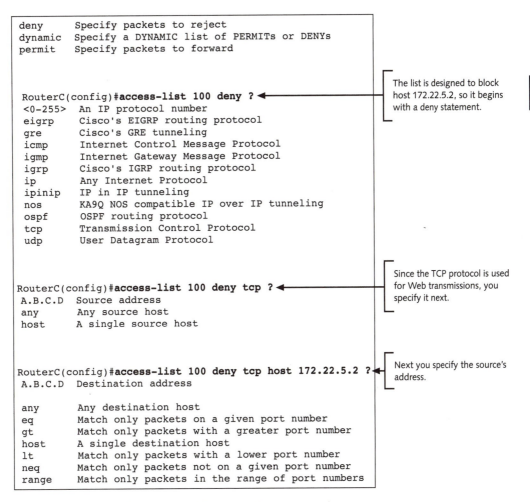

```
deny      Specify packets to reject
dynamic   Specify a DYNAMIC list of PERMITs or DENYs
permit    Specify packets to forward


RouterC(config)#access-list 100 deny ?
<0-255>   An IP protocol number
eigrp     Cisco's EIGRP routing protocol
gre       Cisco's GRE tunneling
icmp      Internet Control Message Protocol
igmp      Internet Gateway Message Protocol
igrp      Cisco's IGRP routing protocol
ip        Any Internet Protocol
ipinip    IP in IP tunneling
nos       KA9Q NOS compatible IP over IP tunneling
ospf      OSPF routing protocol
tcp       Transmission Control Protocol
udp       User Datagram Protocol


RouterC(config)#access-list 100 deny tcp ?
A.B.C.D   Source address
any       Any source host
host      A single source host


RouterC(config)#access-list 100 deny tcp host 172.22.5.2 ?
A.B.C.D   Destination address

any       Any destination host
eq        Match only packets on a given port number
gt        Match only packets with a greater port number
host      A single destination host
lt        Match only packets with a lower port number
neq       Match only packets not on a given port number
range     Match only packets in the range of port numbers
```

The list is designed to block host 172.22.5.2, so it begins with a deny statement.

Since the TCP protocol is used for Web transmissions, you specify it next.

Next you specify the source's address.

Figure 3-19   Extended IP access list example (continued)

Unlike standard IP access lists, extended access lists do not have a default wildcard mask of 0.0.0.0. Therefore, you must specify the wildcard mask for the source IP address. You can use either the standard wildcard mask, or, as in the example in Figure 3-20, you can use short-cuts. The **host** keyword is short for a wildcard mask of 0.0.0.0; in other words, the line will only be applied to packets that match the one source address specified with the host key-word. Figure 3-20 shows a continuation of the access list started in Figure 3-19; note the use of the host keyword.

```
RouterC(config)#access-list 100 deny tcp host 172.22.5.2 host 172.22.2.2 ?
  eq           Match only packets on a given port number
  established  Match established connections
  gt           Match only packets with a greater port number
  log          Log matches against this entry
  lt           Match only packets with a lower port number
  neq          Match only packets not on a given port number
  precedence   Match packets with given precedence value
  range        Match only packets in the range of port numbers
  tos          Match packets with given TOS value
  <cr>



RouterC(config)#access-list 100 deny tcp host 172.22.5.2 host 172.22.2.2 eq ?
  <0-65535>  Port number
  bgp        Border Gateway Protocol (179)
  chargen    Character generator (19)
  cmd        Remote commands (rcmd, 514)
  daytime    Daytime (13)
  discard    Discard (9)
  domain     Domain Name Service (53)
  echo       Echo (7)
  exec       Exec (rsh, 512)
  finger     Finger (79)
  ftp        File Transfer Protocol (21)
  ftp-data   FTP data connections (used infrequently, 20)
  gopher     Gopher (70)
  hostname   NIC hostname server (101)
  ident      Ident Protocol (113)
  irc        Internet Relay Chat (194)
  klogin     Kerberos login (543)
  kshell     Kerberos shell (544)
  login      Login (rlogin, 513)
  lpd        Printer service (515)
  nntp       Network News Transport Protocol (119)
  pop2       Post Office Protocol v2 (109)
  pop3       Post Office Protocol v3 (110)
  smtp       Simple Mail Transport Protocol (25)
  sunrpc     Sun Remote Procedure Call (111)
  syslog     Syslog (514)
  tacacs     TAC Access Control System (49)
  talk       Talk (517)
  telnet     Telnet (23)
  time       Time (37)
  uucp       Unix-to-Unix Copy Program (540)
  whois      Nicname (43)
  www        World Wide Web (HTTP, 80)



RouterC(config)#access-list 100 deny tcp host 172.22.5.2 host 172.22.2.2 eq www
RouterC(config)#access-list 100 permit ip any any
RouterC(config)#
```

> At this point, you have specified your protocol and the source and destination addresses. You must now configure the operator and port. The example list should block WWW and therefore must contain an equal to operator and the WWW port number or name.

> Finally, you place the port number or name and press enter to add the line to the access list.

> The next line you must add is a line that will permit all other IP traffic. If you do not, the implicit deny any at the end of the access list will block all other traffic. Notice that the any keyword is used twice; the first instance corresponds to any source, and the second corresponds to any destination.

Figure 3-20   Extended IP access list example continued

3

Once an extended IP access list is created, it must be applied to an interface, just like a standard list. The difference is the placement of the list. Standard IP access lists examine the source address only. As a result, you must place them as close to the destination as possible to avoid blocking traffic bound for another interface/network. On the other hand, extended IP access lists are able to filter based on source and destination. Therefore, they are placed as close to the source as possible.

In our sample network, the list is best placed as an inbound filter on the Ethernet0 interface of RouterC. Traffic from host 172.22.5.2 destined for the Web server at 172.22.2.2 will be blocked before it has a chance to even enter the network. Because of their placement, extended access lists create less traffic across the internetwork. Figure 3-21 displays the proper commands for adding the extended access list as an inbound list on interface Ethernet0.

```
RouterC(config)#int e0
RouterC(config-if)#ip access-group 100 in
RouterC(config-if)#^Z
RouterC#
%SYS-5-CONFIG_I: Configured from console by console
RouterC#
```

Once in interface configuration mode, you use the ip access-group [list #] [in | out] command to add the list to the interface.

Figure 3-21 Applying an extended ip access list to an interface

If you wish to remove a list from an interface, you enter interface configuration mode and use the no ip access-group [list #] [in | out] command. Figure 3-22 shows this command.

```
RouterC#config t
Enter configuration commands, one per line.  End with CNTL/Z.
RouterC(config)#int e0
RouterC(config-if)#no ip access-group 101 in
RouterC(config-if)#^Z
RouterC#
%SYS-5-CONFIG_I: Configured from console by console
RouterC#
```

Once in interface configuration mode, you use the no ip access-group [list #] [in | out] command to remove the list from the interface.

Figure 3-22 Removing an extended ip access list from an interface

Monitoring Extended IP Access Lists

The same commands used to monitor standard IP access lists are used to monitor extended IP access lists. If you wish to view the access lists configured on your router, you use the show access-lists or show ip access-lists commands. Figure 3-23 shows the show ip access-lists commands.

```
RouterC#show ip  access-lists
Extended IP access list 100
    deny    tcp host 172.22.5.2 host 172.22.2.2 eq www
    permit ip any any (450 matches)
Extended IP access list 101
    deny    tcp host 172.22.5.2 host 172.22.2.2 eq www
    deny    tcp host 172.22.5.2 host 172.22.2.2 eq ftp
    permit ip any any (1445 matches)
RouterC#
```

Extended access lists show the number of matches per line of the access list. The deny statement in list 100 has not been used in this example. In this example, no attempts have been made by host 172.22.5.2 to access the Web server.

450 packets have matched the permit ip any any statement.

Figure 3-23 Show ip access-lists command

To clear the counters, you issue the clear access-list counters *[list #]* command. Figure 3-24 shows the correct syntax for the clear access-list counters command.

```
RouterC#clear access-list counters 101
RouterC#show ip access-list
Extended IP access list 100
    deny    tcp host 172.22.5.2 host 172.22.2.2 eq www
    permit ip any any (450 matches)
Extended IP access list 101
    deny    tcp host 172.22.5.2 host 172.22.2.2 eq www
    deny    tcp host 172.22.5.2 host 172.22.2.2 eq ftp
    permit ip any any (9 matches)
RouterC#
```

Notice that the number of matches on access list 101 has dropped from the previous 1445 matches in Figure 3-23 to 9 because the counters were cleared to 0 (zero).

Figure 3-24   Clear access-list counters command

STANDARD IPX ACCESS LISTS

Standard IPX access lists are very similar to their IP cousins, but they have one distinct difference. While standard IP access lists only filter based on source addresses, **standard IPX access lists** can filter based on source and destination nodes or on networks. In all other respects, they act just like standard IP access lists. In order to configure standard IPX access lists, you must create the list and then apply it to an interface using the following syntax (a detailed explanation of each item is contained in the subsequent bulleted list):

access-list *[list #] [permit | deny] [source network/node address] [destination network/node address]*

- *[list #]*: Standard IPX access lists are represented by a number in the range of 800–899.

- *[permit | deny]*: Used to specify the nature of the access list line. It is either a permit or a deny statement.

- *[source network/node address]*: The IPX address of the source network or node

- *[destination network/node address]*: The IPX address of the destination network or node

Standard IPX Access List Examples

In order to visualize the placement and function of standard IPX access lists, you must have a reference network. Figure 3-25 shows the IPX network used in this section.

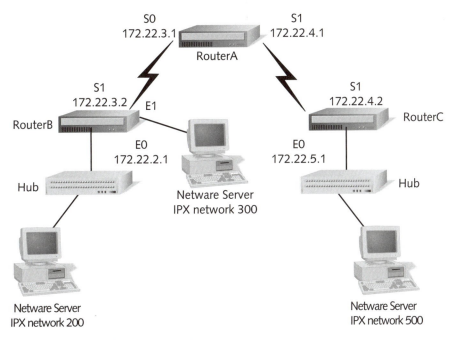

Figure 3-25 Sample IPX Network

Assume that in the sample IPX network in Figure 3-25, you wish to block all traffic from IPX network 500 to IPX network 200. In addition, traffic flow between network 500 and network 300 must remain unaffected. Figure 3-26 shows how you create the access list using context-sensitive help.

```
RouterC(config)#access-list 800 ?
  deny    Specify packets to reject
  permit  Specify packets to permit

RouterC(config)#access-list 800 deny ?
  -1           Any IPX net
  <0-FFFFFFFF> Source net
  N.H.H.H      Source net.host address
  <cr>
RouterC(config)#access-list 800 deny 500 200
RouterC(config)#access-list 800 permit -1 -1 ◄
RouterC(config)#
RouterC(config)#int e0
RouterC(config-if)#ipx access-group ? ◄
  <800-999>  A valid Novell access list number

RouterC(config-if)#ipx access-group 800 ?
  in    inbound packets
  out   outbound packets
  <cr>

RouterC(config-if)#ipx access-group 800 in ◄
RouterC(config-if)#
```

The -1 keyword stands for all IPX networks and all IPX nodes, just as the any keyword stands for all IP addresses in IP access lists. The final line in the access list is necessary because IPX access lists, like all access lists, end with an implicit deny any. Without the final line, you would block traffic between network 500 and networks 200 and 300.

Your next step is to apply the list to an interface. The ipx access-group command accomplishes this task.

Figure 3-26 Standard IPX access list configuration

Monitoring Standard IPX Lists

You can view IPX access lists with the show access-lists command. Figure 3-27 shows the router output when you type this command.

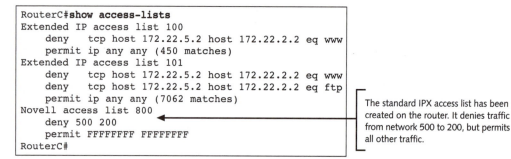

```
RouterC#show access-lists
Extended IP access list 100
    deny    tcp host 172.22.5.2 host 172.22.2.2 eq www
    permit ip any any (450 matches)
Extended IP access list 101
    deny    tcp host 172.22.5.2 host 172.22.2.2 eq www
    deny    tcp host 172.22.5.2 host 172.22.2.2 eq ftp
    permit ip any any (7062 matches)
Novell access list 800
    deny 500 200 ◄
    permit FFFFFFFF FFFFFFFF
RouterC#
```

The standard IPX access list has been created on the router. It denies traffic from network 500 to 200, but permits all other traffic.

Figure 3-27   Show access-lists command

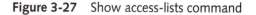

EXTENDED IPX ACCESS LISTS

Extended IPX access lists allow you to filter based on source and destination network or node address, IPX protocol type, and IPX socket number. In order to configure extended IPX access lists, you must create the list and then apply it to an interface using the following syntax (a detailed explanation of each item is contained in the subsequent bulleted list):

access-list *[list#] [permit|deny] [protocol] [source network/node] [socket]*
[destination network/node] [socket]

- *[list#]*: Extended IPX access lists are represented by a number in the range of 900–999.

- *[permit|deny]*: Used to specify the nature of the access list line. It is either a permit or a deny statement.

- *[protocol]*: IPX protocol. A −1 specifies all IPX protocols.

- *[source network/node address]*: The IPX address of the source network or node

- *[socket]*: Similar to the port value in IP access lists. Points to a particular service.

- *[destination network/node address]*: The IPX address of the destination network or node

- *[socket]*: Similar to the port value in IP access lists. Points to a particular service.

Extended IPX Access Lists Example

We can take our standard IPX access list and convert it to an extended list to show the correct format of an extended IPX access list. Figure 3-28 shows how you do this using context-sensitive help.

Monitoring Extended IPX Access Lists

Just as with all other access lists, the show access-lists command will display your extended IPX access lists along with all other access lists on the router. Figure 3-29 shows an example of this command.

```
RouterC(config)#access-list 900 ?
  deny    Specify packets to reject
  permit  Specify packets to permit

RouterC(config)#access-list 900 deny ?
  -1       Any IPX protocol type
  <0-255>  Protocol type number (DECIMAL)
  <cr>

RouterC(config)#access-list 900 deny -1 ?
  -1            Any IPX net
  <0-FFFFFFFF>  Source net
  N.H.H.H       Source net.host address
  <cr>

RouterC(config)#access-list 900 deny -1 500 ?
  <0-FFFFFFFF>  Source Socket (0 for all sockets) HEXIDECIMAL
  <cr>

RouterC(config)#access-list 900 deny -1 500 0 ?
  -1            Any IPX net
  <0-FFFFFFFF>  Destination net
  N.H.H.H       Destination net.host address
  <cr>

RouterC(config)#access-list 900 deny -1 500 0 200 ?
  <0-FFFFFFFF>  Destination Socket (0 for all sockets) HEXIDECIMAL
  <cr>

RouterC(config)#access-list 900 deny -1 500 0 200 0 ?
  <cr>

RouterC(config)#access-list 900 deny -1 500 0 200 0
RouterC(config)# access-list 900 permit -1 -1 0 -1 0
RouterC(config)#
```

> The deny -1 statement will deny any IPX protocol type.

> 500 represents the source IPX network.

> 200 represents the destination IPX network.

> The completed statement blocks all IPX protocols from IPX network 500 to IPX network 200.

> The final line in the access list permits all IPX protocols, from all sockets, on all networks. You must include this line or the implicit deny any will cause problems.

Figure 3-28   Configuring extended IPX access-lists

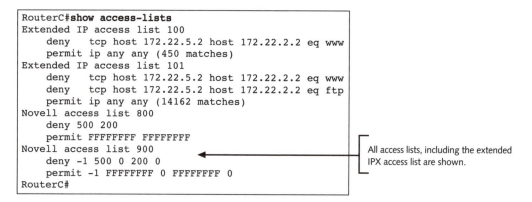

```
RouterC#show access-lists
Extended IP access list 100
    deny   tcp host 172.22.5.2 host 172.22.2.2 eq www
    permit ip any any (450 matches)
Extended IP access list 101
    deny   tcp host 172.22.5.2 host 172.22.2.2 eq www
    deny   tcp host 172.22.5.2 host 172.22.2.2 eq ftp
    permit ip any any (14162 matches)
Novell access list 800
    deny 500 200
    permit FFFFFFFF FFFFFFFF
Novell access list 900
    deny -1 500 0 200 0
    permit -1 FFFFFFFF 0 FFFFFFFF 0
RouterC#
```

> All access lists, including the extended IPX access list are shown.

Figure 3-29   Show access-lists command

IPX SAP FILTERS

IPX SAP filters limit SAP traffic in order to control what resources on the IPX network will be visible to IPX clients. This allows you to limit the "advertising" of particular servers and services to a particular IPX network segment. Since SAP advertisements are broadcast, limiting them reduces network traffic. For instance, you could block the server used for school administration from "advertising" to the router, which in turn blocks the propagation of administration server updates in other SAP tables.

IPX input SAP filters reduce the number of SAP entries that are placed into a router's SAP table. IPX output SAP filters reduce the number of entries in the SAP table that are passed to other connected routers (for an in-depth discussion of SAP and routers, review Chapter 2).

In order to configure IPX SAP filters, you must create the list and then apply it to an interface using the following syntax (a detailed explanation of each item is contained in the subsequent bulleted list):

access-list *[list #] [permit|deny] [source network/node] [service-type]*

- *[list#]*: IPX SAP filters are represented by a number in the range of 1000–1099.
- *[permit|deny]*: Used to specify the nature of the access list line. It is either a permit or a deny statement.
- *[source network/node address]*: The IPX address of the source network or node.
- *[service-type]*: IPX service such as print service, files services, or directory services

IPX SAP Filter Example

In order to create an IPX SAP filter, you must first determine what SAP services you wish to block. Assume that you want to create a SAP filter that blocks all SAP updates on network 200 from being advertised by RouterB in its SAP table updates. Figure 3-30 shows how you do that using context-sensitive help.

```
RouterB(config)#access-list ?
    <1-99>        IP standard access list
    <100-199>     IP extended access list
    <1000-1099>   IPX SAP access list
    <1100-1199>   Extended 48-bit MAC address access list
    <1200-1299>   IPX summary address access list
    <200-299>     Protocol type-code access list
    <700-799>     48-bit MAC address access list
<800-899>     IPX standard access list
    <900-999>     IPX extended access list

RouterB(config)#access-list 1000 ?
    deny    Specify packets to reject
    permit  Specify packets to forward

RouterB(config)#access-list 1000 deny ?
    -1            Any IPX net
    <0-FFFFFFFF>  Source net
    N.H.H.H       Source net.host address

RouterB(config)#access-list 1000 deny 200 ?
    <0-FFFFFFFF>  Service type-code (0 matches all services)
    N.H.H.H       Source net.host mask
    <cr>

RouterB(config)#access-list 1000 deny 200 0
RouterB(config)#access-list 1000 permit -1 0
RouterB(config)#exit
RouterB#
%SYS-5-CONFIG_I: Configured from console by console
RouterB#
```

At this point, you must specify which network you wish to block.

The final permit statement allows SAP updates from all other networks to be advertised.

Figure 3-30   IPX SAP filter example

IPX SAP filters must be applied to interfaces just like all other access lists. To apply IPX SAP filters, you must use the ipx input-sap-filter *[list #]* or ipx output-sap-filter *[list #]* commands. Figure 3-31 shows the ipx input-sap-filter *[list #]* command.

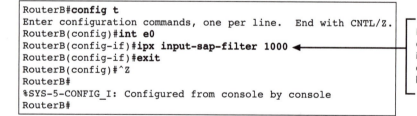

```
RouterB#config t
Enter configuration commands, one per line.  End with CNTL/Z.
RouterB(config)#int e0
RouterB(config-if)#ipx input-sap-filter 1000
RouterB(config-if)#exit
RouterB(config)#^Z
RouterB#
%SYS-5-CONFIG_I: Configured from console by console
RouterB#
```

From interface configuration mode, the ipx input-sap-filter command applies access list 1000 as an input filter.

Figure 3-31   Applying an IPX SAP filter to an interface

The resulting list and application of that list would block all SAP updates from network 200 from being passed to other routers in the internetwork.

Monitoring IPX SAP Filters

Like all other access lists, the show access-lists command displays all SAP filters defined on the router. Refer to other monitoring instructions in this chapter for guidance in experimenting with the monitoring of IPX SAP filters.

CHAPTER SUMMARY

Access lists are one of the most important IOS tools for controlling network traffic and security. Access lists are created in a two-step process. First, you create the list, using the specific syntax of the type of list you wish to create. Then, you apply the list to an interface to make it active. All access lists are created sequentially and applied sequentially to all packets that enter an interface where the list is applied. Access lists, by default, always end in an implicit deny any, which will drop any packet that does not meet an access list criteria. Only one access list per direction (inbound or outbound) per protocol can be applied to an interface.

Standard IP access lists allow you to filter traffic based on the source IP address of a packet. They should be applied to an interface as close to the destination as possible to avoid accidentally blocking valid traffic. Extended IP access lists filter traffic based on source, destination, protocol type, and application type. They allow for more specific control over network traffic. They should be placed as close to the source as possible to keep unnecessary traffic from getting onto the internetwork.

Standard IPX access lists, while more complex than standard IP lists because they can incorporate destination addresses into filtering decisions, behave nearly exactly the same. Extended IPX lists allow you to filter based on IPX protocol type and other IPX parameters. Finally, IPX SAP filters allow you to limit the amount of SAP traffic passed by your routers.

Ranges of numbers represent all access lists. Table 3-2, which follows, summarizes the numbers associated with each type of list.

Table 3-2   Access list number ranges

Access List Type	Number
Standard IP access lists	1–99
Extended IP access lists	100–199
Standard IPX access lists	800–899
Extended IPX access lists	900–999
IPX SAP filters	1000-1099

KEY TERMS

- **access lists** — Permit or deny statements that filter traffic based on criteria such as source address, destination address, and protocol type.

- **any** — A keyword used to represent all hosts or networks; replaces 0.0.0.0 255.255.255.255 in an access list.

- **extended IP access lists** — Filter traffic by source IP address, destination IP address, protocol type, and port number.

- **extended IPX access lists** — IPX access lists that filter traffic based on source and destination IPX nodes or networks, IPX protocol type, and IPX socket number.

- **host** — A keyword that specifies that an address should have a wildcard mask of 0.0.0.0.

- **implicit deny any** — Blocks all packets that do not meet the requirements of the access list.

- **inverse mask** — *See* Wildcard mask.

- **IPX SAP filters** — Access lists that filter SAP traffic on a network.

- **standard IP access lists** — Filter traffic based on source IP address.

- **standard IPX access lists** — Filter traffic based on source and destination IPX nodes or networks.

- **wildcard mask** — Applied to IP addresses to determine if an access list line will act upon a packet. Zeros are placed in positions deemed significant, and ones are placed in nonsignificant positions.

REVIEW QUESTIONS

1. Which wildcard mask would apply an access list line to all packets from network 175.25.0.0?

   a. 255.255.255.0

   b. 255.255.0.0

   c. 255.254.0.0

   d. 0.0.255.255

2. Standard IP access lists filter traffic based on which of the following? (Choose all that apply.)

   a. destination IP address

   b. IP protocol

   c. port number

   d. source IP address

3. Wildcard masks use a _____ to signify which bits of an address are significant.

4. Standard IPX access lists filter traffic based on which of the following? (Choose all that apply.)

   a. IPX protocol

   b. source IPX network

   c. destination IPX network

   d. socket number

5. Which command shows only the IP access lists on a router?

   a. show access-lists

   b. show ipx access-lists

   c. show ip access-lists

   d. show interface

6. Which commands allow you to view the interfaces that have IP access lists applied to them? (Choose all that apply.)

   a. show interfaces

   b. show ip interfaces

   c. show ip traffic

   d. show ip counters

7. Which host and wildcard mask pair does the any keyword represent?

   a. 255.255.255.255   0.0.0.0

   b. 0.0.255.255   0.0.0.0

   c. 0.0.0.0 0.0.0.0

   d. 0.0.0.0 255.255.255.255

8. Which command is used to apply an IP access list to an interface?

   a. ip access-group *[list #] [in | out]*

   b. ip access-group permit 100

   c. ip access-group *[list #] [permit | deny]*

   d. show ip interfaces

9. Access lists are _____. (Choose all that apply.)

   a. used to filter traffic and control network security

   b. applied as either inbound or outbound filters

   c. sequential permit or deny statements

   d. built into the router's firmware

3

10. Standard IP access lists are represented by the _____ number range.

    a. 100–199

    b. 1–99

    c. 1000–1099

    d. 200–299

11. Extended IPX access lists are represented by the _____ number range.

    a. 900–999

    b. 800–899

    c. 1000–1099

    d. 1–99

12. Which command could be used to remove an access list from your router?

    a. no ip access-group in

    b. no ip access-list 1 in

    c. no access-list 1

    d. no ip access-list one

13. Extended IP access lists are represented by the _____ number range.

    a. 100–199

    b. 200–299

    c. 1000–1099

    d. 1–99

14. IPX SAP filters are represented by the _____ number range.

    a. 100–199

    b. 1–99

    c. 800–899

    d. 1000–1099

15. The show access-lists command displays _____.

    a. access lists applied to interfaces

    b. all access lists on the router

    c. only IP access lists on the router

    d. only IPX access lists on the router

16. At which of the following prompts would you create an access list?

    a. RouterC#

    b. RouterC>

    c. RouterC(config-if)#

    d. RouterC(config)#

17. At which of the following prompts would you apply an access list to an interface?

    a. RouterC#

    b. RouterC>

    c. RouterC(config-if)#

    d. RouterC(config)

18. Which of the following host and corresponding wildcard mask pairs represent the same value as host 172.29.2.2?

    a. 0.0.0.0   255.255.255.255

    b. 172.29.2.2   0.0.0.0

    c. 255.255.255.255   0.0.0.0

    d. 0.0.0.0   172.29.2.2

19. Standard IPX access lists are represented by the _____ number range.

    a. 1–99

    b. 800–899

    c. 900–999

    d. 1000–1099

20. A router can have one _____ access list and one _____ access list per protocol on each interface.

CASE PROJECTS

1. Freytech industries has hired you to help with an important network project. They wish to block HTTP traffic from one particular network to their Web server. What type of access list would you have to use to meet their needs? Research the syntax necessary to perform this filtering task.

2. You have been asked to deliver a speech on the SAP traffic filtering capabilities of the Cisco IOS. Prepare a short outline that addresses why SAP filtering is important and the proper techniques for creating and applying SAP filters.

NONROUTABLE, ROUTED, AND ROUTING PROTOCOLS

After reading this chapter and completing the exercises you will be able to:

♦ Differentiate nonroutable, routed, and routing protocols

♦ Define Interior Gateway Protocols, Exterior Gateway Protocols, distance-vector routing protocols and link-state routing protocols

♦ Explain the concepts of count-to-infinity, split horizon, split horizon with poison reverse, and hold-down timers

♦ Describe, configure, and monitor the interior routing protocols RIP and IGRP

In Chapter 4 of *CCNA Guide to Networking Fundamentals*, you were introduced to the concepts of routed versus routing protocols. This chapter is a continuation and expansion of that discussion. In particular, this chapter adds the concept of nonroutable protocols, while at the same time expanding and defining several classes of routed protocols. In addition, you will learn the proper way to configure and monitor Routing Information Protocol (RIP) and Interior Gateway Routing Protocol (IGRP) on Cisco routers.

NONROUTABLE PROTOCOLS

In the beginning, networks were small collections of computers tied together for the purpose of sharing expensive peripherals such as high-end laser printers. Few companies could afford to link all their computers together on a local area network (LAN). Instead, using coaxial cable, computers were hooked together in workgroups. Figure 4-1 shows a typical early network.

Computer A   Computer B   Computer C   Computer D

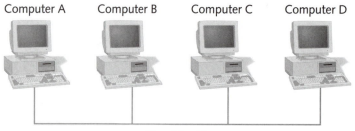

Coaxial cable

Figure 4-1   Early network model using coaxial cable

Early networks were sometimes configured as **peer-to-peer networks**, in which computers communicate with and provide services to their "peers." Peer-to-peer networks do not pass packets between multiple networks. All communication occurs on the one small segment where the peer-to-peer network exists.

Due to the localized nature of traffic on a peer-to-peer network, they do not need protocols that contain network source and destination information, which are large and inefficient. Instead, peer-to-peer networks can use the small and efficient non-routable protocols.

Several **nonroutable protocols** exist in today's networking world, but NetBEUI, short for NetBIOS Enhanced User Interface, is the most common. NetBEUI ships with all Microsoft Windows operating systems. In small, peer-to-peer networks, NetBEUI is easy to configure and use. Since it is very small, it is fast and efficient.

Unfortunately, NetBEUI cannot scale into large internetworks because it cannot hold Network layer information in its frame header. Without this information, packets cannot be routed between multiple network segments. Therefore, if you try to use NetBEUI—or any nonroutable protocol—in a network with multiple networks, communication between the networks will fail.

ROUTED PROTOCOLS

Routed protocols have packet headers that can contain Network layer addresses. Routed protocols were developed to support networks consisting of multiple network segments or multiple networks. Figure 4-2 shows a typical internetwork within which routed protocols, such as TCP/IP or IPX/SPX, are used.

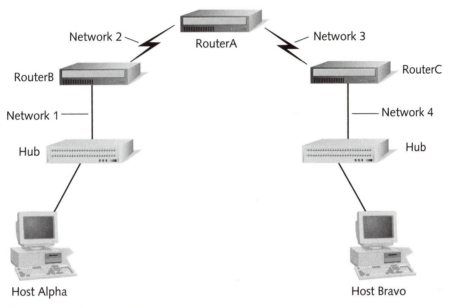

Figure 4-2   Common internetwork

In this sample internetwork, Host Alpha can communicate with Host Bravo only if Host Alpha uses a protocol that can add Network layer addressing to each packet header. With this Network layer addressing, information from Alpha can traverse the internetwork from Network 1 to Network 4. Without the Network layer information, all packets are only able to communicate within Network 1. **Transmission Control Protocol/Internet Protocol (TCP/IP)** and **Internetwork Packet exchange/Sequence Packet exchange (IPX/SPX)** are two protocols that can carry Network layer information. Thus, routers can route them through the internetwork.

For routed protocols to work on a network, every device (computer, printer, and router interface port) must be configured with a unique IP or IPX address. These Network layer, **logical addresses** allow TCP/IP packets to be routed throughout the internetwork. Figure 4-3 shows the sample network with IP addresses assigned to each device.

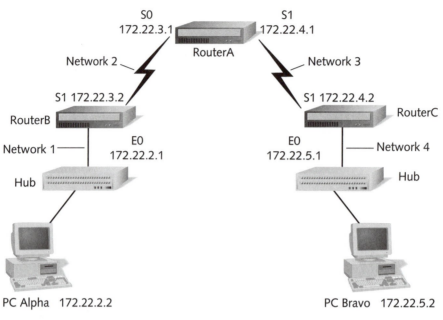

Figure 4-3   Common internetwork with IP addresses

ROUTING PROTOCOLS

For proper network connectivity, you need more than just routed protocols on large internet-works. Because routers must be able to find the correct paths to route routed protocols, they use routing protocols to build route tables that specify exactly where every network in the internetwork is located. **Routing protocols** are protocols used by routers to make path determination choices and to share those choices with other routers. Table 4–1 shows a conceptual route table that RouterB in Figure 4–3 would use to route a TCP/IP packet from Network 1 to Network 4.

Table 4-1   Conceptual route table

Network	Path	Distance
Network 2	Available via RouterB	1 hop
Network 3	Available via RouterA	2 hops
Network 4	Available via RouterC	3 hops

This table shows that RouterB can reach any of the networks in our internetwork. The Distance column refers to hop count as the single metric used in this route table. **Hop count** is the number of routers a packet must pass through to reach a particular network. A **metric** is a value used to define the suitability of a particular route. In other words, routers use metrics to determine which routes are better than other routes.

> TIP   In the internetwork shown in Figure 4-3, routing metrics are simple because of the single path nature of the internetwork. The route to Network 4 from RouterB will be via RouterA and Router C; there is no better path available.

An **autonomous system (AS)**, which uses Interior Gateway Protocols as routing protocols, is a group of routers under the control of a single administration. Figure 4-4 shows Big Tin Inc.'s AS.

4

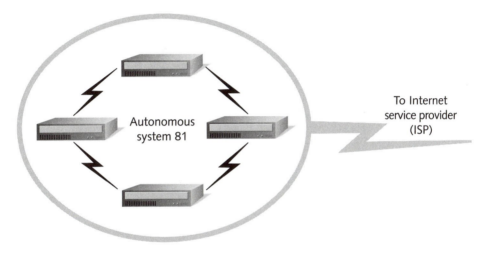

Figure 4-4   Big Tin Inc.'s AS

Big Tin Inc. has an autonomous system consisting of the four routers under the control of local network engineers. In general, AS systems run a single routing protocol. Routing protocols come in two major categories: **Interior Gateway Protocols (IGPs)** are the routing protocols used within an AS, and **Exterior Gateway Protocols (EGP)** are routing protocols used to route between multiple autonomous systems. **Routing Information Protocol (RIP)**, **Interior Gateway Routing Protocol (IGRP)**, **Enhanced Interior Gateway Routing Protocol (EIGRP)**, and **Open Shortest Path First (OSPF)** are examples of IGPs. **Border Gateway Protocol (BGP)** and Exterior Gateway Protocol (EGP) are examples of EGPs. In this book, all discussions will focus on the RIP and IGRP—both of which are basic IGPs.

Two Types of IGP Routing Protocols

Interior Gateway Routing protocols are subdivided into two major types of routing protocols—**distance-vector** and **link-state**. These protocol types accomplish the same job—determining routes within an autonomous system—but they do so via different mechanisms.

Distance-Vector Routing Protocols

Distance-vector routing protocols broadcast their entire routing table to each neighbor router at predetermined intervals (the actual interval rate depends on the distance-vector routing protocol in use, but varies between 30 and 90 seconds). Figure 4-5 shows how this process occurs.

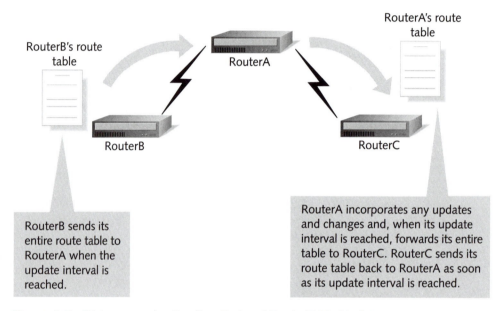

RouterA's route table

RouterB's route table

RouterA

RouterB

RouterC

RouterB sends its entire route table to RouterA when the update interval is reached.

RouterA incorporates any updates and changes and, when its update interval is reached, forwards its entire table to RouterC. RouterC sends its route table back to RouterA as soon as its update interval is reached.

Figure 4-5 Distance-vector Routing Protocol Route Table Update

As the updates propagate throughout the network, RouterC will only receive information about RouterB's route table via RouterA. This is sometimes referred to as routing by rumor. It also is one of the main problems with distance-vector routing protocols. If RouterB and RouterA have an update interval of 30 seconds, RouterC will not learn about network topology changes (changes in router interface states or route metrics) on RouterB for up to a minute. Figure 4-6 shows the types of problems this slow time to **convergence** (a state where all routers on the internetwork share a common view of the internetwork routes) can cause.

Figure 4-6 shows that the time it will take the network to converge depends on the amount of time between update intervals on RouterB and RouterA. In this sample network, given its small size, the amount of time between convergence would be fairly minimal. Still, for a short amount of time, RouterC is working on the assumption that the network is configured differently than it actually is.

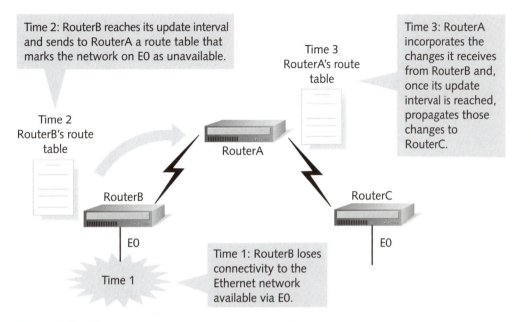

Time 2: RouterB reaches its update interval and sends to RouterA a route table that marks the network on E0 as unavailable.

Time 2 RouterB's route table

Time 3 RouterA's route table

Time 3: RouterA incorporates the changes it receives from RouterB and, once its update interval is reached, propagates those changes to RouterC.

RouterA

RouterB

RouterC

E0

E0

Time 1

Time 1: RouterB loses connectivity to the Ethernet network available via E0.

Figure 4-6 Distance-vector convergence example

Problems, such as routing loops, can occur with distance-vector protocols if control measures are not put in place. **Routing loops** are often referred to as **count-to-infinity** problems because loops, without preventive measures (described next), will cause packets to bounce around the internetwork for an infinite amount of time. Figure 4-7 illustrates the types of problems that can occur with routing loops.

In this internetwork, true loops are not possible because of the linear nature of the network design. Still, the scenario presented in Figure 4-7 shows that the internetwork could, without proper precautions, readvertise a route that was in actuality not accessible. To prevent these problems, techniques such as defining a maximum, split horizon, split horizon with poison reverse, and hold-down timers are used to reduce the chances that incorrect route table information will be propagated.

Defining a maximum is one of the easiest ways to limit count-to-infinity problems. If you assign a packet a maximum hop count, it cannot bounce infinitely around the internetwork. RIP, one of the most common distance-vector protocols, defines a maximum hop count of 15. Therefore, if a routing loop did occur on a RIP internetwork, the packet would only travel through 15 hops before the packet exceeded its **time to live (TTL)** and was dropped. In other words, the 16th router that the packet tried to cross on a RIP internetwork would see that the packet had exceeded its TTL and would drop the packet. For distance-vector routing protocols, in general, the hop count used to define a maximum is also the sole metric used to determine the relative desirability of a particular path.

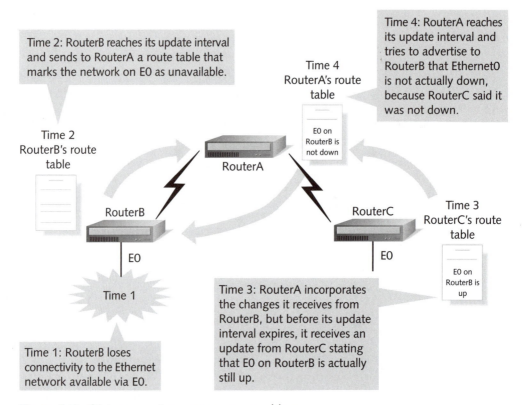

Figure 4-7   Distance-vector convergence problems

Split horizon and **split horizon with poison reverse** are two other common ways to prevent routing loops. Split horizon controls what information a router will send out about particular routes. In short, routers will not send information back through an interface about an advertised route from that interface. For example, if RouterA in Figure 4-7 uses split horizon, it will not accept the update from RouterC at Time 4 (Time 4 in Figure 4-7 represents the time when RouterC's update interval expires and RouterC sends out its update table). It won't accept it because that update would need to be sent out of the interface from which RouterA learned that E0 on RouterB was down in the first place. If RouterA uses split horizon with poison reverse, it not only refuses to send RouterC's update to RouterB, but it also responds to RouterC's attempted update. RouterA will tell RouterC that the route to E0 is no longer available by indicating that the hop count has been exceeded. In other words, it poisons the erroneous route advertised by RouterC so that no other router will see this as a viable route.

Another common technique used to stop routing loops is the **hold-down timer**. Hold-down timers allow a router to place a route in a state where it will not accept any changes to that route. If RouterA uses hold-down timers in Figure 4-7, the update from RouterC is ignored because the route would be in "hold down" for a period of time after it was marked down. This prevents improper route information from being propagated throughout the internetwork.

Link-State Routing Protocols

Link-state routing protocols are the second type of routing protocols you can use to exchange route information between routers in an autonomous system. They behave very differently from distance-vector routing protocols. Routers configured with a link-state routing protocol use **Link-state advertisements (LSAs)** to inform all routers on the internetwork of their route tables.

Link-state packets (LSPs), packets used to send out LSAs, allow every router in the internetwork to share a common view of the **topology** of the internetwork. Also, link-state routing protocols use the **Shortest Path First (SPF) algorithm** to determine the best paths in the internetwork. Figure 4-8 shows how a router configured with a link-state routing protocol **floods** or broadcasts LSPs to the network so that every other router on the internetwork has a common view of the topology of the internetwork.

In the example in Figure 4-8, the network quickly reaches a state of convergence due to the flooding of link-state packets. This is one huge advantage link-state routing protocols have over distance-vector routing protocols. Also, later updates by the routers in the internetwork will be **triggered updates**. These updates occur due to network topology changes, not periodic route table advertisements. In other words, RouterB will only flood the internetwork with LSPs if a change occurs to its route table. This announcement contains only the changes in the route table, not the entire route table. This conserves bandwidth on the internetwork links.

Link-state routing protocols do have some problems, however. Due to the complexity of the Shortest Path First algorithm and the need to hold a view of the entire internetwork topology, routers using link-state protocols must be configured with more memory and processing power than those using distance-vector routing protocols.

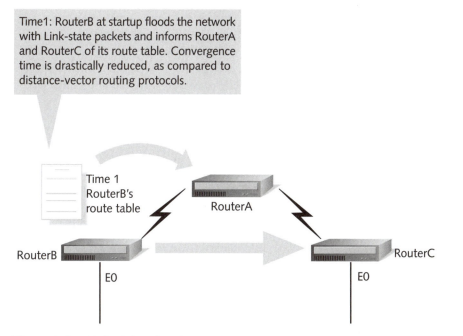

Time1: RouterB at startup floods the network with Link-state packets and informs RouterA and RouterC of its route table. Convergence time is drastically reduced, as compared to distance-vector routing protocols.

Figure 4-8   Link-state advertisements

Table 4-2 summarizes the key characteristics associated with distance-vector and link-state routing protocols.

Table 4-2   Major characteristics of distance-vector and link-state routing protocols

Distance-vector	Link-state
Periodically broadcasts entire routing table to neighbors	Broadcasts entire routing table to all other routers in the AS on start up; all other routing table updates contain only updated routes; updates only occur when a network topology change occurs
Slow to converge	Fast to converge due to link-state advertisements
Prone to routing loops because of their routing by rumor nature	Less prone to routing loops because all other routers share a common view of the network
Easy to configure and administer	Harder to configure; requires greater memory and processing power on each router

Now that you have been introduced to the theory behind routing protocols, you need to learn how to actually configure specific protocols on Cisco routers. RIP and IGRP, both distance-vector protocols, are the two main protocols covered on the Cisco Certified Network Associate exam. In the next two sections, you will learn how to configure each protocol.

ROUTING INFORMATION PROTOCOL

The first Interior Gateway Protocol you must know how to configure is RIP. RIP is a distance-vector routing protocol that broadcasts entire routing tables to neighbors every 30 seconds, out of every interface on which it is configured. RIP uses hop count as its sole metric. Also, RIP has a maximum hop count of 15. As a result, RIP does not work in large internetworks. In addition, RIP is susceptible to all the problems normally associated with distance-vector routing protocols. It is slow to converge and forces routers to learn network information only from neighbors. Still, RIP is an easy to install and configure protocol. To install RIP on a Cisco router using TCP/IP, you must perform the following two tasks:

- Enable RIP
- Enable RIP routing for each major network you wish to use

You need only to configure major network numbers with RIP because RIP does not maintain subnet mask information within the route tables it produces. As you go through the following text, remember that there are actually two versions of RIP. This section focuses on RIP version 1. RIPv1 does not pass subnet mask information with its route table updates.

Enabling RIP Routing

For the following discussion of RIP, we will use the network in Figure 4-9. In the discussion, for brevity, we will only focus on enabling RIP on RouterB. You can assume that RIP has already been enabled on RouterA and RouterC.

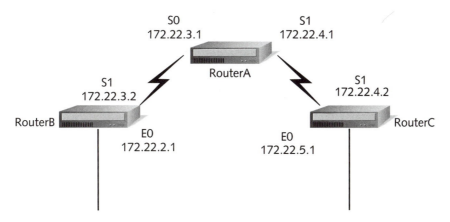

Figure 4-9   Sample IP network

To start configuring RIP, you must first enter privileged mode and then global configuration mode on your router. Once you type the enable command and config terminal command to enter global configuration mode, router output similar to that in Figure 4–10 should appear.

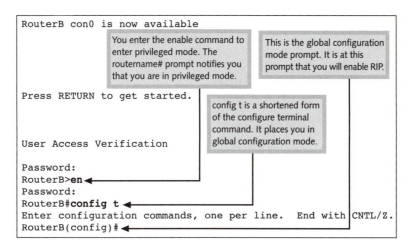

Figure 4-10   Global configuration mode

Once in global configuration mode, you must enable RIP with the router rip command. The commands to enable RIP are displayed in Figure 4-11.

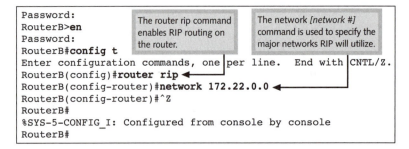

Figure 4-11   Configuring RIP

Enabling RIP Routing for Each Major Network

Figure 4-11 also displays the commands necessary to turn RIP routing on for a particular major network. The network *[network #]* command in Figure 4-11 turns RIP routing on for the major class B network 172.22.0.0. If you have multiple major networks configured on a router, an individual network *[network #]* command must be issued for each separate network.

After you have enabled RIP routing globally and configured each major network that the router will advertise with RIP updates, RIP is fully configured on the router. After the update interval of 30 seconds passes on each router, RouterB will learn of all networks. You type the show ip route command to display the routes learned via RIP (this command actually displays all ip routes on the router). Figure 4-12 shows the output from the show ip route command on RouterB.

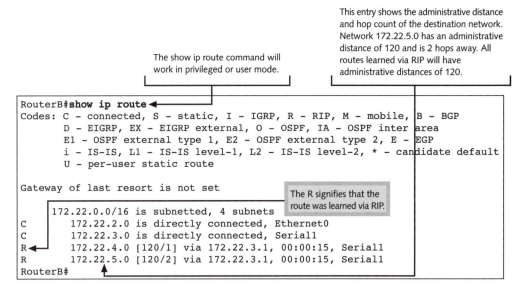

Figure 4-12 Output from the show ip route command

The output in Figure 4-12 illustrates an extremely important concept called administrative distance. **Administrative distance** is a value used to determine the reliability of a particular route. Table 4-3 shows common routing protocols and their administrative distances.

Table 4-3 Administrative distances

Route Learned Via:	Administrative Distance
Direction connection	0
Static route	1
IGRP	100
OSPF	110
RIP	120

Therefore, if a route is being discovered using both RIP and a directly connected interface, the route available via the directly connected interface will be the preferred route because it has a lower administrative distance. Likewise, if both IGRP and RIP advertise a route for a particular network, the IGRP route will be used because it is considered more reliable due to its lower administrative distance.

show ip protocol and debug ip Commands

You can use the show ip protocol and debug ip rip commands to monitor RIP. You can type the show ip protocol command in either user mode or privileged mode. When you type the show ip protocol command, you will receive output similar to that found in Figure 4-13.

```
RouterB>show ip protocol
Routing Protocol is "rip"
  Sending updates every 30 seconds, next due in 6 seconds
  Invalid after 180 seconds, hold down 180, flushed after 240
  Outgoing update filter list for all interfaces is not set
  Incoming update filter list for all interfaces is not set
  Redistributing: rip
  Default version control: send version 1, receive any version
    Interface        Send  Recv   Key-chain
    Ethernet0         1    1 2
    Serial1           1    1 2
  Routing for Networks:
    172.22.0.0
  Routing Information Sources:
    Gateway          Distance     Last Update
    172.22.3.1            120     00:00:27
  Distance: (default is 120)

RouterB>
```

The show ip protocol command will work in privileged or user mode.

All RIP timers are dislpayed via this command.

Figure 4-13 Output from the show ip protocol command

In Figure 4-13, you can see the timers associated with RIP. RIP updates on TCP/IP networks, as stated previously, occur every 30 seconds. A route is considered invalid if six consecutive update intervals pass without an update from that route. The hold-down time of 180 seconds allows the router to stabilize its route table to help prevent routing loops when a network path does go down. Finally, the flush interval is the time at which a route will be totally removed from the route table if no updates are received.

The debug ip rip command, like all debug commands, should only be used when troubleshooting RIP. This command places very high processing demands on your router and could affect network performance. Figure 4-14 shows the output of the debug ip rip command.

```
RouterB>en
Password:
RouterB#debug ip rip        ◄────   The debug ip rip command
RIP protocol debugging is on        only works in privileged mode.
RouterB#
RIP: received v1 update from 172.22.3.1 on Serial1
     172.22.4.0 in 1 hops
     172.22.5.0 in 2 hops
RouterB#
RIP: sending v1 update to 255.255.255.255 via Ethernet0 (172.22.2.1)
     subnet  172.22.3.0, metric 1
     subnet  172.22.4.0, metric 2
     subnet  172.22.5.0, metric 3
RIP: sending v1 update to 255.255.255.255 via Serial1 (172.22.3.2)
     subnet  172.22.2.0, metric 1
RIP: ignored v1 update from bad source 172.22.5.1 on Ethernet0
RIP: received v1 update from 172.22.3.1 on Serial1
     172.22.4.0 in 1 hops
     172.22.5.0 in 2 hops
RouterB#
RIP: sending v1 update to 255.255.255.255 via Ethernet0 (172.22.2.1)
     subnet  172.22.3.0, metric 1
     subnet  172.22.4.0, metric 2
     subnet  172.22.5.0, metric 3
RIP: sending v1 update to 255.255.255.255 via Serial1 (172.22.3.2)
     subnet  172.22.2.0, metric 1
RIP: ignored v1 update from bad source 172.22.5.1 on Ethernet0
RouterB#no debug ip rip    ◄──────   The no debug ip rip command
RIP protocol debugging is off        turns RIP debugging off.
RouterB#
```

Figure 4-14   Output from the debug ip rip command

RIP, like most distance-vector routing protocols is slow to converge. If RouterC loses its connection to subnet 172.22.5.0 on Ethernet0, RouterB will learn about the route status changing. However, it could take at least a minute for the changes to propagate throughout the network (30 seconds maximum for the update interval on RouterC and RouterA). Once RouterB learns of the change in status for network 172.22.5.0, it marks the route as being possibly down and initiates a hold-down timer. You can type the show ip route command to display this change in status. Figure 4-15 shows the results of the show ip route command after Ethernet0 on RouterC becomes inaccessible.

```
RouterB#show ip route
Codes: C - connected, S - static, I - IGRP, R - RIP, M - mobile, B - BGP
       D - EIGRP, EX - EIGRP external, O - OSPF, IA - OSPF inter area
       E1 - OSPF external type 1, E2 - OSPF external type 2, E - EGP
       i - IS-IS, L1 - IS-IS level-1, L2 - IS-IS level-2, * - candidate default
       U - per-user static route

Gateway of last resort is not set

     172.22.0.0/16 is subnetted, 4 subnets
C        172.22.2.0 is directly connected, Ethernet0
C        172.22.3.0 is directly connected, Serial1
R        172.22.4.0 [120/1] via 172.22.3.1, 00:00:19, Serial1
R        172.22.5.0/24 is possibly down,
            routing via 172.22.3.1, Serial1
```

The route to subnet 172.22.5.0 is in hold down and marked as possibly down.

Figure 4-15   Output from the show ip route command

Eventually, the route will be flushed from the route table. Still, with a hold-down time of 180 seconds and a flush timer of 240 seconds, the time it takes for the internetwork to converge can become excessive. If you issue the show ip route command after the route has been flushed from the route table, you will get the router output displayed in Figure 4-16.

```
RouterB#show ip route
Codes: C - connected, S - static, I - IGRP, R - RIP, M - mobile, B - BGP
       D - EIGRP, EX - EIGRP external, O - OSPF, IA - OSPF inter area
       E1 - OSPF external type 1, E2 - OSPF external type 2, E - EGP
       i - IS-IS, L1 - IS-IS level-1, L2 - IS-IS level-2, * - candidate default
       U - per-user static route

Gateway of last resort is not set

     172.22.0.0/16 is subnetted, 3 subnets
C        172.22.2.0 is directly connected, Ethernet0
C        172.22.3.0 is directly connected, Serial1
R        172.22.4.0 [120/1] via 172.22.3.1, 00:00:10, Serial1
RouterB#
```

The route to subnet 172.22.5.0 has been removed from the route table.

Figure 4-16   New output from the show ip route command

Note that RIP relies on hop count as its single metric. In the network in Figure 4-17, a router configured to use RIP would always route packets to the subnet 172.22.5.0 via the 56-Kbps link between RouterB and RouterC, because of the hop count of one.

As this network is configured, it may actually be faster to route packets along the T1 lines. This route, with a hop count of two, will not be used by RIP as the best route even though it may be the best route. To combat this problem associated with distance-vector protocols such as RIP, Cisco developed its own proprietary distance-vector protocol: IGRP.

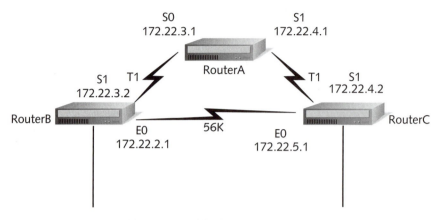

Figure 4-17   RIP problems caused by hop count reliance

Interior Gateway Routing Protocol

IGRP is a proprietary distance-vector routing protocol created by Cisco to solve some of the problems associated with RIP. A larger hop count metric allows IGRP to be used on larger networks. In fact IGRP supports a hop count of 255. On the 256th hop, IGRP will return an ICMP destination network unreachable message. Also, IGRP uses the following additional metrics:

- Load: The measure of the greatest load on a link in the route

- Bandwidth: The slowest link in the route

- Reliability: Measures reliability with a scale of 0 to 255

- Delay: Delay of all links on a route

- **Maximum transmission unit (MTU)**: The smallest MTU along the path is used to find the route

By default, IGRP computes the best available route using only bandwidth and delay, but it can be configured to use all of the metrics mentioned previously. The ability to use bandwidth as a factor in the route selection process, along with reliability and delay, allows IGRP to make more intelligent route choices than RIP. IGRP also has the ability to use multiple, different cost paths to allow for redundancy and load balancing. IGRP can support up to four different cost paths.

Configuring IGRP on a Cisco router using TCP/IP is a simple process accomplished with the router igrp *[autonomous system #]* and network *[network #]* commands. Figure 4-18 shows the router commands necessary to configure IGRP.

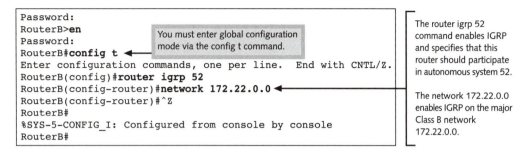

Figure 4-18   Commands used to configure IGRP

Once IGRP is configured throughout the internetwork, you can issue the show ip route command to monitor all available IGRP routes. Figure 4-19 shows the results of this command.

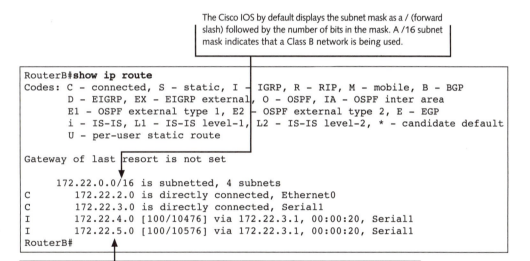

Figure 4-19   The show ip route command with IGRP

If you wish to see the IGRP timers, you can type the show ip protocol command. It will present output similar to that found in Figure 4-20.

```
RouterB#show ip protocol
Routing Protocol is "rip"
  Sending updates every 30 seconds, next due in 21 seconds
  Invalid after 180 seconds, hold down 180, flushed after 240
  Outgoing update filter list for all interfaces is not set
  Incoming update filter list for all interfaces is not set
  Redistributing: rip
  Default version control: send version 1, receive any version
    Interface       Send  Recv   Key-chain
    Ethernet0       1     1 2
    Serial1         1     1 2
  Routing for Networks:
    172.22.0.0
  Routing Information Sources:
    Gateway         Distance        Last Update
    172.22.3.1          120         00:00:12
  Distance: (default is 120)                       IGRP sends updates
                                                   every 90 seconds.
Routing Protocol is "igrp 52"  ◄──────────────
  Sending updates every 90 seconds, next due in 68 seconds
  Invalid after 270 seconds, hold down 280, flushed after 630
  Outgoing update filter list for all interfaces is not set
  Incoming update filter list for all interfaces is not set
  Default networks flagged in outgoing updates
  Default networks accepted from incoming updates
  IGRP metric weight K1=1, K2=0, K3=1, K4=0, K5=0
  IGRP maximum hopcount 100
  IGRP maximum metric variance 1
  Redistributing: igrp 52
  Routing for Networks:
    172.22.0.0
  Routing Information Sources:
    Gateway         Distance        Last Update
    172.22.3.1          100         00:00:36
  Distance: (default is 100)

RouterB#
```

Figure 4-20   The show ip protocol command with IGRP

IGRP sends out routing table updates every 90 seconds. This reduces the amount of broadcast traffic used to maintain routing tables. In Figure 4-20, you can see that the router is running multiple routing protocols, RIP and IGRP. In the real world, you would normally not configure your routers to run both RIP and IGRP on the same interfaces. Doing so would waste network bandwidth on RIP updates that will always be considered inferior to IGRP updates.

A final command available to monitor IGRP is the debug ip igrp command. Figure 4-21 shows the correct syntax for typing the command and some common router output from the command.

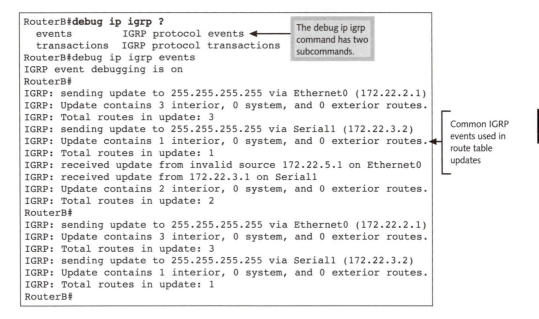

```
RouterB#debug ip igrp ?
  events         IGRP protocol events          The debug ip igrp
  transactions  IGRP protocol transactions     command has two
RouterB#debug ip igrp events                   subcommands.
IGRP event debugging is on
RouterB#
IGRP: sending update to 255.255.255.255 via Ethernet0 (172.22.2.1)
IGRP: Update contains 3 interior, 0 system, and 0 exterior routes.
IGRP: Total routes in update: 3
IGRP: sending update to 255.255.255.255 via Serial1 (172.22.3.2)
IGRP: Update contains 1 interior, 0 system, and 0 exterior routes.
IGRP: Total routes in update: 1
IGRP: received update from invalid source 172.22.5.1 on Ethernet0
IGRP: received update from 172.22.3.1 on Serial1
IGRP: Update contains 2 interior, 0 system, and 0 exterior routes.
IGRP: Total routes in update: 2
RouterB#
IGRP: sending update to 255.255.255.255 via Ethernet0 (172.22.2.1)
IGRP: Update contains 3 interior, 0 system, and 0 exterior routes.
IGRP: Total routes in update: 3
IGRP: sending update to 255.255.255.255 via Serial1 (172.22.3.2)
IGRP: Update contains 1 interior, 0 system, and 0 exterior routes.
IGRP: Total routes in update: 1
RouterB#
```

Common IGRP events used in route table updates

Figure 4-21   Output from the debug ip igrp command

CHAPTER SUMMARY

Protocols vary in their functions. Some protocols are designed to be used in small networks without the need for Network layer addressing. These protocols are described as nonroutable protocols. Other protocols were designed with the ability to move between multiple networks via Network layer addressing. These protocols are routed protocols. Finally, protocols must be available that can find the best path throughout an internetwork and relay that information to routers. Routing protocols serve this function on modern networks.

Furthermore, routing protocols are classed in two major groups: Interior Gateway Protocols and Exterior Gateway Protocols. Interior Gateway Protocols are routing protocols that function within a single autonomous system. Exterior Gateway Protocols function as routing protocols between autonomous systems.

Routing protocols are further divided into distance-vector routing protocols and link-state routing protocols. These two types of Interior Gateway Protocols use very different methods to determine the best path in an internetwork. Distance-vector protocols periodically broadcast entire routing tables to neighbor routers. Link-state protocols broadcast updates to all other routers on the internetwork upon startup and when network topology changes.

Two common distance-vector IGPs are the Routing Information Protocol and the Interior Gateway Routing Protocol. RIP is an easy-to-install routing protocol that uses hop count as its sole metric. RIP has a hop count limit of 15. RIP uses split horizon, split horizon with poison reverse, and hold-down timers to help limit routing loops.

IGRP is also a distance-vector routing protocol. IGRP has a maximum hop count of 255. IGRP is not limited to using hop count as its sole metric. IGRP can also use load, bandwidth, reliability, delay, and maximum transmission unit when determining best path.

KEY TERMS

administrative distance — A value used to determine the reliability/desirability of a particular route table update.

autonomous system (AS) — A group of routers under the control of a single administration.

Border Gateway Protocol (BGP) — An exterior gateway protocol used to route between multiple autonomous systems.

convergence — The point at which all routers on a network agree upon the correct routes for that network and share a similar view of the network.

count-to-infinity — A routing loop whereby packets bounce infinitely around an internetwork.

defining a maximum — Defining a maximum hop count, so that packets cannot bounce infinitely throughout an internetwork.

distance-vector routing protocol — A routing protocol that functions by sending out periodic route table updates to all connected neighbors; examples include RIP and IGRP.

Enhanced Interior Gateway Routing Protocol (EIGRP) — A proprietary Cisco distance-vector protocol developed to overcome some of the limitations associated with distance-vector protocols.

Exterior Gateway Protocol (EGP) — An exterior gateway protocol used to route between multiple autonomous systems.

floods — The process of broadcasting packets onto a network.

hold-down timers — Used by routers to stabilize route tables and to prevent erroneous route table updates.

hop count — A count of the number of routers a packet must pass through in order to reach a destination network.

Interior Gateway Routing Protocol (IGRP) — A proprietary Cisco distance-vector routing protocol that uses hop count, delay, bandwidth, reliability, and maximum transmission unit as metrics.

Internetwork Packet exchange/Sequence Packet exchange (IPX/SPX) — Routed protocol stack developed by Novell for use with the Netware network operating system.

link-state advertisement (LSA) — Advertisement used by link-state routing protocols to advertise their route tables to all other routers in an internetwork.

link-state packets (LSP) — Used to send out link-state advertisements.

link-state routing protocols — Routing protocols that function via link-state advertisements using link-state packets to inform all routers on the internetwork of route tables.

logical addresses — Layer 3 addresses (also referred to as Network layer addresses) that allow routed protocols to determine which network a particular host is on.

maximum transmission unit (MTU) — The largest packet size allowed to pass across a network.

metric — A value used to define the suitability or desirability of a particular route.

nonroutable protocols — Protocols that do not contain Network layer addressing and therefore cannot pass between multiple networks.

Open Shortest Path First (OSPF) — A link-state routing protocol based upon open (nonproprietary) standards.

peer-to-peer networks — Small networks, normally consisting of fewer than 10 computers, in which each computer can give and receive network services.

routed protocols — Protocols that do contain Network layer addressing and therefore can pass between multiple networks.

routing loops — A network state in which packets are continually forwarded from one router to another in an attempt to find another path from a source network to a destination network.

Routing Information Protocol (RIP) — A distance-vector routing protocol that uses hop count as its primary metric.

routing protocols — Used by routers to define and exchange route table information in an internetwork.

Shortest Path First (SPF) algorithm — Complex algorithm used by link-state routing protocols to determine the best path in an internetwork.

split horizon — A technique used by routers to prevent routing loops. In short, a router will not send an update for a route via an interface from which it has received knowledge of that route.

split horizon with poison reverse — A split horizon in which the router responds to attempts to update a route with an update that marks the route in contention as unreachable.

time to live (TTL) — Normally, the same as the hop count. A packet with a TTL of 15 can pass through 15 routers before it is dropped.

Transmission Control Protocol/Internet Protocol (TCP/IP) — Routed protocol stack developed in the late 1960s for use on the precursor to the Internet; protocol stack of the modern-day Internet.

triggered updates — Occur due to network topology changes, not periodic route table advertisements.

topology — The physical or logical structure of an internetwork.

REVIEW QUESTIONS

1. Which of the following is necessary to add IGRP to a router? (Choose all that apply.)

   a. router rip

   b. router igrp [*autonomous system #*]

   c. network [*major network #*]

   d. router network igrp

2. What is the administrative distance of RIP?
   a. 100
   b. 110
   c. 120
   d. 90

3. Link–state routing protocols _____. (Choose all that apply.)
   a. use link-state advertisements to notify all routers of route changes
   b. send route table updates only to neighbors
   c. reach convergence faster than distance–vector routing protocols
   d. determine the best path via the hop count algorithm

4. RIP has a maximum hop count of _____.
   a. 255
   b. 16
   c. 15
   d. 254

5. Which command enables RIP on a router?
   a. router network RIP
   b. router rip
   c. router igrp
   d. router ospf

6. Which command will show the IP route table of a router?
   a. show ip route
   b. show ip protocol
   c. debug ip igrp events
   d. show run

7. True/False: Nonroutable protocols are able to pass packets among multiple networks.

8. IGRP can use which of the following as metrics? (Choose all that apply.)
   a. hop count
   b. bandwidth
   c. delay
   d. split horizon

9. Which of the following is a routed protocol? (Choose all that apply.)
   a. NetBEUI
   b. TCP/IP
   c. IPX/SPX
   d. RIP

10. Which of the following helps to prevent routing loops? (Choose all that apply.)

    a. split horizon

    b. count-to-infinity

    c. hold-down timers

    d. split horizon with poison reverse

11. At which router prompt can you use the router rip and router igrp command?

    a. RouterB#

    b. RouterB>

    c. RouterB(config)#

    d. RouterB(config-router)#

12. At which router prompt can you issue the network [*network #*] commands?

    a. RouterB#

    b. RouterB>

    c. RouterB(config)#

    d. RouterB(config-router)#

13. True/False: The debug ip rip command can be used in user mode and privileged mode.

14. Which of the following routing protocols can route between autonomous systems? (Choose all that apply.)

    a. IGRP

    b. RIP

    c. BGP

    d. EGP

15. What type of routing protocol is used within autonomous systems?

    a. Exterior Gateway Protocols

    b. TCP/IP

    c. NetBEUI

    d. Interior Gateway Protocols

16. RIP and IGRP both advertise a route to a particular network. Which route will be added to the route table?

    a. the RIP route

    b. the IGRP route

    c. NetBEUI

    d. BGP-enhanced IGRP

17. What command is used to display RIP timers?

    a. show ip route

    b. show run

    c. debug ip rip

    d. show ip protocol

18. What two commands are needed to enable RIP on a router? (Choose all that apply.)

    a. network rip

    b. router rip

    c. router network rip

    d. network [*network #*]

19. True/False: A metric is a variable used to determine the suitability of a route.

20. A major drawback of link-state routing protocols is _____.

    a. routing by rumor

    b. increased memory and processing on routers

    c. slow time to convergence

    d. inability to adapt to network topology changes

CASE PROJECTS

1. Antonia and Merlin have been hired by Big Tin Inc. to redesign Big Tin's network. Currently, the network consists of 14 routers with a potential growth of 3 routers in the next four months. They suggest the company implement RIP for internetwork routing. Is this the best possible solution for Big Tin Inc? Justify your answers.

2. Hogan's, an international food services conglomerate, wishes to implement wide area network links between their 25 plants spread across 13 countries. You have been brought in to act as a consultant on the project. Hogan's wishes for convergence to be as quick as possible, and, due to slow WAN links in some undeveloped countries, must reduce routing table updates to the absolute minimum. Hogan's wishes to use a distance-vector routing protocol because of their ease of use. Create a network design using the distance-vector protocol you feel will meet Hogan's needs. Support your answers in a one-page description of your design.

5

PPP AND ISDN

After reading this chapter and completing the exercises you will be able to:

♦ Describe Cisco's PPP encapsulation

♦ Configure PPP encapsulation and its options

♦ Describe and enable PPP multilink

♦ Explain how to implement ISDN BRI on Cisco routers

♦ Configure an ISDN BRI connection

In Chapter 9 of *CCNA Guide to Cisco Networking Fundamentals*, you received an overview of WAN technologies such as **Frame Relay**, **X.25**, and Integrated Services Digital Network (ISDN). You also learned about WAN connectivity terminology such as **channel service unit/digital service unit** (**CSU/DSU**), terminal adapter (TA), Central Office (CO), and **Regional Bell Operating Companies** (**RBOC**). WAN protocols, such as Point-Point Protocol (PPP) and High-level Data Link Control (HDLC), and WAN standards were also introduced. In this chapter, expanded coverage is given to PPP and ISDN. Then, you will revisit and learn more about each of these WAN technologies. Last, you will learn how to configure a Cisco router to support PPP and ISDN.

PPP

Point-to-Point Protocol (PPP) is an Internet standard protocol defined in RFCs 2153, 1661, and 3132. The **Internet Engineering Task Force (IETF)** defined PPP to provide router-to-router, host-to-router, and host-to-host connections. PPP is commonly used over dial-up or leased lines to provide connections into IP networks. PPP also supports other Network layer protocols such as Novell IPX and AppleTalk. Due to its flexibility, PPP is the most widely used WAN connection method today.

The **Serial Line Internet Protocol (SLIP)** was the predecessor to PPP; it only supported IP connections. Other advantages offered by PPP are the capability to handle **asynchronous** as well as **synchronous** communication. It also handles error correction. PPP is also more efficient and supports more protocols and interfaces. PPP can be used over several different physical interfaces, including:

- Asynchronous serial
- ISDN synchronous serial
- High-Speed Serial Interface (HSSI)

Asynchronous serial connections are typically used with analog modems, which connect directly to the existing phone lines and outlets that are wired in residential areas throughout the United States. ISDN **synchronous serial** connections require the use of **ISDN modem** equipment in order to interface with the Integrated Services Digital Network (ISDN) provided by many public carriers. (ISDN is described in greater detail later in this chapter.) **High-Speed Serial Interface (HSSI)** is a type of serial device that was developed by Cisco and T3Plus Networking. It defines a serial connection that operates at speeds of up to 52 Mbps over distances of up to 15 meters (50 feet).

PPP in the Protocol Stack

As mentioned, you can use PPP over both asynchronous and synchronous connections at the Physical layer of the OSI reference model. However, PPP also provides functions at the Data Link layer of the OSI reference model and relies on Network layer services called **Network Control Protocols (NCPs)**. NCPs are required for each protocol that utilizes PPP. Examples of NCPs include **IP Control Protocol (IPCP)**, **IPX Control Protocol (IPXCP)**, and **AppleTalk Control Protocol (ATCP)**. Figure 5-1 illustrates the location of PPP in the protocol stack; notice that the NCPs function at the Network layer.

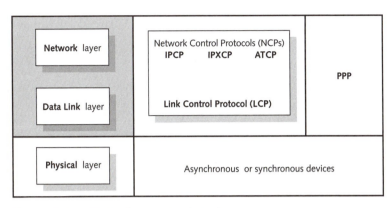

Figure 5-1   PPP in the protocol stack

5

Frame Format

PPP, like most WAN technologies, uses a variation of the **High-level Data Link Control (HDLC)** protocol. The difference between PPP frames and HDLC frames is that PPP frames contain protocol and **Link Control Protocol (LCP)** fields, as shown in Figure 5-2. The Protocol field allows PPP to support multiple protocols by allowing it to indicate which protocol it is encapsulating. PPP uses the LCP field to establish, configure, maintain, and terminate connections.

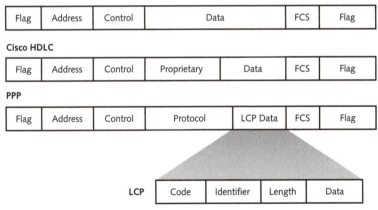

Figure 5-2   HDLC and PPP packet structure

Figure 5-2 also shows the Cisco proprietary HDLC frame. Cisco HDLC has proprietary fields that support the encapsulation of multiple protocols. Cisco's HDLC is the default encapsulation type for serial interfaces on Cisco routers. The elements of the PPP frame are as follows:

- **Flag**: Binary sequence 01111110, which indicates the beginning of the frame

- **Address**: Binary sequence 11111111; since PPP is used to create a point-to-point connection, there is no need for PPP to assign an individual address for each host.

- **Control**: Binary sequence 00000011, which indicates that the transmission of user data will not be sequenced and is to be delivered over a connectionless link

- **Protocol**: Two bytes used to identify the protocol that is encapsulated

- **LCP or Data**: The LCP field is also known as the Data field. This location contains the LCP information and the data that has been encapsulated from the higher layers. The default size of this field is 1500 bytes, but PPP implementations can negotiate a larger size for this field. LCP is explained in greater detail in the following section.

- **Frame Check Sequence (FCS)**: Two bytes by default, but can be as large as four bytes; uses a **cyclical redundancy check (CRC)** to verify the integrity of the frame to ensure that it was not corrupted during transmission

- **Flag**: Binary sequence 01111110, which identifies the end of the data frame

LCP

LCP is described in RFCs 1548, 1570, 1661, 2153, 1570, and 2484. RFC 1661, which made RFC 1548 obsolete, describes PPP organization and methodology, including basic LCP extensions. RFC 1661 was later updated by RFC 2153, which explains PPP Vendor extensions. RFC 1570 and its update, RFC 2484, further expand the definition of LCP extensions. The LCP field of the PPP packet can contain many different pieces of information, including:

- **Asynchronous character map**: Allows PPP to encode its transmission properly for the recipient host

- **Maximum receive unit size**: Sets the receive buffer size for the LCP connection, typically 1500 bytes

- **Compression**: Data compression that can be performed on the PPP packet at the source and then uncompressed at the destination; typically improves the speed of data transfer over slow serial connections because less data has to traverse the connection

- **Authentication**: Can be enabled to require a password in order to establish the PPP connection; two authentication protocols are available: **Password Authentication Protocol (PAP)** and **Challenge Handshake Authentication Protocol (CHAP)**. Authentication is described in greater detail in the following section.

- **Magic number**: Aids in detecting links that are in the looped-back condition. When interfaces are looped-back, data that is sent out the interface is immediately received on that interface. Magic numbers are unique numbers added by the router to a packet, which allow it to detect a looped-back link. If the router receives a packet that contains its own unique magic number, it detects that the interface is looped back. Loopback is typically used for testing interfaces to ensure they are sending and receiving data. The **loopback command** can be run from the interface configuration prompt. Although good for testing, looped-back interfaces are undesirable in production environments. In a production environment, you can use the **down-when-looped** command from interface configuration mode, which will automatically shut down that interface when looping is detected.

- **Link Quality Monitoring (LQM)**: Checks the reliability of the link by monitoring the number of errors, latency between requests, connection retries, and connection failures on the PPP link

- **Multilink**: Allows multiple transmission devices to send data over separate physical connections. The benefit of multilink is that you can combine the bandwidth of two separate devices over one logical connection. For example, two 64-Kbps ISDN channels can be combined to provide an effective throughput of 128 Kbps. PPP will fragment, sequence, and reassemble these packets in order to provide faster throughput over multiple slow serial connections. Multilink is defined in RFC 1717, and you can enable multilink with the ppp multilink command from the interface configuration mode.

LCP Link Configuration

The **LCP link configuration** process modifies and/or enhances the default characteristics of a PPP connection. This part of the link configuration process manages the link, controls the authentication, and can be used to set link quality. The LCP link configuration process includes the following actions: link establishment, authentication (optional), link-quality determination (optional), Network layer protocol configuration negotiation, and link termination. Each of these link configuration actions is described in the bulleted list below:

- **Link establishment**: PPP must open and configure the PPP connection before any data can be transferred over the link.

- **Authentication** (optional): CHAP or PAP can be used to verify the identity of the devices that are establishing the connection. CHAP and PAP are discussed in greater detail later in this chapter.

- **Link-quality determination** (optional): Checks the quality of the link and monitors its reliability

- **Network layer protocol configuration negotiation**: Identifies the appropriate Network layer protocol for the connection; the devices negotiate to use a protocol that is common to both.

- **Link termination**: When the call is complete, or the specifications defining the call are no longer met, the call is terminated.

Establishing PPP Communications

There are three phases in the establishing process: link establishment, authentication, and Network-layer protocol encapsulation. The link establishment phase involves the configuration and testing of the data link. As mentioned earlier, PPP connections may use the information contained in the LCP portion of the PPP packet to configure the link by passing requirements for maximum transmission units and compression.

The second phase of the establishing process is optional. The authentication process can use two authentication types with PPP connections: PPP and CHAP. Most network administrators configure their devices to use CHAP because it is the stronger authentication method of the two. RFC 1994, which made RFC 1334 obsolete, documents the PAP and CHAP authentication protocols.

PAP uses a simple two-way handshake method to establish the link. In this link, PPP transmits a clear text user name and password across the link between hosts in order to establish the link. The device attempting to establish the link transmits the user name and password, so that the destination host will allow the PPP session. PPP only conducts PAP authentication during initial link establishment.

Compared to PAP, CHAP provides a much more sophisticated authentication process. Like PAP, CHAP provides username and password authentication service during the initial link establishment. However, instead of stopping there, CHAP employs a three-way handshake. Once the link is established, the local router queries the remote host with a packet known as a **challenge**. The challenge is in the form of a unique encryption key. The remote host uses the encryption key to encode the username and password. The router compares the decrypted username and password and looks for a match with its username and password. It then either accepts or drops the connection based on whether the comparison yields a matching username and password.

After the connection is made, CHAP can continue this query process, using a different encryption key each time and do so using unique and unpredictable intervals. This further ensures that connections are legitimate because it prevents someone from capturing the data packets that are exchanged during the initial authentication process between two authorized systems and then playing those data packets from an unauthorized system in an attempt to gain PPP access to the server.

> The router typically controls the authentication process but a **Terminal Access Controller Access Control System (TACACS)** or third-party authentication server can also be used to centralize management of CHAP authentication and other security features.

PPP is an encapsulation type for serial interface communications. Therefore, to configure a PPP connection, you must access the interface configuration mode for the specific interface you wish to configure. For example, if you want to configure PPP on the first serial interface of the router (S0), you would use the commands shown in Figure 5-3 (assuming that the router was already in enable mode):

```
router#config t
router(config)#int s0
router(config-if)#encap ppp
```

Figure 5-3   Enabling PPP

Configuring PPP Authentication

Using authentication with PPP connections is optional. Therefore, you must specifically configure PPP authentication on each PPP host in order for the host to utilize PPP. You can choose to enable CHAP and/or PAP on your PPP connection, in either order. For example, to set the router to first use CHAP, and then to go to PAP (assuming that CHAP is not available), you would type the commands in Figure 5-4.

```
router(config-if)#ppp authentication chap pap
```

Figure 5-4   Enabling both CHAP and PAP authentication

If you entered that command, your local router would request CHAP authentication during the connection, but if the other device did not support CHAP or attempted PAP authentication instead, then PAP would be tried. You could also decide to use just CHAP or just PAP by omitting the undesired method from the command line. Also, if you reversed the authentication protocol order on the command line, then PAP would be the requested authentication type, and CHAP would be the alternate authentication type.

Once you set the authentication type, you must still configure a username and password for the authentication. To do so, you must exit interface configuration mode and enter global configuration mode. Then, type "username" followed by the hostname of the remote router; after that, type "password" followed by the password for that connection. Ensure that each router uses the same password, but place the other router's hostname after username of the connection. Figure 5-5 illustrates a configuration and the commands required for that configuration to operate using CHAP authentication.

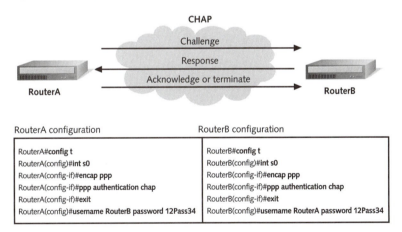

Figure 5-5   Configuring CHAP

If you want to configure the same hostname and password for CHAP authentication on several routers, you can do so via the interface configuration mode prompt. For example, if you wanted to configure the hostname flagstaff and set the password to lumberjack for all routers, you would enter the commands in Figure 5-6 on all router's PPP interfaces:

```
router(config-if)#ppp chap hostname flagstaff
router(config-if)#ppp chap password lumberjack
```

Figure 5-6   Configuring PPP and CHAP

In this example, the flagstaff hostname sets the alternate CHAP hostname to flagstaff. The lumberjack password part of the command sets the default CHAP password to lumberjack. This type of configuration is easier to implement than the one shown in Figure 5-5, in which you must configure each router with the same password, but with opposite hostnames.

 TIP   If you are using PAP authentication with Cisco IOS Releases 11.1 or later, you must enable PAP on the interface of the router to receive the PAP request.

Confirming PPP Communications

Once you have completed configuring your PPP interface, you can verify your changes using the show interface command. You must be in privileged EXEC mode in order to view the interfaces. For example, if you want to view your configuration on the Serial 1 interface, type the following:

Router#**sh int S1**

ISDN

Integrated Services Digital Network (ISDN) is a circuit-switched service provided by telecommunications providers to allow voice, data, video, and audio transmissions over existing digital telephone lines. ISDN is often used as a lower-cost alternative to Frame Relay or T1 connections, while still offering a higher connection speed than does an analog modem. The service is offered at two different levels: **Basic Rate Interface (BRI)** and **Primary Rate Interface (PRI)**. BRI is typically used in small offices or for home connections, and PRI is used in larger environments because it provides higher bandwidth.

Telecommunications providers offer digital connections via ISDN as channels. BRI connections offer three channels: two at 64 Kbps and one at 16 Kbps. The 64-Kbps channels are known as **bearer** or **B-channels**, because they carry the data for the connection. ISDN BRI connections use the 16-Kbps **signaling channel**, which is also called a **D-channel**, to control the communications on the link. PRI connections offer 23 B-channels and one 64-Kbps D-channel.

European ISDN PRI service offers 30 64-Kpbs B-channels and one 64-Kbps D-channel.

In both ISDN BRI and PRI, a single D-channel is used for signaling information, and the B-channels are used to carry the data. Because the control communications are conducted on a channel that is separate from the data transfer, ISDN is said to use **out of band signaling**.

ISDN Standards

The **International Telecommunications Union (ITU)** maintains several standards on ISDN. These standards are organized into ITU-T groups. The ITU-T groups are organized by three different letter designations: I, E, and Q. Each group is then subdivided into specific protocols, preceded by the group designator. For example, protocols I.430 and I.431 are part of the I-series protocol group. Protocols within each group define a related set of standards. Table 5-1 lists and describes the relationship between the protocol designators and the concepts that they define.

Table 5-1   ISDN protocol series

Protocol Series	Description	Examples
E	Telephone and network standards	E.163 – Telephone numbering E.164 – ISDN addressing
I	Methods, terminology, concepts, and interfaces	I.100 – Terminology, structure, and concepts I.300 – Networking recommendations
Q	Signaling and switching standards	Q.921 – Data Link layer LAPD procedures (explained later in this chapter) Q.931 – Network layer functions

ISDN Operations

ISDN uses both PPP and the **Link Access Procedure D-channel (LAPD)**. ISDN uses LAPD to pass the signaling messages between the router and the ISDN switch at the local CO. The data travels between routers on the B-channels via HDLC or PPP encapsulation, as shown in Figure 5-7.

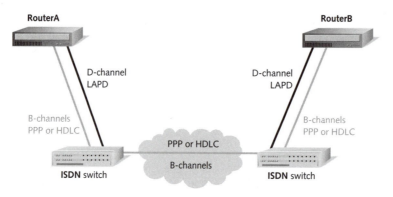

Figure 5-7   ISDN operations

Functions and References

ISDN standards use **function groups** and **reference points** to describe the various components that can be utilized in making an ISDN connection. Function groups describe a set of functions that are implemented by a device and software. For example, a **terminal adapter (TA)** converts network signals to a format appropriate for the ISDN connection. The TA is an example of a function group because it describes a device that provides a set of conversion functions to make ISDN communication possible. The connection between two function groups (including the cabling) is called a reference point. Not all function groups and reference points are required for each ISDN connection. Figure 5-8 shows the variety of different connection types that may exist.

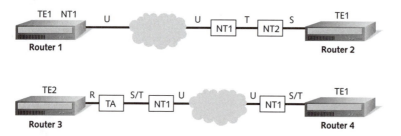

Figure 5-8   ISDN function groups and reference points

The function groups shown in the graphic are as follows:

- **Terminal adapter**: A converter device that allows non–ISDN devices to operate on an ISDN network

- **Terminal Equipment 1 (TE1)**: A device that supports ISDN standards and that can be connected directly to an ISDN network connection. For example, ISDN telephones, personal computers, or videophones could function as TE1s.

- **Terminal Equipment 2 (TE2)**: A non-ISDN device, such as an analog phone or modem, which requires a TA in order to connect to an ISDN network

- **Network Termination 1 (NT1)**: A small connection box that is attached to ISDN BRI lines. This device terminates the connection from the **Central Office (CO)**. In the graphic, the CO would be located inside the cloud, which represents the telephone company network.

- **Network Termination 2 (NT2)**: A device that provides switching services for the internal network. This type of interface is typically used with PRI lines, when they need to be divided for several functions. For example, some channels may be used for WAN data communications and others for the telephone system and/or video teleconferencing.

The reference points in Figure 5-8 include the following:

- **U**: The point that defines the demarcation between the user network and the telecommunications provider's ISDN facility. The **U-interface** is the actual two-wire cable, also called the **local loop**, that connects the customer's equipment to the telecommunications provider.

- **R**: The point between non-ISDN equipment (TE2) and the TA. The **R-interface** is the wire or circuit that connects TE2 to the TA.

- **S**: The point between the ISDN customer's TE1 or TA and the network termination (NT1 or NT2). The **S-interface** is a four-wire cable from TE1 or TA to the NT1 or NT2, which is a two-wire termination point.

- **T**: The point between NT1 and NT2, which is also the **T-interface**. This four-wire cable is used to divide the normal telephone company two-wire cable into four wires, which then allows the connection of up to eight ISDN devices.

- **S/T**: When NT2 is not used on a connection that uses NT1, the connection from the router or TA to the NT1 connection is typically called S/T. This is essentially the combination of the S and T reference points.

SPID

Many telecommunications providers utilize ISDN switches, which require **Service Profile Identifiers (SPIDs)** for dial-in access. SPIDs are frequently referred to as **ISDN phone numbers** because their functions are similar.

An ISDN device can access each ISDN channel via its SPID number. You can configure the router to utilize a single or multiple SPIDs when making a connection to the ISDN provider. The ISDN provider must assign the SPID numbers for each channel, which is normally an 8- to 14-digit numeric. Then, you can use those numbers to configure your ISDN dialer connections. You must also define the type of switch that is used at the Central Office to which you are connecting. The commands shown in Figure 5-9 illustrate an ISDN configuration.

```
router(config)#isdn switch-type dms-100
router(config)#interface bri 0
router(config-if)#isdn spid1 52069145231010
router(config-if)#isdn spid2 52069145241010
```

Figure 5-9   ISDN switch configuration

In this figure, the commands illustrate the configuration for a BRI connection over two channels. The switch type will usually be a Northern Telecom DMS-100 or an AT&T 5ess or 4ess. Notice in the first line that the switch type is a DMS-100. You will have to obtain the switch type and the SPID numbers from the ISDN providers. Potential switch types include the following:

- **dms-100**: Northern Telecom DMS-100 (as described above)

- **ni1**: National ISDN-1; used in North America

- **net3**: Net3 switch; used in Europe and the United Kingdom

- **ntt**: Switch from NNT; used in Japan

- **1tr6**: 1TR6 switch; used in Germany

- **ts013**: TS013 Australian switch

- **none**: Used when a switch has not been specified

If you want your Cisco router to answer incoming calls over your ISDN line, you can configure an ISDN subaddress. The subaddress is configured as subordinate to one of the ISDN SPIDs. For example, to define a subaddress for ISDN SPID2, the command would look like this:

Router(config-if)#**isdn answer 152069145241010 5551212**

Multilink PPP

RFC 1717 defines multilink PPP, which allows you to combine the individual bandwidth of several modems and/or several ISDN channels to increase the bandwidth of a single connection. Multilink provides load balancing, packet fragmentation and reassembly, and sequencing for packets sent across WAN links. Since multilink is a capability available in PPP connections, it can function over synchronous or asynchronous serial connections, such as analog modems or ISDN channels. The command to enable multilink is:

router(config-if)#**ppp multilink**

Each serial interface that is to be enabled with multilink must also be configured for PPP encapsulation and DDR.

DDR

The **Dial-on-demand routing (DDR)** feature that is available on Cisco routers allows you to use bandwidth as needed. This feature can save organizations money on connections because DDR automatically connects and disconnects the line and/or ISDN channels as needed to support requested bandwidth. A DDR connection will only be made when **interesting traffic** reaches a certain level. Interesting traffic is network traffic that you feel is worthy of activating or maintaining the link.

There are many different and important configuration commands to know for configuring a DDR connection. The following commands, shown in Figure 5-10, define the DDR connection parameters and define the connection link.

```
router(config-if)#dial wait-for-carrier time 15
router(config-if)#dialer idle-timeout 300
router(config-if)#dialer load-threshold 50 either
router(config-if)#dialer map ip 192.168.52.1 name FLG speed 56 5205551212
```

Figure 5-10   ISDN settings

The first command tells the dialer to wait no longer than 15 seconds for the ISDN provider to answer during a DDR connection attempt. The second command tells the dialer to hang-up the connection if the connection does not pass any interesting traffic for 300 seconds. The third command tells the dialer to only dial additional lines (assuming that you have configured multiple ISDN channels for the connection) when any channel is transferring at 50% of the available bandwidth, either inbound or outbound. In addition, load-threshold does allow you to specify a percentage load for inbound traffic, outbound traffic, or traffic in either direction. The fourth command maps the dialer to a specific hostname (FLG), IP address (192.168.52.1), speed (56 Kbps), and phone number (520551212). If you don't configure a speed, the default is assumed to be 64 Kbps.

In order to define what type of traffic is considered interesting, you must use dialer group commands. The commands in Figure 5-11 illustrate how you can use a dialer group and access lists to permit IP traffic on your link, but deny IGRP traffic.

```
router(config-if)#dialer-group 1
router(config-if)#exit
router(config)#dialer-list 1 protocol ip list 110
router(config)#access-list 110 deny igrp any any
router(config)#access-list 110 permit ip any any
```

Figure 5-11   ISDN and access lists

ISDN BRI Configuration Example

Now that you have seen the configuration parameters individually in the sections above, it is useful to consider a sample configuration. Figure 5-12 shows two routers that will be used to create a temporary ISDN BRI connection. The group utilizes up to two channels for IP traffic. The routers will not use a routing protocol because link use is to be minimized for this

DDR connection. (The point of DDR is to reduce the money spent on connection time.) In addition, routing updates are unimportant in this configuration because it is a point-to-point connection.

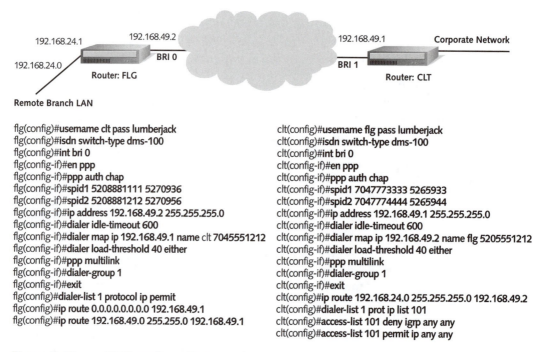

flg(config)#username clt pass lumberjack
flg(config)#isdn switch-type dms-100
flg(config)#int bri 0
flg(config-if)#en ppp
flg(config-if)#ppp auth chap
flg(config-if)#spid1 5208881111 5270936
flg(config-if)#spid2 5208881212 5270956
flg(config-if)#ip address 192.168.49.2 255.255.255.0
flg(config-if)#dialer idle-timeout 600
flg(config-if)#dialer map ip 192.168.49.1 name clt 7045551212
flg(config-if)#dialer load-threshold 40 either
flg(config-if)#ppp multilink
flg(config-if)#dialer-group 1
flg(config-if)#exit
flg(config)#dialer-list 1 protocol ip permit
flg(config)#ip route 0.0.0.0.0.0.0 192.168.49.1
flg(config)#ip route 192.168.49.0 255.255.0 192.168.49.1

clt(config)#username flg pass lumberjack
clt(config)#isdn switch-type dms-100
clt(config)#int bri 0
clt(config-if)#en ppp
clt(config-if)#ppp auth chap
clt(config-if)#spid1 7047773333 5265933
clt(config-if)#spid2 7047774444 5265944
clt(config-if)#ip address 192.168.49.1 255.255.255.0
clt(config-if)#dialer idle-timeout 600
clt(config-if)#dialer map ip 192.168.49.2 name flg 5205551212
clt(config-if)#dialer load-threshold 40 either
clt(config-if)#ppp multilink
clt(config-if)#dialer-group 1
clt(config-if)#exit
clt(config)#ip route 192.168.24.0 255.255.255.0 192.168.49.2
clt(config)#dialer-list 1 prot ip list 101
clt(config)#access-list 101 deny igrp any any
clt(config)#access-list 101 permit ip any any

Figure 5-12   ISDN configuration sample

Note that the routers in the graphic are both using PPP with CHAP authentication. The username has been set for the opposite router in each configuration, and the password is the same so that CHAP will authenticate properly. Each router has the ability to dial the other router. The CLT router is located at the corporate network, which has other connections and uses IGRP to transfer routing tables on the corporate network. However, IGRP is not desired on the ISDN connection, so the CLT router has an access list specifically denying IGRP on the ISDN link.

Further note that both routers do permit all IP traffic on the ISDN link and all IP traffic will be considered interesting or worthy of activating the ISDN link. Multilink is enabled on both routers, and they will dial their additional lines when there is 40% or more utilization on the first channel. The link will be terminated if there is no interesting traffic for 600 seconds (10 minutes). The IP routes are configured such that all traffic destined from the corporate network to 192.168.24.0 will be sent to the FLG router. Since the FLG router is a remote branch with no other connections, all traffic that is not specifically destined for 192.168.24.0 will be sent to the CLT router. Notice that each router has its dialer mapped to the IP address of the other router.

Monitoring ISDN

You can use the following commands to view your ISDN configuration, manage the link, and view statistics. All the commands are available via the privileged EXEC mode (enable mode) prompt.

- **clear interface**: Disconnects all current connections
- **show dialer**: Shows the current dialer status, including the time that the link has been active
- **debug dialer**: Displays the configuration and operation of the dialer
- **debug q921**: Shows the call connection establishment and disconnection
- **show isdn active**: Displays the status of the ISDN connection while the call is in progress
- **show isdn status**: Gives status information for ISDN connections
- **show int bri 0**: Shows you the configuration statistics and speed of your ISDN BRI interface

You can also use the show ip route command to view the routing table to ensure that the IP packets are being routed properly on your system. If you have all IP traffic enabled on the link, you can use the ping or telnet command to test the link.

Digital Lines

ISDN is only one type of connection that you can obtain from a telecommunications provider. Other types of digital connections are available. The following list contains some currently available services:

- **T1**: North American, 24-channel digital line capable of supporting data transmissions of up to 1.544 Mbps
- **T1C**: North American, 48-channel digital line capable of supporting data transmissions of up to 3.152 Mbps
- **T2**: North American, 96-channel digital line capable of supporting data transmissions of up to 6.312 Mbps
- **T3**: North American, 672-channel digital line capable of supporting data transmissions of up to 44.376 Mbps
- **T4**: North American, 4032-channel digital line capable of supporting data transmissions of up to 274.176 Mbps
- **E1**: Also known as **DS1**, this European 30-channel digital line is capable of supporting data transmissions up to 2.048 Mbps.
- **DS2**: European 120-channel digital line capable of supporting data transmissions of up to 8.448 Mbps

- **DS3**: European 480-channel digital line capable of supporting data transmissions of up to 34.368 Mbps

- **DS4**: European 1920-channel digital line capable of supporting data transmissions of up to 139.268 Mbps

- **DS5**: European 7680-channel digital line capable of supporting data transmissions of up to 565.148 Mbps

- **Fractional E1** and **fractional T1**: Some telecommunications providers allow organizations to order fractional T1 or E1 connections. A Fractional T1 or E1 occurs when less than the full bandwidth is available. For example, a Fractional T1 might be a 512-Kbps connection, instead of the full 1.544 Mbps.

- **Digital Subscriber Line (DSL)**: Services that offer high bandwidth over existing copper lines. DSL connections are generically referred to as **xDSL** because there are several different DSL technologies, such as **Asymmetric Digital Subscriber Line (ADSL)**, **High-bit-rate Digital Subscriber Line (HDSL)**, **ISDN Digital Subscriber Line (IDSL)**, **Symmetrical Digital Subscriber Line (SDSL)**, and **Very-high-data-rate Digital Subscriber Line (VDSL)**.

CHAPTER SUMMARY

There are many different WAN connectivity options available for modern networks. These options include digital lines, Frame Relay, and analog modems. WAN technologies typically define Data Link and Physical layer standards.

The Point-to-Point Protocol (PPP) is the most widely used WAN protocol in use today. On Cisco routers, PPP is used mainly as a Data Link layer encapsulation method; however, it does provide an interface to the Network layer via specific Network Control Protocols (NCPs). PPP provides link establishment, quality determination, Network layer protocol encapsulation, and link termination services. PPP is often used over Integrated Digital Service Network (ISDN) connections.

ISDN is a digital service provided by several telecommunications companies worldwide. ISDN was developed as a faster WAN connection to replace analog modems, and as a cheaper alternative to Frame Relay and full T1 connections. ISDN service comes in Basic Rate Interface (BRI) and Primary Rate Interface (PRI). BRI offers connections of up to 128 Kbps for data transfer, and PRI offers up to 24 channels in the United States, each with the ability to transfer data at 64 Kbps. Connections over ISDN can take advantage of dial-on-demand routing (DDR) and multilink services offered through PPP connections. DDR allows the router using an ISDN connection to dial additional channels as needed to support given traffic levels. Multilink allows ISDN to utilize mutliple channels evenly by spreading the load across those channels.

KEY TERMS

AppleTalk Control Protocol (ATCP) — PPP interface protocol for AppleTalk; *See* **Network Control Protocol**.

Asymmetric Digital Subscriber Line (ADSL) — DSL service that provides from 1.536-Mbps to 6.144-Mbps connections in the United States. Outside the U.S. connections are either 2.048 or 4.096 Mbps.

asynchronous — Communication technique that relies on start and stop bits to define the end points of a transmission. The implication of asynchronous communication is that timing mechanisms are not needed to maintain clock synchronization between the source and destination (as they are in synchronous communication).

asynchronous serial — Serial connections that are employed in most modems connected to residential phone lines.

authentication — The process of verifying the right to complete a connection.

Basic Rate Interface (BRI) — An ISDN service that provides two B-channels for data transfers up to 128 Kbps and one D-channel to control the communications.

B-channel — *See* **bearer channel**.

bearer channel — ISDN channel used to transfer data; typically supports 64-Kbps bandwidth.

Central Office (CO) — The telecommunications company location that is the point of entry to the toll network from the demarcation.

challenge — The query packet, or the action of sending the query packet over a CHAP connection, that is used to verify the participants of the PPP connection.

Challenge-Handshake Authentication Protocol (CHAP) — PPP authentication protocol that provides better security than PAP in authenticating devices on PPP connections.

channel service unit/digital service unit (CSU/DSU) — A device that provides connectivity between the WAN service provider network and the customer's LAN.

cyclical redundancy check (CRC) — A mathematical computation that is used to verify the integrity of a data packet.

D-channel — *See* **signaling channel**.

dial-on-demand routing (DDR) — A feature available on Cisco routers that allows you to use bandwidth as needed.

Digital Subscriber Line (DSL) — Telecommunications services that offer high bandwidth over existing copper lines. DSL connections are generically referred to as xDSL because there are several different DSL technologies.

down-when-looped — A Cisco router command that shuts down an interface when looping is detected; used to prevent testing scenarios from causing troubleshooting problems in a production environment.

DS1 — *See* **E1**.

DS2 — European 120-channel digital line capable of supporting up to 8.448-Mbps data transmissions.

DS3 — European 480-channel digital line capable of supporting up to 34.368-Mbps data transmissions.

DS4 — European 1920-channel digital line capable of supporting up to 139.268-Mbps data transmissions.

DS5 — European 7680-channel digital line capable of supporting up to 565.148-Mbps data transmissions.

E1 — European 30-channel digital line capable of supporting up to 2.048-Mbps data transmissions.

flag — Marks the beginning and ending of the frame.

Frame Check Sequence (FCS) — A mathematical computation placed at the end of the frame that is used to ensure that the frame was not corrupted during transmission.

fractional E1 — A service that offers some number of channels less than the 30 (64-Kbps) digital channels provided by a full E1 connection.

fractional T1 — A service that offers some number of channels less than the 24 (64-Kbps) digital channels provided by a full T1 connection.

Frame Relay - Frame Relay is purely a Data Link Layer protocol that relies on high-speed, highly reliable connections; it can operate between 56 Kbps and 1.544 Mbps over a WAN connection.

function groups — Used in ISDN communication to describe a set of functions that are implemented by a device and its software; a terminal adapter (TA) is a function group.

High-bit-rate Digital Subscriber Line (HDSL) — Symmetric digital communication service capable of 1.536 Mbps in the United States and 2.048 Mbps in Europe.

High-level Data Link Control (HDLC) — A Data Link layer encapsulation protocol that is a superset of the SDLC protocol. HDLC is a WAN protocol that can be used for both point-to-point and multipoint connections.

High-Speed Serial Interface (HSSI) — A type of serial device that was developed by Cisco and T3Plus Network that operates at speeds of up to 52 Mbps over distances of 15 meters.

Integrated Services Digital Network (ISDN) — A service provided by most major telecommunications carriers, such as AT&T, Sprint, and RBOCs; operates over existing phone lines and transfers both voice and data.

interesting traffic — Network traffic for which you feel it is worth activating or maintaining an ISDN link that is configured with DDR.

International Telecommunications Union (ITU) — Recommends telecommunications standards worldwide; implemented the Integrated Services Digital Network (ISDN).

Internet Engineering Task Force (IETF) — Researches and defines standards related to Internet communication; defined the serial line protocols PPP and SLIP.

IP Control Protocol (IPCP) — PPP interface protocol for IP; *see* **Network Control Protocol**.

IPX Control Protocol (IPXCP) — PPP interface protocol for IPX; *see* **Network Control Protocol**.

ISDN Digital Subscriber Line (IDSL) — A telecommunications service that makes an ISDN connection into a 128-Kbps DSL connection. Unlike ISDN, IDSL only supports data communications (not analog voice or video).

ISDN modem — *See* **terminal adapter**.

ISDN phone number — *See* **Service Profile Identifier (SPID)**.

LCP link configuration — A process that modifies and/or enhances the default characteristics of a PPP connection; includes the following actions: link establishment, authentication, link-quality determination, Network layer protocol configuration negotiation, and link determination.

Link Access Procedure D-channel (LAPD) — A WAN protocol adapted from HDLC; used in communication over ISDN lines.

Link Control Protocol (LCP) — Used in PPP connections to establish, configure, maintain, and terminate PPP connections.

link establishment — The process of opening and configuring a PPP connection before any data can be transferred over the link.

link-quality determination — The process of checking the quality of a PPP link and monitoring its reliability.

Link Quality Monitoring (LQM) — PPP feature that checks the reliability of the link by monitoring the number of errors, latency between requests, connection retries, and connection failures on the PPP link.

link termination — The process of disconnecting a PPP connection when the call is complete, which is determined by the PPP hosts that made the connection.

local loop — The connection between the demarcation point and the telephone company (WAN service provider) office.

loopback command — A Cisco router command that places an interface in a looped back state, which means that all outgoing data will be redirected as incoming data without going out on the network; used for testing purposes.

magic number — Unique numbers added by the router to a packet, which allows it to detect a looped-back link.

multilink — Allows multiple transmission devices (such as two modems) to send data over separate physical connections; defined in RFC 1717.

Network Control Protocol (NCP) — Allows PPP to encapsulate multiple protocols including IP, IPX, and AppleTalk. NCPs are functional fields that contain codes, which indicate the type of protocol that is encapsulated.

Network layer protocol configuration negotiation — The process of determining a Network layer protocol to use over a PPP connection that is common to both PPP hosts.

Network Termination 1 (NT1) — A small connection box that is attached to ISDN BRI lines. This device terminates the connection from the Central Office (CO).

Network Termination 2 (NT2) — A device that provides switching services for the internal network.

5

out of band signaling — The practice of controlling an ISDN connection on a channel other than the channel(s) on which data is transferred.

Password Authentication Protocol (PAP) — PPP authentication protocol that provides some security in verifying the identity of devices using PPP connections.

Point-to-Point Protocol (PPP) — An Internet standard WAN protocol defined in RFCs 2153, 1661, and 3132; used to provide router-to-router, host-to-router, and host-to-host WAN connections; a Data Link and Network layer encapsulation method.

Primary Rate Interface (PRI) — An ISDN service that provides 23 B-channels for data transfers up to 1.544 Mbps and one D-channel for controlling communications.

R — The point between non-ISDN equipment (TE2) and the TA.

reference points — Used in ISDN communications to identify specific connection points along the ISDN connection, including the cable that form those connections; *See* **U** and **U-interface**.

Regional Bell Operating Company (RBOC) — A company that was originally part of AT&T until antitrust laws caused their desolution. Examples of RBOCs are Pacific Bell, SouthWestern Bell, and NorthWestern Bell.

R-interface — The wire or circuit that connects TE2 to the TA.

S — The point between the ISDN customer's TE1 or TA and the network termination, NT1 or NT2.

Serial Line Internet Protocol (SLIP) — Originally used for IP connections over serial lines. However, since PPP is more efficient, supports more protocols, and can be used over more physical interfaces, it has replaced SLIP.

Service Profile Identifier (SPID) — A reference number assigned to ISDN channels; functions like a phone number.

signaling channel — Used for controlling ISDN connections; the D-channel is usually 16 Kbps in ISDN BRI and 64 Kbps in ISDN PRI connections.

S-interface — A four-wire cable from TE1 or TA to the NT1 or NT2, which is a two-wire termination point.

S/T — When NT2 is not used on a connection that uses NT1, the connection from the router or TA to the NT1 connection is typically called S/T. This is essentially the combination of the S and T reference points.

Symmetrical Digital Subscriber Line (SDSL) — A symmetric digital communication service that utilizes a combination of HDSL and the regular telephone system.

synchronous — Communications that are synchronous rely on a clock. The clock of the source and destination must be synchronized so that the destination can pick up and interpret the transmitted frames correctly.

synchronous serial — The type of serial connection that is used with ISDN lines.

T — The point between NT1 and NT2, which is also the T-interface; a four-wire cable that is used to divide the normal telephone company two-wire cable into four wires, which then allows you to connect up to eight ISDN devices.

T1 — North American 24-channel digital line capable of supporting up to 1.544-Mbps data transmissions.

T1C — North American 48-channel digital line capable of supporting up to 3.152-Mbps data transmissions.

T2 — North American 96-channel digital line capable of supporting up to 6.312-Mbps data transmissions.

T3 — North American 672-channel digital line capable of supporting up to 44.376-Mbps data transmissions.

T4 — North American 4032-channel digital line capable of supporting up to 274.176-Mbps data transmissions.

Terminal Access Controller Access Control System (TACACS) — An authentication protocol that allows Cisco routers to offload user administration to a central server. TACACS and Extended TAXACS (XTACACS) are defined in RFC 1492.

terminal adapter (TA) — A converter device that allows non-ISDN devices to operate on an ISDN network.

Terminal Equipment 1 (TE1) — A device that supports ISDN standards and can be connected directly to an ISDN network connection.

Terminal Equipment 2 (TE2) — A non-ISDN device, such as an analog phone or modem, which requires a TA in order to connect to an ISDN network.

T-interface — *See* **T**.

U — The point that defines the demarcation between the user network and the telecommunications provider ISDN facility.

U-interface — The actual two-wire cable, also called the local loop, which connects the customer's equipment to the telecommunications provider.

Very-high-data-rate Digital Subscriber Line (VDSL) — A digital subscriber technology that supports 51.84-Mbps connections over unshielded twisted-pair cable.

X.25 — A standard that defines a packet switching network; a packet switching WAN service provided by telecommunications providers such as MCI, Sprint, and AT&T.

xDSL — *See* **Digital Subscriber Line**.

REVIEW QUESTIONS

1. What do ISDN protocols that begin with E define?

   a. methods, terminology, concepts, and interfaces

   b. telephone and network standards

   c. encapsulation

   d. signaling and switching

2. The standards defined in the ISDN I.100 protocol cover which of the following?

   a. signaling and switching

   b. telephone and network standards

   c. ISDN addressing

   d. methods, terminology, concepts, and interfaces

3. If you want to use CHAP authentication, which protocol would you employ?

   a. multilink

   b. PAP

   c. Frame Relay

   d. PPP

4. Which of the following is the correct syntax to set the switch type to dms–100?

   a. router>isdn switch-type dms–100

   b. router#en switch-type dms–100

   c. router(config)#isdn switch-type dms–100

   d. router(config-if)#isdn switch-type dms–100

5. If you are configuring an ISDN connection and want to enable multilink, which of the following is the correct prompt and command?

   a. router(config)#ena multilink

   b. router(config-if)#ppp multilink

   c. router>ppp multilink

   d. router#enable multilink

6. Which of the following is typically used as a cheap alternative to Frame Relay or a T1 connection, but typically offers better performance than an analog modem?

   a. ISDN BRI

   b. T2

   c. E1

   d. DS5

7. What does the reference point R in ISDN communications indicate?

   a. demarcation point between the user network and the telecommunications company

   b. point between the non-ISDN equipment and the terminal adapter

   c. point between the ISDN customer's TE1 or TA and the network termination NT1

   d. point between NT1 and NT2

8. In ISDN communications, what does the functional group TE2 represent?

   a. terminal adapter

   b. a non-ISDN device

   c. a device often used with ISDN PRI service

   d. connection box that is attached to ISDN BRI lines, which terminates the connection from the CO

9. What is the ISDN indicator for a converter device that allows non–ISDN devices to operate on an ISDN network?

   a. TE2

   b. NT1

   c. U

   d. TA

10. What do ISDN protocols that begin with Q define?

   a. methods, terminology, concepts, and interfaces

   b. telephone and network standards

   c. encapsulation

   d. signaling and switching

11. What does the reference point U in ISDN communications indicate?

   a. a demarcation point between the user network and the telecommunications company

   b. a point between the non–ISDN equipment and the terminal adapter

   c. a point between the ISDN customer's TE1 or TA and the network termination NT1

   d. a point between NT1 and NT2

12. In ISDN communications, what does the functional group NT1 represent?

   a. a terminal adapter

   b. a small connection device attached to ISDN BRI lines, which terminates the connection from the CO

   c. a non–ISDN device

   d. device often used with ISDN PRI service, which provides switching services for the internal network

13. What does the reference point S in ISDN communications indicate?

   a. a demarcation point between the user network and the telecommunications company

   b. a point between the non–ISDN equipment and the terminal adapter

   c. a point between the ISDN customer's TE1 or TA and the network termination NT1

   d. a point between NT1 and NT2

14. Which of the following protocols would you use when establishing a connection over ISDN?

   a. SLIP

   b. PPP

   c. PAP

   d. CHAP

5

15. What does the reference point T in ISDN communications indicate?

    a. demarcation point between the user network and the telecommunications company

    b. point between the non–ISDN equipment and the terminal adapter

    c. point between the ISDN customer's TE1 or TA and the network termination NT1

    d. point between NT1 and NT2

16. Which portion of a PPP frame indicates the higher layer encapsulated protocol?

    a. Protocol

    b. Address

    c. Control

    d. LCP

17. To check your LCP and NCP states for PPP connections, you must run the show interface command from which prompt?

    a. router#

    b. router>

    c. router(config)#

    d. router(config-if)#

18. What is the default encapsulation type on serial interfaces of Cisco routers?

    a. PPP

    b. HDLC

    c. SDLC

    d. Frame Relay

19. Which of the following is an NCP? (Choose all correct answers.)

    a. IPXCP

    b. HDLC

    c. SDLC

    d. ATCP

    e. IPCP

20. PPP was derived from _____.

    a. Frame Relay

    b. HDLC

    c. RBOC

    d. ISDN

21. What is a common reason for looping an interface?

    a. to achieve greater bandwidth

    b. to drop nonessential frames

    c. to increase packet size

    d. testing

22. Which of the following is a unique number that helps devices discover looped interfaces?

    a. MAC

    b. LCP

    c. magic number

    d. bandwidth

23. Which of the following employs the strongest encryption technique?

    a. plaintext

    b. PAP

    c. CHAP

    d. clear text

24. If you want your router to use CHAP and then PAP authentication, which of the following commands would be correct?

    a. router>ppp au chap pap

    b. router#ppp authentication chap pap

    c. router(config-if)#ppp au pap chap

    d. router(config-if)#ppp au chap pap

    e. router(config)#ppp authentication chap pap

CASE PROJECTS

1. Rob and Mike are network administrators for a company that has offices in Greensboro and Charlotte, North Carolina. Each office has a few users that must communicate with each other and across the WAN link. All network users utilize a database that is located in Charlotte. They need to connect the two offices via some type of WAN link. The link is not expected to get heavy use, but they do need something faster than the 56K modem, which is what they are using now. Assume that you have been brought in as a consultant for this scenario. Consider the questions that you would have for Rob and Mike about their connectivity requirements. What type of information would you need to collect? What equipment might be part of the connectivity solution? How would you configure the connectivity equipment?

2. Dave is an employee of a large dry goods manufacturer in Phoenix, Arizona, but he lives and works 140 miles north of Phoenix in Flagstaff. Currently Dave uses an ISDN BRI connection to connect to the main intranet. Dave also uses one of the BRI channels to routinely transfer files to the main office in Phoenix. The information that Dave transfers to the main office is typically text file order forms, not more than 30K each, and no more than 10 forms per day are usually submitted. However, Dave maintains the company's Web site which is on his Web server in Flagstaff. Lately, some of the distributors have been complaining that the large product catalogs they require from the company's Web site are downloading quite slowly. In an attempt to keep the distributors happy, Dave is considering ordering a faster connection to the Internet from his telecommunications provider. Assume that you have been sent to help Dave investigate his connectivity options. What information would you collect? Which type of WAN connections would you consider?

3. Your network consulting team has been brought in by XYZ Corporation to solve a WAN connectivity problem. The customer has reported that the ISDN BRI connections it has in three different locations are not functioning properly. The remote office in Lexington, MO, won't connect at all. The router does dial, but the connection is dropped before it ever has a chance to connect. The main office in New York, NY, seems to maintain a connection all the time, even though it is supposed to be dial on demand. The branch office in Los Angeles, CA, doesn't seem to utilize both of its channels no matter how much data is being transmitted across the link. What type of information would you collect from each of these locations? What specific configuration parameters would you be interested in seeing for each location?

6

FRAME RELAY

After reading this chapter and completing the exercises, you will be able to:

- ♦ Understand Frame Relay standards and equipment
- ♦ Describe the role of virtual circuits and performance parameters in Frame Relay
- ♦ Understand the Frame Relay topologies
- ♦ Configure and monitor Frame Relay

WAN technologies typically define the Physical and Data Link layer connections. **Frame Relay** is both a Data Link layer encapsulation type implemented on the router and a Physical service provided by a telecommunications company. In this chapter, you will learn about Frame Relay terms, specifications, and service types. In addition, you will see how to implement and configure Frame Relay connections on Cisco routers.

FRAME RELAY STANDARDS AND EQUIPMENT

Frame Relay is a packet switching and encapsulation technology that functions at the Physical and Data Link layers of the OSI reference model. Frame Relay is a communications technique for sending data over high-speed digital connections operating anywhere from 56 Kbps to 44.736 Mbps or higher. The **International Telecommunication Union-Telecommunications Standardization Sector (ITU-T)** and the **American National Standards Institute (ANSI)** define Frame Relay as a connection between the **data terminal equipment (DTE)** and the **data communications equipment (DCE)**. DCE is switching equipment, supplied by a telecommunications provider, that serves as a connection to the **public data network (PDN)**. DTE is also known as **customer premises equipment (CPE)**, because it is the equipment that belongs to, and is maintained by, the PDN customer. For example, if you connect your Cisco router to a **Frame Relay switch** (which is provided by the phone company), the Cisco router is the CPE and the Frame Relay switch is the DCE, as shown in Figure 6-1.

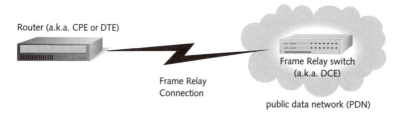

Figure 6-1   CPE to DCE connection

> **TIP** The ITU-T was formerly known as the **Consultative Committee on International Telephony and Telegraphy (CCITT)**, which is the primary international organization for fostering cooperative standards for telecommunications equipment and systems.

The physical equipment that is used on a network may vary from one organization to another. For example, some networks may use a separate router and **channel service unit/digital service unit (CSU/DSU)** to make their WAN connections. In Figure 6-2, you can see a CSU/DSU that is used with a Cisco 2501 router to make the connection. The CSU/DSU is located at the customer location of the digital connection. The unit is used for encoding, filtering, and translating communications to and from the digital line.

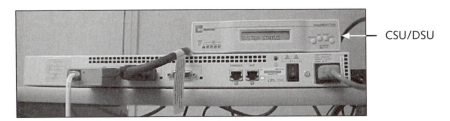

Figure 6-2 CSU/DSU and router

Some routers have built-in cards that allow them to make WAN connections. For example, in Figure 6-3, you can see a T1 CSU/DSU card built into the router. The router in the picture is a Cisco 1600 series router. Notice that a T1 line connects directly to the CSU/DSU on the back of the router.

6

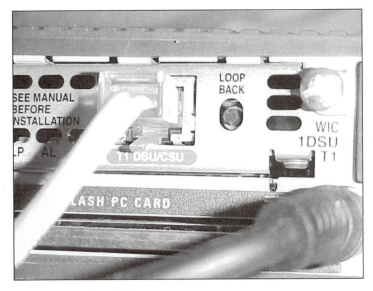

Figure 6-3 CSU/DSU connection

 TIP The order of the acronym—CSU/DSU or DSU/CSU—is unimportant, because both forms refer to the same device. The correct ordering of the three-letter acronyms is a matter of personal preference.

In Frame Relay connections, the network device that connects to the Frame Relay switch is also known as a **Frame Relay access device (FRAD)**; you may also see this defined as **Frame Relay assembler/disassembler**. The Frame Relay switch is also called the **Frame Relay network device (FRND)**, which is pronounced "friend." The network administrator typically handles the local connection up to the point that it enters the PDN. Items that are part of the PDN, including the Frame Relay switch, fall under the control and responsibility of the telecommunications provider.

VIRTUAL CIRCUITS

You can use Frame Relay with nearly any serial interface. It operates by multiplexing, which means that it combines multiple data streams onto one physical link. Frame Relay separates each data stream into logical (software-maintained) connections called **virtual circuits**, which carry the data transferred on the connection. Two types of virtual circuits, **switched virtual circuits** (**SVC**) and **permanent virtual circuits** (**PVC**), connect Frame Relay ports. SVCs, which are the less common of the two, are controlled by software and are only active while a connection to the WAN is active. The SVC software automatically dials the WAN, establishing and terminating the connection as required to transfer data over the Frame Relay service. PVCs, which are the more common of the two, remain permanently connected to the WAN. The network administrator manually defines the PVC; it remains until the network administrator removes it.

DLCI

Frame Relay connections identify virtual circuits by **Data Link Connection Identifier** (**DLCI**) numbers. The DLCI (pronounced *dell-see*) numbers map virtual circuits to layer 3 protocol addresses. For example, a DLCI number associates an IP address with a specific virtual circuit. DLCI numbers are not unique identifiers on the network; instead, they have only local significance, which means they are important only to the local router and Frame Relay switch.

Frame Relay Map

DLCI numbers are mapped, or assigned, to a specific interface. Each router that supports Frame Relay will have a **Frame Relay map**, which is a table that defines the specific interface to which a specific DLCI number is mapped. The definition will contain a DLCI number and an interface identifier.

Figure 6-4 shows a sample Frame Relay configuration. RouterA has two serial interfaces configured for Frame Relay. The first serial interface (S0) on RouterA is configured for DLCI 9, in order to form a virtual circuit between itself and RouterB. The second serial interface (S1) is configured for DLCI 12. It refers to a virtual circuit between RouterA and RouterB. The Frame Relay map shows which destination IP addresses are used with which DLCI numbers.

Notice that the **Frame Relay switching table** is configured to map its ports (P0, P1, and P2) to the correct DLCI numbers for the virtual connection. Each switching table entry consists of four elements: the incoming port on the switch, the incoming DLCI number, the outgoing port on the switch, and the outgoing DLCI number. The switching table in this example is simplified; in reality, the switch would be more complex and involve additional Frame Relay switches.

In the example, only the mapping table for RouterA is shown. In reality, however, each router will have its own mapping table. Remember that DLCI numbers are only locally significant, so it would be possible for RouterA and RouterB to use the same DLCI number to specify a virtual circuit.

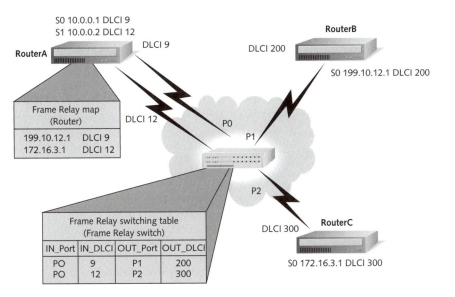

Figure 6-4   Sample Frame Relay configuration

Subinterfaces

In Figure 6-4, RouterA has two different serial interfaces, each configured for one virtual connection. In early implementations of Frame Relay, each PVC required its own dedicated serial interface. With current technology, however, a single router serial interface can now service multiple PVCs through a single physical serial interface. In order to allow a single serial interface to support multiple PVCs, the IOS divides the interface into logical **subinterfaces**.

By dividing a single physical interface into several logical subinterfaces, the cost of implementing multiple Frame Relay virtual circuits is reduced because only one port is required on the router. Also, the network administrator has to configure and maintain fewer physical connections. You learned in Chapter 5 that decimal numbers following the physical interface identifier reference the subinterfaces defined on Cisco routers. For example, if Serial 0 (S0) had three subinterfaces, they would be referenced as S0.1, S0.2, and S0.3.

LMI

Frame Relay engineers designed **Local Management Interface (LMI)** to exchange information about PVC status and to ensure that the link between two points was operating correctly. LMI is a standard signaling mechanism between the CPE (usually a router) and the Frame Relay connection. It provides the CPE with a local DLCI number and gives that DLCI number network-wide, or global, significance. Providing DLCI numbers that are globally rather than just locally significant makes automatic configuration of the Frame Relay map possible (as explained in the following section).

LMI uses **keepalive packets** (sent every 10 minutes by default) to verify the Frame Relay link and to ensure the flow of data. The Frame Relay switch in turn provides to the Frame Relay connectivity device the status of all virtual circuits that the device can utilize. Each virtual circuit, represented by its DLCI number, can have one of three connection states:

- **Active**: The connection is working and routers can use it to exchange data.

- **Inactive**: The connection from the local router to the switch is working, but the connection to the remote router is not available.

- **Deleted**: No LMI information is being received from the Frame Relay switch; this can indicate that the connection between the CPE and DCE is not functional.

The Frame Relay switch reports this status information to the Frame Relay map on the local router. The status information is used by the Frame Relay connectivity devices to determine whether data can be transmitted over the configured virtual circuits.

Inverse ARP

As previously mentioned and illustrated in Figure 6-4, a Frame Relay map includes DLCIs and their corresponding remote IP addresses. Routers use the protocol **Inverse ARP** to send a query using the DLCI number to find an IP address. As other routers respond to the Inverse ARP queries, the local router can build its Frame Relay map automatically. In order to maintain the Frame Relay map, routers exchange Inverse ARP messages every 60 seconds, by default.

 If the remote router does not support Inverse ARP, the Frame Relay map will have to be maintained statically (built and updated manually by the network administrator). Do not confuse Inverse ARP with **Reverse Address Resolution Protocol (RARP)**; RARP is used primarily on LANs to provide hosts that only have MAC addresses with IP addresses.

Encapsulation Types

LMI has several different protocol encapsulation types that it can use for management communications. Different Frame Relay switches, CPE, and Frame Relay connectivity equipment employ or support different types of LMI encapsulation. Cisco routers, for example, support these types of LMI encapsulation:

- cisco: This LMI type was originally defined by four companies: DEC, Nortel, Stratac, and Cisco. It allows for 992 virtual circuit addresses and uses DLCI 1023 as a management circuit, which transfers link and DLCI status messages.

- ansi: ANSI standard T1.617 Annex-D provides for 976 virtual circuit addresses and uses DLCI 0 as the management circuit.

- q933a: ITU-T Q.933 Annex A, similar to ANSI T1.617 Annex-D, uses DLCI 0 as a management circuit.

Cisco routers (using IOS Release 11.2 or later) can autosense the LMI type used by the Frame Relay switch. If the Frame Relay responds with more than one LMI type, the Cisco router will automatically configure itself to use the last LMI type received. The network administrator can also manually configure the LMI type. This manual configuration is explained later in the chapter.

The basic LMI type has three information elements: report type, keepalive, and PVC status. The report type indicates whether the message is just a keepalive frame or a full status message. The Frame Relay devices send keepalive frames every 5–30 seconds (10 by default) to ensure that the link is still active. Full status messages contain DLCI status in addition to the keepalive information.

As stated, management circuits transfer DLCI status messages. Depending on your Frame Relay provider, these messages may contain all or some of the following pieces of information concerning the status of the virtual circuit:

- New: Used if a new DLCI connection has been configured

- Active: Used to indicate whether the virtual circuit is available for data transfer

- Receiver not ready: Used for flow control to indicate that the virtual circuit is congested. This option is not available in the q933a LMI type.

- Minimum bandwidth: Indicates the minimum available bandwidth

- Global addressing: Used to give DLCI global significance, as described earlier

- Multicasting: Used to configure a group of destination addresses rather than a single address. The IEEE has reserved DLCI numbers 1019 through 1022 for this purpose. Frame Relay devices use multicasting to make DLCI numbers globally significant by advertising them across the Frame Relay network.

- Provider-Initiated Status Update: Normally, the Frame Relay switch obtains PVC status information only when the CPE sends a full status message and requests status information for the other DLCI connections. This option allows the provider to initiate a status inquiry.

Not all Frame Relay providers support every piece of link status information. All current implementations provide the New and Active information, but support for other information varies by provider.

Frame Relay does not provide error checking, as do other network protocols such as **Synchronous Data Link Control (SDLC)**. This makes Frame Relay connections more efficient, but it also means that Frame Relay must rely on the upper-layer protocols, such as TCP, to provide error correction.

Split Horizon

Split horizon is a routing technique that reduces the chance of **routing loops** on a network. A split horizon implementation prevents routing update information received on one physical interface from being rebroadcast to other devices through that same physical interface. People also refer to this rule as **nonbroadcast multiaccess (NBMA)**.

Although split horizon is useful for reducing routing loops, it can cause problems for Frame Relay routing updates. For example, consider a router (RouterA), which is connected to two other routers (RouterB and RouterC) through a single physical interface configured for different virtual circuits (see Figure 6-5). Assuming that RouterA is not using subinterfaces, it would not be able to send router updates received from RouterB to RouterC, and vice versa.

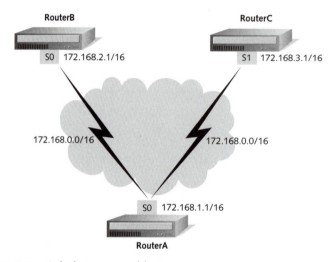

Figure 6-5 Split horizon problem

If the network is using IP, split horizon could be disabled on RouterA, which would solve the problem. However, disabling split horizon is not an option for IPX/SPX or AppleTalk. Furthermore, if the network administrator disables split horizon, the chance of getting routing loops on the network will be increased. The best solution is to configure subinterfaces for each virtual connection, because the individual virtual circuits can be maintained and split horizon can remain on. Routing update information that is received through one subinterface can be propagated to other subinterfaces.

As an example of this use of subinterfaces, examine Figure 6-6. It is the same as Figure 6-5, except that now the division of serial zero (S0) into subinterfaces S0.1 and S0.2 allows a different subnet identifier to be assigned to each virtual circuit. This allows router updates going from RouterB to be transmitted to RouterC, and vice versa.

6

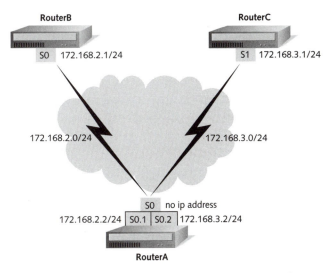

Figure 6-6   Subinterfaces in use in a point-to-point configuration

The network administrator can set each subinterface as a point-to-point connection or a multipoint connection. Point-to-point connections allow you to divide a single serial interface into multiple subinterfaces, each supporting a separate virtual connection. The network administrator must configure each subinterface with its own subnet identifier in a point-to-point configuration, as shown in Figure 6-6. In a multipoint configuration, the network administrator can configure a single subinterface to support multiple connections to physical or logical interfaces on other routers. A multipoint configuration on a subinterface is still subject to the split horizon rule, but it does allow you to configure a single network identifier for all of your routers, as shown in Figure 6-7.

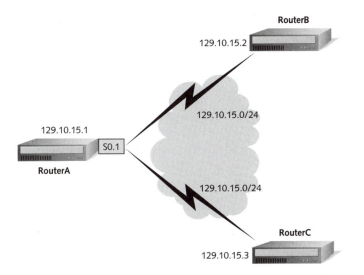

Figure 6-7   Single subinterface configured for multiport connection

Notice that in Figure 6-7, the network uses the same subnet identifier for both virtual circuit connections. Note also that the routers all share the same subnet, identified by their first three octets.

PERFORMANCE PARAMETERS

When organizations contract Frame Relay services from a telecommunications provider such as MCI, Sprint, AT&T, or one of the Regional Bell Operating Companies (RBOCs), the contract specifies parameters by which the connection is expected to function. Terms that appear in the contract may include:

- **Access rate**: The speed of the line, which indicates transfer rate. Common U.S. access rates are 56 Kps, and 64 and 128 Kbps, which are provided by Integrated Service Digital Network (ISDN) connections, and 1.544 Mbps, which is provided by T1 connections. Access rate is also known as the **local access rate**.

- **Committed information rate (CIR)**: The minimum transfer rate that the Frame Relay customer negotiates with the Frame Relay service provider. The service provider agrees to always allow the customer to transfer information at no less than the transfer rate specified by the CIR. This is usually lower than the access rate because the transfer rate may exceed the CIR during short bursts.

- **Committed Burst Size (CBS)**: The maximum amount of data bits that the service provider agrees to transfer in a set time period under normal conditions.

- **Excess Burst Size (EBS)**: The amount of excess traffic (over the CBS) that the network will attempt to transfer during a set time period. The network can discard EBS data, if necessary.

- **Oversubscription**: When the sum of the data arriving over all virtual circuits exceeds the access rate, the situation is called oversubscription. This can occur when the CIR is exceeded by burst traffic from the virtual circuits. Oversubscription results in dropped packets. In such a case, the dropped packets must be retransmitted.

Congestion

Frame Relay switches attempt to control congestion on the network. When the Frame Relay switch recognizes congestion, it sends a **forward explicit congestion notification (FECN)** message to the destination router. This message tells the router that congestion was experienced on the virtual circuit. In addition, the switch sends a **backward explicit congestion notification (BECN)** message to the transmitting, or source, router. The router's reaction to the BECN should be to reduce the amount of traffic it is sending.

A network administrator can configure certain types of traffic at the router as **discard eligible (DE)**. Thus, during times of congestion, the router can discard DE frames in order to provide a higher, more reliable, service to those frames that are not discard eligible.

FRAME FORMAT

Frame Relay devices can utilize different Frame Relay frame formats. Since this course is focused on Cisco devices, this section will focus on the Cisco proprietary Frame Relay frame format, its Frame Relay frame structure, and the Address field of the frame.

Figure 6-8 shows the Frame Relay frame format, the basic frame structure, and an expanded look at the Address field of that structure.

Flag	Address	Ethertype	Data	Frame Check Sequence	Flag
1 byte	2–4 bytes	2 bytes	Variable	2 bytes	1 byte

	8	7	6	5	4	3	2	1
1st byte	DLCI, high-order bits						CR	EAO
2nd byte	DLCI, low-order bits				FECN	BECN	DE	EA1

Figure 6-8   Frame Relay frame format

The Frame Relay frame format has specific parts, as discussed below:

- **Flag**: An eight-bit binary sequence (01111110) that indicates the start of the data frame

- **Address**: Two to four bytes that contain several pieces of Frame Relay information

- **Ethertype**: Identifies the type of higher-layer protocol being encapsulated (IP, IPX, or AppleTalk); this data field is specific to the Cisco proprietary frame format.

- **Data**: A variable length field that contains the information from the higher layers encapsulated in the Frame Relay frame

- **FCS**: **frame check sequence (FCS)**, or **cyclical redundancy check (CRC)**, is a mathematical computation placed at the end of the frame and is used to ensure that the frame was not corrupted during transmission.

- **Flag**: An eight-bit binary sequence (01111110) that indicates the end of the data frame

Although the Address portion of the Frame Relay frame can contain up to four bytes, Figure 6-8 displays only two bytes because that is the most common format. Three- and four-byte addressing varies only slightly from the structure of two-byte addressing. Refer back to Figure 6-8 as you read the descriptions for the bits of the Address field.

- **CR**: A command or response bit that is used for sending connection management and frame acknowledgement information between stations

- **FECN**: Setting used to alert receiving devices if the frame experiences congestion

- **BECN**: Setting used on frames traveling away from the congested area to warn source devices that congestion has occurred on that path

- **DE**: Discard eligible bit that is used to identify frames that are first to be dropped when the CIR is exceeded. Cisco routers allow you to set the DE bit for a particular virtual connection by DLCI number.

- **EA**: Extension address bits that are used to extend the address field from two bytes to either three or four bytes. It allows you to create additional DLCI numbers. For each EA bit that is turned on, one byte is added to the address field.

Although the Frame Relay frame formats vary slightly, the above information provides a thorough description. In addition to variety in Frame Relay formats, there is some variation in the topology that Frame Relay can utilize. In the next section you will explore different Frame Relay topologies.

FRAME RELAY TOPOLOGIES

You can use different topologies to create Frame Relay connections. These topologies are the **star**, the **partial mesh**, and the **full mesh**. Figure 6-9 depicts the three topologies.

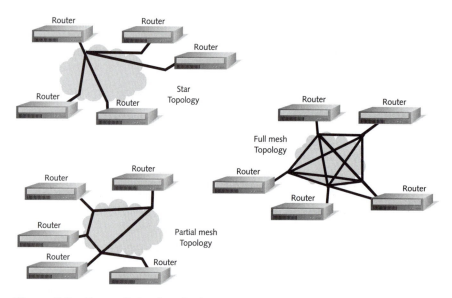

Figure 6-9   Frame Relay topologies

The star is the most popular Frame Relay topology. This configuration is also called the **hub-and-spoke** topology because one router functions as a central point, or hub, in a simple hierarchical configuration. All other devices are connected to the central router as spokes would connect to a hub. Typically the network administrator will configure the central router with a single interface that makes a multipoint connection to all other routers. The star is also the least expensive topology because it requires the least number of virtual circuits.

The full mesh is the most expensive topology to implement because each router has a direct connection to every other router. However, this topology is the most fault-tolerant because there are always at least two routes to every router on the network. The more routers added to the full mesh, the more expensive the topology becomes, because multiple routes are required for each router.

The partial mesh is a compromise between the hierarchy of the star and the expense of the full mesh. A partial mesh is not as expensive as a full mesh because the principle of connecting every router to every other router is not required. Instead, connections are made according to need and traffic flow. If there is heavy traffic flow to one router, multiple virtual circuits may be established between that router and the routers sending the most traffic to it. The partial mesh does not follow the hierarchical structure of the star, in that all routers do not have to be connected to a single central router. Essentially, any Frame Relay topology that isn't a star or a full mesh is a partial mesh.

FRAME RELAY CONFIGURATION

In this section, you will learn how to configure Frame Relay over serial interfaces, using IP as the Network layer protocol. To implement such a configuration, you must configure the serial interfaces or subinterfaces to IP addresses, map the DLCI numbers to the correct IP addresses, and then configure the desired options for the virtual circuit.

Basic Configuration

Begin with configuring the easiest Frame Relay connection: the local and remote routers that will support LMI and Inverse ARP. In this case, LMI will notify the router about the available DLCI numbers.

Look at Figure 6-10 and assume that you are responsible for configuring RouterA. RouterA is a Cisco router running IOS version 11.2, so it has the ability to autosense the LMI type. In addition, it automatically receives the DLCI information by querying the network. You only have to configure the serial interface for the correct IP address (129.10.15.1) and the subnet mask (255.255.255.0), and then configure it to support Frame Relay. Assume that the negotiated bandwidth of this connection is 56 Kbps and that you want to use the Routing Information Protocol (RIP) to pass the routing table updates between the routers.

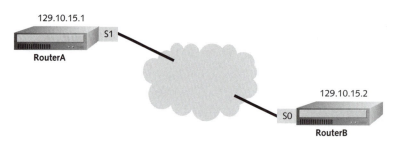

Figure 6-10   Simple Frame Relay configuration

Table 6-1 lists the Cisco router prompts and commands that you will need to complete this configuration.

Table 6-1   Basic router prompts and commands for configuring the multipoint example shown in Figure 6-10

Router prompts this:	You type this:	Description
router>	en	Allows you to enter privileged EXEC (a.k.a. enable) mode. You will be prompted to enter the appropriate password after this command.
router#	config t	Allows you to configure the router from the terminal line
router(config)#	int s1	Tells the router to access interface serial 1 for configuration
router(config-if)#	ip address 129.10.15.1 255.255.255.0	Maps the interface serial 1 to the IP address and subnet mask shown
router(config-if)#	en fr	Sets the encapsulation for this port to Frame Relay using Cisco (the default). The other option is ietf.
router(config-if)#	ban 56	Sets the bandwidth for this port to 56 Kbps
router(config-if)#	exit	Exits interface configuration mode
router(config)#	router rip	Enables the RIP for routing table updates
router(config-router)#	net 129.10.15.0	Enables RIP on the specified network address

The commands in Table 6-1 successfully configure RouterA for the connection shown in Figure 6-10.

Now, assume that you are the network administrator for RouterB and all the same information applies, except that your router is using IOS release version 11.0, which does not support automatic LMI sensing. To accommodate this new fact, you would have to enter the LMI type and, of course, different IP addresses. Last, for this example, assume that the LMI type is ansi.   With all these conditions, the configuration commands for RouterB are shown in Figure 6-11.

```
router#config t
router(config)#int sl
router(config-if)#ip address 129.10.15.2 255.255.255.0
router(config-if)#en fr
router(config-if)#ban 56
router(config-if)#frame-relay lmi-type ansi
router(config-if)#ex
router(config)# router rip
router(config-router)# net 129.10.15.0
```

Figure 6-11   RouterB configuration

Subinterface Configuration

Configuring subinterfaces for Frame Relay requires a little more work than just configuring interfaces. You have to configure each subinterface and virtual circuit in order to do it successfully.

To configure a multipoint subinterface, you map it to multiple remote routers using the same subnet mask, but different DLCI numbers. For example, assume that you are the administrator for RouterA in Figure 6-12 and you want to configure subinterface S1.2, which has IP address 192.168.51.1 and subnet mask 255.255.255.0, to connect over three different virtual connections to the remote Routers B, C, and D.

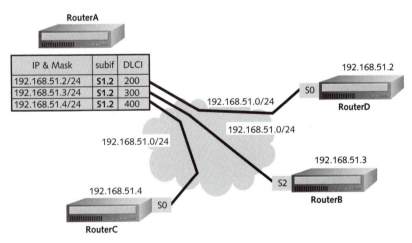

Figure 6-12   Multipoint subinterface configuration on S1.2

Table 6-2 outlines the steps to configure Router A.

Table 6-2   Subinterface configuration prompts and commands

Router prompts this:	You type this:	Description
router#	config t	Allows you to configure the router from the terminal line
router(config)#	int s1	Tells the router to access interface serial 1 for configuration
router(config-if)#	no ip address	When you are configuring a subinterface, you do not want the main interface to have an IP address; this command removes any configured IP address for the S1 interface.
router(config-if)#	en fr	Sets the encapsulation for this port to Frame Relay using Cisco (the default). The other option is ietf.
router(config-if)#	exit	Exits interface configuration mode
router(config)#	int s1.2 multipoint	Configures subinterface S1.2 for a multipoint connection
router(config-subif)#	ip ad 192.168.51.1 255.255.255.0	Sets S1.2 for the IP address shown
router(config-subif)#	ban 64	Sets the bandwidth for this port to 64 Kbps
router(config-subif)#	fr map ip 192.168.51.2 200 b	Maps subinterface to DLCI 200 and enables broadcast routing updates
router(config-subif)#	fr map ip 192.168.51.3 300 b	Maps subinterface to DLCI 300 and enables broadcast routing updates
router(config-subif)#	fr map ip 192.168.51.4 400 b	Maps subinterface to DLCI 400 and enables broadcast routing updates
router(config-subif)#	exit	Leaves subinterface configuration mode
router(config)#	router rip	Enables RIP
router(config-router)#	network 192.168.51.0	Sets RIP to be used on the network

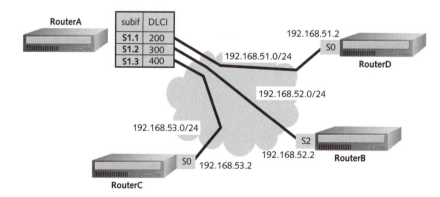

Figure 6-13   Point-to-point configuration sample using subinterfaces

The previous commands define a multipoint connection. You could, however, make a point-to-point connection by assigning different IP addresses to each connection on RouterA and creating separate subnets for each virtual circuit. Assuming that you decide to use 192.168.52.1 and 192.168.53.1 for the additional serial interfaces, the point-to-point configuration illustrated in Figure 6-13 is created by the commands in Figure 6-14.

```
router(config)#int s1
router(config-if)#no ip address
router(config-if)#en fr
router(config-if)#exit
router(config)#int s1.1 point-to-point
router(config-subif)#ip ad 192.168.51.1 255.255.255.0
router(config-subif)#ban 64
router(config-subif)#frame-relay interface-dlci 200 b
router(config-if)#exit
router(config)#int s1.2 point-to-point
router(config-subif)#ip ad 192.168.52.1 255.255.255.0
router(config-subif)#ban 64
router(config-subif)#frame-relay interface-dlci 300 b
router(config-if)#exit
router(config)#int s1.3 point-to-point
router(config-subif)#ip ad 192.168.53.1 255.255.255.0
router(config-subif)#ban 64
router(config-subif)#frame-relay interface-dlci 400 b
router(config-subif)#exit
router(config)#router rip
router(config-router)#network 192.168.51.0
router(config-router)#network 192.168.52.0
router(config-router)#network 192.168.53.0
```

Figure 6-14   Point-to-point configuration commands

Notice that the frame-relay interface-dlci 200b command is used in the command set shown in Figure 6-14. With point-to-point subinterfaces, this is the command you must use to associate the interface to a DLCI number. The frame-relay interface-dlci command can be abbreviated "fr int".

Frame Relay Static Mapping

As shown in Figure 6-14, you sometimes have to define the DLCI numbers manually. This is called making a **static address to DLCI Frame Relay map**. You statically configure your DLCI entries in the following situations:

- The remote router doesn't support Inverse ARP.
- You need to assign specific subinterfaces to specific DLCI connections.
- You want to reduce broadcast traffic.
- You are configuring **Open Shortest Path First (OSPF)** over Frame Relay.

To configure the Frame Relay map manually, you must use the frame-relay map command. The command has the following syntax:

frame-relay map protocol address dlci *[broadcast] [ietf : cisco] [payload-compress packet-by-packet]*

You have not seen the last two optional parameters in the previous examples. The Frame Relay encapsulation type can be selected as either ietf or cisco. If you do not make a choice, the cisco encapsulation type is the default. You should only select ietf when connecting to a non-Cisco router. Payload-compress packet-by-packet is a Cisco proprietary compression method that is off by default.

Keepalive Configuration

By default, keepalive packets are sent out every 10 seconds to the Frame Relay switch. Keepalive packets, as previously described, are used to maintain the connection and inform the router of the connection status. You can change the keepalive period by typing "keepalive" followed by the time in seconds of the keepalive period at the the router(config-if)# interface configuration prompt. The keepalive period can be set from as low as zero to as high as 32,767 seconds. For example, if you want to set the keepalive period to 64 seconds, type "keepalive 64" at the interface configuration prompt.

EIGRP Bandwidth

If you configure **Enhanced IGRP (EIGRP)** on your Frame Relay connection, you can set the percentage of bandwidth that can be used for EIGRP routing traffic. The percentage is based on the bandwidth number that was configured with the bandwidth command (as shown in previous examples). If no bandwidth number was set, the default is 1.544 Mbps. A sample command for configuring EIGRP bandwidth is:

Router(config-if)#**ip bandwidth-percent eigrp 6750 50**

This command allows EIGRP to use up to 50% of the available bandwidth for its connection. The number 6750 is the autonomous system number, which is used to help EIGRP construct a consistent picture of the routed environment.

Monitoring Frame Relay

You can check your Frame Relay configuration by using show commands. These commands allow you to verify that the commands you entered above produced the desired effect on your router. Figures 6-15, 6-16, 6-17, and 6-18 show the commands and their output.

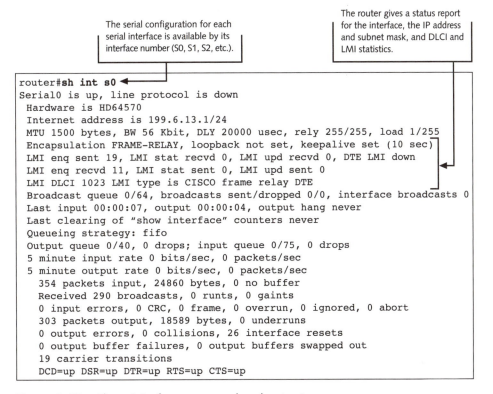

The serial configuration for each serial interface is available by its interface number (S0, S1, S2, etc.).

The router gives a status report for the interface, the IP address and subnet mask, and DLCI and LMI statistics.

```
router#sh int s0
Serial0 is up, line protocol is down
  Hardware is HD64570
  Internet address is 199.6.13.1/24
  MTU 1500 bytes, BW 56 Kbit, DLY 20000 usec, rely 255/255, load 1/255
  Encapsulation FRAME-RELAY, loopback not set, keepalive set (10 sec)
  LMI enq sent 19, LMI stat recvd 0, LMI upd recvd 0, DTE LMI down
  LMI enq recvd 11, LMI stat sent 0, LMI upd sent 0
  LMI DLCI 1023 LMI type is CISCO frame relay DTE
  Broadcast queue 0/64, broadcasts sent/dropped 0/0, interface broadcasts 0
  Last input 00:00:07, output 00:00:04, output hang never
  Last clearing of "show interface" counters never
  Queueing strategy: fifo
  Output queue 0/40, 0 drops; input queue 0/75, 0 drops
  5 minute input rate 0 bits/sec, 0 packets/sec
  5 minute output rate 0 bits/sec, 0 packets/sec
    354 packets input, 24860 bytes, 0 no buffer
    Received 290 broadcasts, 0 runts, 0 gaints
    0 input errors, 0 CRC, 0 frame, 0 overrun, 0 ignored, 0 abort
    303 packets output, 18589 bytes, 0 underruns
    0 output errors, 0 collisions, 26 interface resets
    0 output buffer failures, 0 output buffers swapped out
    19 carrier transitions
    DCD=up DSR=up DTR=up RTS=up CTS=up
```

Figure 6-15   Show interface command and output

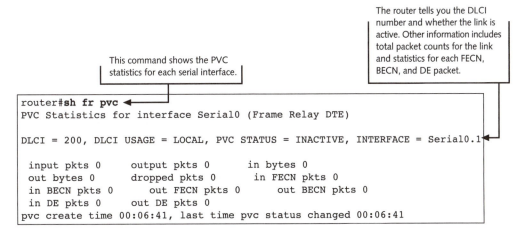

This command shows the PVC statistics for each serial interface.

The router tells you the DLCI number and whether the link is active. Other information includes total packet counts for the link and statistics for each FECN, BECN, and DE packet.

```
router#sh fr pvc
PVC Statistics for interface Serial0 (Frame Relay DTE)

DLCI = 200, DLCI USAGE = LOCAL, PVC STATUS = INACTIVE, INTERFACE = Serial0.1

  input pkts 0       output pkts 0       in bytes 0
  out bytes 0        dropped pkts 0       in FECN pkts 0
  in BECN pkts 0      out FECN pkts 0       out BECN pkts 0
  in DE pkts 0       out DE pkts 0
pvc create time 00:06:41, last time pvc status changed 00:06:41
```

Figure 6-16   Show Frame Relay permanent virtual circuit command and output

6

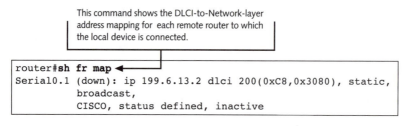

Figure 6-17   Show Frame Relay map command and output

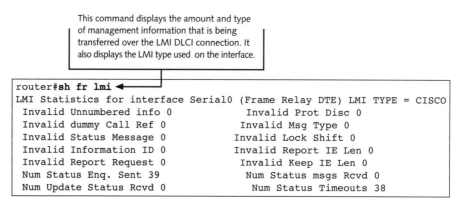

Figure 6-18   Show Frame Relay Local Management Interface command output

---

CHAPTER SUMMARY

Frame Relay is a flexible WAN technology that can be used to connect two geographically separate LANs. Frame Relay is both a service and type of encapsulation. The service parameters must be discussed with the Frame Relay provider (telecommunications company). Service parameters for Frame Relay include the access rate, committed information rate (CIR), Committed Burst Size (CBS), and Excess Burst Size (EBS).

Frame Relay connections employ virtual circuits that can be either permanent or switched. Virtual circuit connections across Frame Relay connections are defined by Data Link Connection Identifier (DLCI) numbers. The DLCI numbers can be associated with Network layer addresses; however, they are only locally significant unless the Local Management Interface (LMI) is available. Most Frame Relay providers support LMI, which allows Frame Relay maps to be dynamically created via Inverse ARP. Static mappings of DLCI numbers to remote IP addresses can be configured when routers do not support Inverse ARP. Inverse ARP is on by default for multipoint configurations. Inverse ARP is not enabled on point-to-point links because there is only one path. Frame Relay circuits can be established over serial interfaces or subinterfaces on Cisco routers.

KEY TERMS

access rate — The speed of the line that indicates transfer rate. Common U.S. access rates are 56, 64, and 128 Kbps provided by Integrated Service Digital Network (ISDN) connections and 1.544 Mbps provided by T1 connections.

American National Standards Institute (ANSI) — A standards organization based in the United States involved with various WAN standards.

backward explicit congestion notification (BECN) — A message sent to the source router when congestion is discovered on the link. The recipient router's reaction to the BECN should be to reduce the amount of traffic it is sending.

channel service unit/digital service unit (CSU/DSU) — A telecommunications device that provides connectivity between the WAN service provider network and the customer's LAN.

Committed Burst Size (CBS) — The maximum amount of data bits that the service provider agrees to transfer in a set time period under normal conditions.

committed information rate (CIR) — The minimum transfer rate that the Frame Relay customer negotiates with the Frame Relay service provider.

Consultative Committee on International Telephony and Telegraphy (CCITT) — The former name of **International Telecommunication Union - Telecommunications Standardization Sector (ITU-T)**.

customer premises equipment (CPE) — Equipment located at the WAN customer's location that is maintained by the customer; also known as **data terminal equipment (DTE)**.

cyclical redundancy check (CRC) — A mathematical computation that is used to verify the integrity of a data packet.

data communications equipment (DCE) — Equipment that is supplied by the telecommunications provider as the connection to their network, such as a Frame Relay or ISDN switch.

Data Link Connection Identifier (DLCI) — Pronounced *dell-see*, it is configured on the router and used to identify which path leads to a specific Network layer address (i.e., IP address). The DLCI is not a network-wide unique address (like a MAC address); instead, the DLCI is only locally significant, meaning that it can, and usually does, change on each physical link.

data terminal equipment (DTE) — Device located at the WAN customer's location that is maintained by the customer and used to make the WAN connection; also known as **customer provided equipment (CPE)**.

discard eligible (DE) — During times of congestion, DE frames are discarded in order to provide a higher, more reliable, service to those frames that are not DE.

Enhanced IGRP (EIGRP) — A protocol that provides more efficient convergence and data transfer than the previous IGRP.

Excess Burst Size (EBS) — The amount of excess traffic (over the CBS) that the network will attempt to transfer during a set time period. EBS data can be discarded by the network, if necessary.

flag — Flags or delimiters mark the beginning and ending of the frame.

6

forward explicit congestion notification (FECN) — A Frame Relay message that tells a router that congestion was experienced on the virtual circuit.

frame check sequence (FCS) — A mathematical computation placed at the end of the frame that is used to ensure that the frame was not corrupted during transmission.

Frame Relay — A Data Link layer protocol that relies on high-speed, highly reliable connections. This protocol can operate between 56 Kbps and 1.544 Mbps over a WAN connection.

Frame Relay access device (FRAD) — The device that the Frame Relay customer utilizes to connect to a Frame Relay network; also known as the **Frame Relay assembler/disassembler**.

Frame Relay assembler/disassembler — *See* **Frame Relay access device (FRAD)**.

Frame Relay map — A table that defines the interface to which a specific DLCI number is mapped.

Frame Relay network device (FRND) — The device that the Frame Relay provider supplies as the connection to the Frame Relay network; the acronym FRND is pronounced *friend*.

Frame Relay switch — A telecommunications company device that is used to support Frame Relay connections from customer locations; used to route Frame Relay traffic inside the public data network.

Frame Relay switching table — A table that is maintained on a Frame Relay switch; used to route Frame Relay traffic via virtual circuit DLCI numbers.

full mesh — The most expensive and most fault-tolerant Frame Relay topology. This topology ensures that each Frame Relay device on the network has an individual router to every other Frame Relay device on the network.

hub-and-spoke topology — *See* **star topology**.

International Telecommunication Union - Telecommunications Standardization Sector (ITU-T) — A standards organization based in Europe, but with membership worldwide; involved in telecommunications standardization.

Inverse ARP — A protocol that allows a router to send a query using the DLCI number to find an IP address.

keepalive packets — Data packets sent between devices to confirm that a connection should be maintained between them.

local access rate — *See* **access rate**.

Local Management Interface (LMI) — A standard signaling mechanism between the CPE and the Frame Relay connection. The LMI can provide the network server with a local DLCI; it can also give DLCI global (network-wide) significance rather than just local significance, and it can provide keepalive and status information to the Frame Relay connection. The LMI also uses Inverse ARP to automatically determine the protocol address of remote devices.

nonbroadcast multiaccess (NBMA) — A rule used in Frame Relay that does not allow broadcasts to be sent to multiple locations from a single interface.

Open Shortest Path First (OSPF) — A link-state IGP used to route information between internal routers while taking into account the load, congestion, distance, bandwidth, security, and reliability of the link.

oversubscription — When the sum of the data arriving over all virtual circuits exceeds the access rate.

partial mesh — A compromise between the full mesh and star topologies for Frame Relay. The partial mesh provides for some redundant routes between certain devices, but not all devices.

permanent virtual circuit (PVC) — A connection to the WAN that is established by the network administrator at the customer location. PVC connections are not expected to be terminated and therefore remain active.

public data network (PDN) — A telecommunications network that connects telephones around the country. These services can be provided by AT&T, Sprint, MCI, and RBOCs.

Reverse Address Resolution Protocol (RARP) — Used to resolve the IP address to the MAC address for the final leg of communication between an IP source and destination. In this way, it is similar to ARP.

routing loops — These packets are sent in endless loops around the network, forwarded from one router to another because no router has an entry that correctly applies to the packet.

split horizon — A technique used by Frame Relay to help prevent routing loops by preventing a single interface from advertising multiple addresses and DLCI numbers.

star topology — The least expensive Frame Relay topology to implement; in this topology, one router serves as the central hub for the entire Frame Relay network; this is also called the hub-and-spoke topology.

static address to DLCI Frame Relay map — A Frame Relay map that has been manually created by a network administrator.

subinterface — A logical division of an interface; for example, a single serial interface can be divided into multiple logical subinterfaces.

switched virtual circuit (SVC) — A temporary virtual circuit that is created when a network device calls the WAN to establish a connection. The SVC is terminated when the connection is terminated.

Synchronous Data Link Control (SDLC) — A protocol developed by IBM in the 1970s to allow IBM host systems to communicate over WAN connections. The SDLC protocol can be used for point-to-point or point-to-multipoint connection between remote devices and a central mainframe.

virtual circuit — Point-to-point connections through a switched network.

6

REVIEW QUESTIONS

1. Which protocol is utilized to automatically build the Frame Relay map along with LMI?

   a. ARP

   b. RARP

   c. Inverse ARP

   d. DLCI

2. In order to make DLCI numbers globally significant, the Frame Relay LMI interface causes routers to issue _____ that advertise the DLCI numbers.

   a. unicasts

   b. keepalives

   c. broadcasts

   d. multicasts

3. When negotiating a data transfer rate for Frame Relay with a telecommunications provider, the rate agreed upon is the _____.

   a. keepalive rate

   b. CIR

   c. EBS

   d. DDR

4. The Address portion of the Frame Relay frame contains which of the following pieces of information? (Choose all that apply.)

   a. DLCI

   b. FECN

   c. flag

   d. BECN

   e. FCS

5. The line speed of a Frame Relay connection is known as the _____.

   a. access rate

   b. CBS

   c. EBS

   d. CIR

6. _____ numbers are locally significant in Frame Relay connections and are used to identify specific virtual circuits.

   a. DLCI

   b. PDN

   c. ARP

   d. LMI

7. In order to prevent routing loops, Frame Relay utilizes _____.

   a. loopback attack

   b. split horizon

   c. event horizon

   d. DLCI numbers

8. Frame Relay is more efficient than older WAN encapsulation methods because error correction is handled by _____ in Frame Relay communications.

   a. lower layers

   b. DLCI

   c. LMI

   d. upper layers

9. Frame Relay uses _____ to combine multiple data streams on one connection.

   a. duplexing

   b. simplexing

   c. multiplexing

   d. encoding

10. What is the purpose of keepalive packets?

   a. to reduce data transfer rates

   b. to keep PVCs active

   c. to increase data transfer rates

   d. to negotiate connection speed

11. Which of the following layers do WAN specifications typically define? (Choose all that apply.)

   a. Physical

   b. Data Link

   c. Network

   d. Transport

   e. Presentation

12. In Frame Relay, what would be considered the DCE?

   a. customer's router

   b. terminal adapter

   c. PPP

   d. Frame Relay switch

13. Which of the following was formerly CCITT?

    a. ASCII

    b. ANSI

    c. ITU-T

    d. EBCDIC

14. What is another acronym used to describe a Frame Relay switch?

    a. FRND

    b. FRAD

    c. PDN

    d. PSTN

15. Which of the following would be a subinterface for Serial 1?

    a. S0.1

    b. S0.2

    c. S1.2

    d. S2.1

16. What does LMI stand for?

    a. Logical Management Interface

    b. Local Management Interface

    c. Logical Maintenance Interconnect

    d. Logical Maintenance Interface

17. What are the three possible connection states for a DLCI? (Choose all that apply.)

    a. interactive

    b. active

    c. inactive

    d. disconnected

    e. deleted

18. Which of the following does not allow broadcasts to be sent to multiple destinations through a single interface?

    a. LMI

    b. subinterfaces

    c. LCP

    d. MBA

    e. NBMA

19. Which of the following is a type of virtual circuit? (Choose all that apply.)

    a. MVC

    b. PVC

    c. SVC

    d. QVC

20. Which of the following are LMI encapsulation types supported by Cisco routers? (Choose all that apply.)

    a. LMI 2

    b. cisco

    c. ansi

    d. v923i

    e. q933a

21. Which of the following is the default LMI encapsulation type for a Cisco router?

    a. LMI 2

    b. cisco

    c. ansi

    d. v923i

    e. q933a

22. What does the router(config-if) #en fr command do?

    a. sets the enable mode prompt to FR

    b. enables Frame Relay on the first serial interface

    c. sets the encapsulation to Frame Relay

    d. sets the language to French

23. Which of the following commands would show statistics for a virtual circuit?

    a. router>sh fr map

    b. router#sh fr map

    c. router#sh fr pvc

    d. router(config-if)#sh fr pvc

24. What does the "6950" stand for in the following command?

    router(config-if) #ip bandwidth-percent eigrp 6950 40

    a. percentage of bandwidth allowed for the connection

    b. percentage of bandwidth disallowed for the connection

    c. percentage of existing bandwidth remaining

    d. autonomous system number

25. How often are Frame Relay keepalive packets sent, by default?

    a. every 30 seconds

    b. every 10 seconds

    c. once every hour on the half-hour

    d. once every hour on the hour

    e. once every 30 minutes

CASE PROJECTS

1. Your company has decided to use Frame Relay to connect several different locations. You are in Austin, Texas, and will be connecting PVCs to Dallas, San Antonio, and Houston. You are expected to have a conference call with the network administrators at the other locations to discuss the Frame Relay configuration. What type of information will have to be coordinated among the various locations? What type of information would you require in order to configure your Cisco 2500 series router to support your Frame Relay connection?

2. Your consulting team is working on a multilocation Frame Relay configuration. There are five locations, all using LMI and globally significant DLCI numbers. Each location has been configured with multipoint connections to the other sites. The network administrator is located in Mobile, Alabama, with remote locations in Key West, Florida; San Diego, California; San Angelo, Texas; and Napa Valley, California. You are consulting with the network administrator for the configuration, and he wants to know the differences between multipoint and point-to-point connections. How could you explain the differences to him using his network as an example?

3. You have been informed that the Frame Relay connection between Lexington, Missouri, and Athens, Georgia, has gone down. Someone has already contacted the phone company and determined that the Frame Relay switches are operating properly. Someone told you that the connection may be misconfigured. You decide to verify the Frame Relay configuration between the two locations. What type of information would you require? What type of configuration problems might you expect to find? What commands would you use to check the configuration?

CHAPTER

7

SWITCHING AND VLANS

After reading this chapter and completing the exercises, you will be able to:

- ◆ Explain the features and benefits of Fast Ethernet
- ◆ Describe the guidelines and distance limitations of Fast Ethernet
- ◆ Define full- and half-duplex Ethernet operation
- ◆ Distinguish between cut-through and store-and-forward LAN switching
- ◆ Define the operation of the Spanning Tree Protocol and its benefits
- ◆ Describe the benefits of virtual LANs

In this chapter, you will revisit some of the concepts surrounding Ethernet operations. Specifically, you will learn about Ethernet performance and methods for improving it. Standard and Fast Ethernet will be part of this discussion, as will half- and full-duplex Ethernet operations. The concepts central to LAN switching—such as switch operations, forwarding techniques, and VLANs—will also be explained.

ETHERNET OPERATIONS

As you have learned, **Ethernet** is a **network access method** (or **media access method**) originated by the University of Hawaii, later adopted by Xerox Corporation, and standardized as IEEE 802.3 in the early 1980s. Today, Ethernet is the most pervasive network access method in use and continues to be the most commonly implemented media access method in new LANs. Many companies and individuals are continually working to improve the performance and increase the capabilities of Ethernet technology.

In the following sections, you will revisit the Ethernet access method, discuss Ethernet errors, investigate latency problems, and learn ways in which Ethernet performance can be improved. Becoming comfortable with these concepts will help you troubleshoot and improve the performance of your LAN.

CSMA/CD

Ethernet uses **carrier sense multiple access with collision detection (CSMA/CD)** as its **contention method**. This means that any station connected to the network can transmit any time that there is not already a transmission on the wire. After each transmitted signal, each station must wait a minimum of 9.6 microseconds before transmitting another packet. This is called the **interframe gap**, or **interpacket gap (IPG)**, which provides sufficient spacing between frames so that network interfaces have time to process a packet before receiving another.

Collisions

Even though stations must listen to the wire before sending a transmission, two stations could listen to the wire simultaneously and not sense a **carrier signal**. In such a case, both stations might begin to transmit their data simultaneously. Shortly after the simultaneous transmissions, a collision would occur on the network wire. The stations would detect the collision as their transmitted signals collided with one another.

Once a collision is detected, the first station to detect the collision transmits a 32-bit **jam signal** that tells all other stations not to transmit for a brief period (9.6 microseconds or slightly more). The jam signal is used to ensure that all stations are aware that a collision has occurred. After the first station to detect the collision transmits the jam signal, the two stations that caused the collision use an algorithm to enter a **backoff period**, which causes them not to transmit for a random interval. The backoff period is an attempt to ensure that those two stations do not immediately cause another collision.

Collision Domain

A **collision domain** is the physical area in which a packet collision might occur. You need to understand this concept in order to understand network segmentation, which is essentially the division of collision domains. Repeaters do not segment the network and therefore do not divide collision domains. Routers, switches, bridges, and gateways do segment networks and thus create separate collision domains.

If a station transmits at the same time another station in the same collision domain transmits, there will be a collision. The 32-bit jam signal that is transmitted when the collision is discovered prevents all stations on that collision domain from transmitting. If the network is segmented, the collision domain is also divided, and the 32-bit jam signal will only affect those stations that operate within that collision domain. Stations that operate within remote segments (other collision domains) are not subject to the collisions or frame errors that occur on the local segment.

Latency

The time that a signal takes to travel from one point to another point on the network affects the performance of the network. **Latency**, or **propagation delay**, is the length of time that is required to forward, send, or otherwise propagate a data frame. Latency differs depending on the resistance offered by the transmission medium and, in the case of a connectivity device, the amount of processing that must be done on the packet. For instance, sending a packet across a copper wire does not introduce as much latency as sending a packet across an Ethernet switch.

The amount of time it takes for a packet to be sent from one device and received at another device is called the **transmission time**. The latency of the devices and media between the two hosts affects the transmission time; the more processing a device must perform on a data packet, the higher the latency. The maximum latency for a repeater can be as high as 140 bit times. The maximum propagation delay for an electronic signal to traverse a 100-meter section of Category 5 unshielded twisted-pair (UTP) or shielded twisted-pair (STP) cable is 111.2 bit times.

A **bit time** is the duration of time to transmit one data bit on the network, which is 100 nanoseconds on a 10-Mbps Ethernet network and 10 nanoseconds on a 100-Mbps Ethernet network.

Table 7-1 illustrates the maximum propagation delays for various media and devices on an Ethernet network. The propagation delays shown illustrate the maximum allowable round-trip delays for cabling and devices on a 100-Mbps Ethernet network.

Table 7-1   Propagation delay for Ethernet media and devices

Media or Device	Maximum Propagation Delay (bit times)
Two Ethernet stations using two-pair UTP or fiber-optic cable	100
Two Ethernet stations using 100Base-T4	135
1-meter segment of Category 3 or 4 UTP cable	1.14
1-meter segment of Category 5 UTP or STP cable	1.112
10-meter segment of fiber-optic cable	1.0
Class I repeater	140
Class II repeater	92

Repeaters can take anywhere from less than 8 bit times up to 140 bit times to propagate a signal.

Slot time (512 bit times) is an important specification because it limits the physical size of each Ethernet collision domain. Slot time specifies that all collisions should be detected from anywhere in the network in less time than is required to place a 64-byte frame on the network. Slot time is the reason that the IEEE created the **5-4-3 rule**, which limits collision domains to five segments, four repeaters, and three populated segments between any two stations on a 10-Mbps network. Violating those design parameters could cause network errors. For example, if a station at one end of the Ethernet network didn't receive the jam signal before transmitting a frame on the network, another collision could occur as soon as the jam signal and newly transmitted frame crossed paths. Theoretically, this situation could occur repeatedly and prevent any useful data from being transmitted on the wire.

Ethernet Errors

Different errors and different causes for errors exist on Ethernet networks. Most errors are caused by defective or incorrectly configured equipment. Errors impede the performance of the network and the transmission of useful data. In this section, you will learn about several Ethernet packet errors and their potential causes.

Frame Size Errors

An Ethernet packet sent between two stations should be between 64 bytes and 1518 bytes. Frames that are shorter or longer are, according to Ethernet specifications, considered errors. The following list names and describes several frame size errors that occur on Ethernet networks:

- **Short frame** or **runt**: A frame that is shorter than 64 bytes, which is the smallest legal Ethernet frame allowed. A collision, a faulty network adapter, corrupt NIC software drivers, or a repeater fault can cause this error.

- **Long frame**: A frame that is larger than 1518 bytes, but under 6000 bytes. Since 1518 is the largest legal frame size, a long frame is too large to be valid. A collision, a faulty network adapter, an illegal hardware configuration, a transceiver or cable fault, a termination problem, corrupt NIC software drivers, a repeater fault, or noise can cause this error.

- **Giant**: An error similar to the long frame, except that its size exceeds 6000 bytes. The same situations that cause a long frame can cause a giant frame.

- **Jabber**: This is another classification for giant or long frames. This frame is longer than Ethernet standards allow (1518 bytes) and has an incorrect **frame check sequence (FCS)**.

In addition to frame size errors, other packet errors might be seen on an Ethernet network. For example, a **frame check sequence (FCS) error**, which indicates that bits of the frame were corrupted during transmission, can be caused by any of the previously listed errors. An

FCS error is detected when the calculation at the end of the packet doesn't conform correctly to the number and sequence of bits in the frame, which means there was some type of bit loss or corruption. An FCS error can be present even if the packet is within the accepted size parameters for Ethernet transmission. If a frame with an FCS error also has an octet missing, it is called an **alignment error**.

Collision Errors

Network administrators should expect collisions to occur on an Ethernet network. However, most administrators consider collision rates above 5% to be high for an Ethernet network. The more devices on a collision domain, the higher the chance that there will be a significant number of collisions. Reducing the number of devices per collision domain will usually solve the problem. You can reduce the number of devices per collision domain by segmenting the network with a router, a bridge, or a switch.

A transmitting station will attempt to send its packet 16 times before discarding it as a **NIC error**. Thus, a network with a high rate of collisions, which prompts multiple retransmissions, may also have a high rate of NIC errors, and vice versa.

Another Ethernet error related to collisions is called a **late collision**. A late collision occurs when two stations transmit more than 64 bytes of their data frames without detecting a collision. This can occur when there are too many repeaters on the network or when the network cabling is too long. A late collision means that the slot time of 512 bytes has been exceeded. The only way a station can distinguish between a late and normal collision is by determining that the collision occurred after the first 64 bytes of the frame had been transmitted.

The solution for eliminating late collisions is to determine which part of the Ethernet configuration violates design standards by having too many repeaters or populated segments, or by exceeding maximum cable lengths. Occasionally, a network device malfunction could cause late collisions. When such problems are located, they must be resolved.

Broadcasts

Stations on the network **broadcast** packets to other stations to make their presence known on the network and to carry out normal network tasks such as IP address to MAC address resolution. However, when there is too much broadcast traffic on a segment, utilization increases and network performance in general suffers. People may experience slower file transfers, e-mail access delays, and slower Web accesses when broadcast traffic is above 10% of the available network bandwidth.

One simple way to reduce broadcast traffic is to reduce the number of services that servers provide on your network and to limit the number of protocols in use on your network. Limiting the number of services will help because each computer that provides a service, such as file sharing, broadcasts its service at a periodic interval over each protocol it has configured. Many operating systems will allow you to selectively bind the service to only a specific protocol, which will reduce broadcast traffic on the network. You can also eliminate unnecessary protocols in order to eliminate broadcast traffic on the network. An example of an unnecessary protocol is the IPX protocol on a server in an IP-only network. In this case, services would be advertised on both IP and IPX, when other stations would only be communicating via IP. IPX advertisements and the use of the IPX protocol is unnecessary in this case because no other stations on the network would be using IPX.

 Network users who share files may be sharing them over multiple different protocols. Broadcast messages typically advertise these file sharing services on each network protocol configured. Therefore, limiting the number of protocols in use on stations that share files can reduce the amount of broadcast traffic on the network.

If a broadcast from one computer causes multiple stations to respond with additional broadcast traffic, it could result in a **broadcast storm**. Broadcast storms will slow down or completely stop network communications, because no other traffic will be able to be transmitted on the network. A broadcast storm occurs on an Ethernet collision domain when there are 126 or more broadcast packets per second.

Software faults with network card drivers or computer operating systems are the typical causes of broadcast storms. You can use a **protocol analyzer** to locate the device causing the broadcast storm. Once the device is identified, you can correct the configuration error or apply an appropriate software driver update to correct the problem.

Half- and Full-Duplex Communications

In **half-duplex** communications, devices can send and receive signals, but not simultaneously. In **full-duplex** communications, devices can send and receive signals simultaneously. As an analogy of these communication types, consider the walkie-talkie and the telephone. When two people use walkie-talkies, one person must finish speaking before the other can transmit. This is half-duplex communication. When two people communicate over the telephone, both people can speak simultaneously, and both transmissions will be heard at the opposite end. This is full-duplex communication.

10Base-T, 10Base-F, 100Base-FX, and 100Base-TX Ethernet networks can utilize equipment that supports half- and full-duplex communications. In half-duplex Ethernet communications, when a twisted-pair NIC sends a transmission, the card loops back that transmission from its transmit wire pair onto its receive pair. The transmission is also sent out of the card. It travels along the network through the hub to all other stations on the collision domain (see Figure 7-1). Half-duplex NICs cannot transmit and receive simultaneously, so all stations on the collision domain (including the transmitting station) will listen to the transmission before sending another.

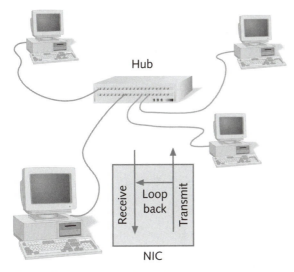

Figure 7-1   Half-duplex Ethernet communications

Full-duplex Ethernet components can send and receive signals at the same time. Full-duplex communications use one set of wires to send and a separate set to receive. Since full-duplex network devices conduct the transmit and receive functions on different wire pairs and do not loop back transmissions as they are sent, collisions cannot occur in full-duplex Ethernet communications. Furthermore, full-duplex Ethernet effectively doubles the throughput capability between devices because there are two separate communication paths. This means that 10BaseT full-duplex network cards are capable of transferring data at a rate of 10 Mbps in each direction, as compared to half-duplex 10BaseT cards. The benefits of using full-duplex are listed below:

- Time is not wasted retransmitting frames, because there are no collisions.

- The full bandwidth is available in both directions because the send and receive functions are separate.

- Stations do not have to wait until other stations complete their transmissions, because there is only one transmitter for each twisted pair.

Fast Ethernet

When a 10BaseT network is experiencing congestion, upgrading to **Fast Ethernet** can reduce congestion considerably. Fast Ethernet uses the same network access method (CSMA/CD) as common 10BaseT Ethernet, but provides 10 times the data transmission rate—100 Mbps. That means that frames can be transmitted in 90% less time with Fast Ethernet than with standard Ethernet.

When you upgrade from 10BaseT to Fast Ethernet, all the network cards, hubs, and other connectivity devices that are now expected to operate at 100 Mbps per second must be upgraded. If the 10BaseT network is using Category 5 or higher cable, however, that cable can still be used for Fast Ethernet operations. Also, a 10-Mbps Ethernet adapter can function on a Fast Ethernet network because the Fast Ethernet hub or switch to which the 10-Mbps device attaches will automatically negotiate a 10-Mbps connection. The Fast Ethernet hub will continue to operate at 100 Mbps with the other Fast Ethernet devices. Last, Fast Ethernet devices are also capable of full-duplex operation, which allows them to obtain a transmission rate of 100 Mbps in each direction.

Fast Ethernet, which is defined under the **IEEE 802.3u** standard, has three defined implementations:

- **100Base-TX**: Uses two pairs of either Category 5 unshielded twisted-pair (UTP) or shielded-twisted pair (STP); one pair is used for transmit (TX), and the other is used for receive (RX). The maximum segment length is 100 meters; two Class II repeaters and a five-meter patch cable can be used to create a maximum distance of 205 meters between stations, per each collision domain.

- **100Base-T4**: Uses four pairs of either Category 3, 4, or 5 UTP cable; one pair is used for TX, one pair for RX, and two pairs are used as bidirectional data pairs. The maximum segment length is 100 meters; as with 100Base-TX, two Class II repeaters and a five-meter patch cable can be used to create a maximum distance of 205 meters between stations, per each collision domain.

- **100Base-FX**: Uses **multimode fiber-optic (MMF) cable** with one TX and one RX strand per link. The maximum segment length is 412 meters.

IEEE 802.3u specifies two types of repeaters: Class I and Class II. Class I repeaters have higher latency than Class II repeaters, as shown in Table 7-1. When two Class II repeaters are deployed on a twisted-pair network (100Base-TX or 100Base-T4), the specification allows for an additional 5-meter patch cord to connect the repeaters. This patch cord is in addition to the normal 200-meter segment length. This means that the maximum distance between two stations can be up to 205 meters. When repeaters are used on networks with fiber-optic cable (i.e., 100Base-FX), the maximum segment lengths are actually reduced because the repeaters introduce latency. Latency increases the propagation delay, which means that the maximum distance possible between stations must be reduced to ensure that the slot time is maintained.

LAN SEGMENTATION

As mentioned, you can improve the performance of your Ethernet network by reducing the number of stations per collision domain. Typically, network administrators implement bridges, switches, or routers to segment the network and divide the collision domains. This division reduces the number of devices per collision domain.

In your previous studies, you learned about using bridges, switches, and routers to segment a network. In this section of the chapter, you will review the concepts behind segmenting a LAN with bridges and routers. In the following section, you will learn—in detail—how to use switches to segment a LAN.

Segmenting with Bridges

A bridge segments the network by filtering traffic at the Data Link layer. It divides a network into two segments and only forwards a packet from one segment to another if the packet is a broadcast or has the MAC address of a station on the opposite segment. Bridges learn MAC addresses by reading packets as the packets are passed across the bridge. As you have already learned, the MAC addresses are contained in the header information inside each packet. If the bridge does not recognize a MAC address, it will forward the packet to all segments.

The bridge maintains a **bridging table** to keep track of the different hardware addresses on each segment. The bridging table maps the MAC addresses learned to the port on the bridge that is connected to the segment where that MAC address is located. Bridges increase latency by 10 to 30%, but since they effectively divide the collision domain, this does not affect slot time.

When you segment a LAN with one or more bridges, remember these points:

- Bridges reduce collisions by segmenting the LAN and filtering traffic.

- A bridge does not reduce broadcast and **multicast** traffic.

- A bridge can extend the useful distance of the Ethernet LAN because distance limitations apply to collision domains, and a bridge separates collision domains.

- The bandwidth for the new individual segments is increased because they can operate separately at 10 Mbps or 100 Mbps, depending on the technology.

- Bridges can be used to limit traffic for security purposes by keeping traffic segregated; traffic between two hosts on one side of the bridge will not be propagated to the other side of the bridge.

Segmenting with Routers

A router operates at layer 3 of the OSI reference model. It interprets the Network layer protocol and makes forwarding decisions based on the layer 3 address. Routers typically do not propagate broadcast traffic; thus, they reduce network traffic even more than do bridges. Routers maintain routing tables that include the Network layer addresses of different segments. The router forwards packets to the correct segment or another router, based on those Network layer addresses. Since the router has to read the layer 3 address and determine the best path to the destination station, latency is higher than with a bridge or repeater.

Keep in mind that when you segment a LAN with routers, routers will:

- Decrease collisions by filtering traffic

- Reduce broadcast and multicast traffic by blocking or selectively filtering packets

- Support multiple paths and routes between them

- Provide increased bandwidth for the newly created segments

- Increase security by preventing packets between hosts on one side of the router from propagating to the other side of the router

- Increase the effective distance of the network by creating new collision domains

- Provide layer 3 routing, packet fragmentation and reassembly, and traffic flow control

- Have a higher latency than do bridges, because routers have more to process. Faster processors in the router can reduce some of this latency.

LAN SWITCHING

Although **switches** are similar to bridges in several ways, using a switch on the LAN has a different effect on the way network traffic is propagated. This difference happens because switches do quite a bit more than merely segment the LAN; they truly change the way in which communication is carried out on the LAN.

The remainder of this chapter focuses on the ways in which a switch can affect LAN communications. First, you will learn how a switch segments the LAN. The benefits and drawbacks of using a switch on the LAN also will be described. Then, you will learn how a switch operates and the switching components that are involved. Then, the final section of the chapter will explain how you can use switches to create virtual LANs.

Segmentation with Switches

Bridges and switches are similar—so much so that switches are often called **multiport bridges**. The main difference between a switch and a bridge is that the switch typically connects multiple stations individually, thereby segmenting the LAN into separate ports. A bridge typically only separates two segments.

Although a switch propagates broadcast and multicast traffic to all ports, it does still perform microsegmentation on **unicast** traffic, as shown in Figure 7-2. **Microsegmentation** means that the switch sends a packet with a specific destination directly to the port to which the destination host is attached.

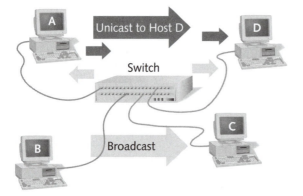

Figure 7-2   Microsegmentation on unicast traffic

In the figure, when Host A sends a unicast to Host D, the switch (which operates at the Data Link layer of the OSI reference model) receives the unicast packet on the port to which Host A is attached, opens the data packet, reads the destination MAC address, and then passes the packet directly to the port to which Host D is attached. However, when Host B sends a broadcast packet, the switch forwards the packet to all devices attached to the switch. Figure 7-3 shows the inherent logic structure of this process.

Given the number of steps that a switch must perform on each packet, its latency is typically higher than that of a repeater. Although switches do slightly more work than bridges, faster processors and a variety of switching techniques make many switches faster than bridges. In general, however, you can count on a switch adding approximately 21 microseconds of latency to network communications.

7

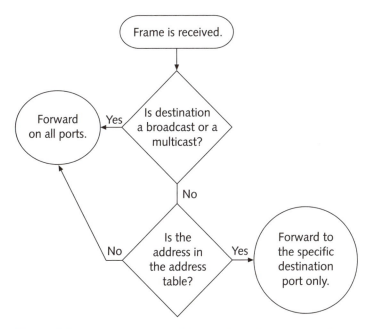

Figure 7-3   Logic structure of forwarding decisions made by a switch

Since switches microsegment most traffic, there is a better utilization of the available bandwidth. When one host is communicating directly with another host, the hosts can utilize the full bandwidth of the connection. For example, with a 10-Mbps switch on a 10BaseT LAN, the switch can often provide 10-Mbps connections for each host that is attached. If a non-switching half-duplex hub were used instead of a switch, all devices on the collision domain would share the 10-Mbps connection.

Switches provide the following benefits:

- Reduction in network traffic and collisions
- Increase in available bandwidth per station, because stations can communicate in parallel

- Increase in the effective distance of the LAN by dividing it into multiple collision domains

- Increased security, because unicast traffic is sent directly to its destination and not to all other stations on the collision domain

Switch Operations

A switch learns the hardware address of devices to which it is attached by reading the source address of packets as they are transmitted across the switch. The switch matches the source MAC address with the port from which the frame was sent. The MAC-to-switch-port mapping is stored in the switch's **content-addressable memory (CAM)**. The switch refers to the CAM when it is forwarding packets, and it updates the CAM continuously. Each mapping receives a time stamp every time it is referenced. Old entries, which are ones that are not referenced frequently enough, are removed from the CAM.

The switch uses a memory buffer to store frames as it determines to which port(s) the frame will be forwarded. There are two different types of memory buffering that a switch can use: **port-based memory buffering** and **shared memory buffering**. In port-based memory buffering, each port has a certain amount of memory that it can use to store frames. If a port is inactive, then its memory buffer is idle. However, if a port is receiving a high volume of traffic (near network capacity), the traffic may overload its buffer, and other frames may be delayed or require retransmission.

Shared memory buffering offers an advantage over port-based memory buffering in that any port can store frames in the shared memory buffer. The amount of memory that each port uses in the shared memory buffer is dynamically allocated according to the port's activity level and the size of frames transmitted. Shared memory buffering works best when a few ports receive a majority of the traffic. This situation occurs in client/server environments, because the ports to which servers are attached will typically see more activity than the ports to which clients are attached.

Some switches can interconnect network interfaces of different speeds. For example, the switch might have a mix of 10-Mbps and 100-Mbps devices attached. These switches use **asymmetric switching** and, typically, a shared memory buffer. The shared memory buffer allows switches to store packets from the ports operating at higher speeds (100 Mbps) when it is necessary to send that information to ports operating at lower speeds (10 Mbps). Asymmetric switching is also better for client/server environments when the server is configured with a network card that is faster than the network cards of the clients. The switch allows the server's NIC to operate at 100 Mbps and all the clients' NICs to operate at 10 Mbps, if necessary. This allows the server to handle the clients' requests more quickly than if it were limited to 10 Mbps.

Switches that require all attached network interface devices to use the same transmit/receive speed are using **symmetric switching**. For example, a symmetric switch could require all ports to operate at 100 Mbps per second or maybe at 10 Mbps, but not at a mix of the two speeds.

Switching Methods

All switches base packet-forwarding decisions on the packet's destination MAC address. However, all switches do not forward packets in the same way. There are actually two main methods for processing and forwarding packets. One is called cut-through, and the other is called store-and-forward. From those two methods, two additional forwarding methods were derived: fragment-free and adaptive cut-through. Cisco switches come with a menu system that allows you to choose from the available switch options, as shown in Figure 7-4 below.

```
Catalyst 2820 - System Configuration
System Revision: 0 Address Capacity: 2048
System UpTime: 2day(s) 21hour(s) 15 minute(s) 4second(s)
----------Settings-----------
[N] Name of system
[C] Contact name
[L] Location
[S] Switching mode                        FragmentFree
[U] Use of store-and-forward for multicast   Disabled
[A] Action upon address violation          Suspend
[G] Generate alert on address violation    Enabled
[I] Address aging time                     300 seconds
[P] Network Port                           None
[H] Half duplex back pressure (10-mbps ports) Disabled
[E] Enhanced Congestion Control (10 Mbps Ports) Disabled
-------------Actions-------------
[R] Reset system              [F] Reset to factory defaults
----------Related Menus-------------
[B] Broadcast storm control     [X] Exit to Main Menu
Enter Selection:
```

Figure 7-4   Catalyst 2820 configuration menu

The figure illustrates the configuration menu for a Cisco Catalyst 2820. Notice that the menu option [S] will allow you to toggle switching modes and that, right now, the switch is set for fragment-free.

The four methods are based on varying levels of latency (delay) and error reduction in forwarding packets. For example, cut-through offers the least latency and least reduction in error propagation, whereas store-and-forward switching offers the best error reduction services, but also the highest latency. Each of these switching methods is described in greater detail in the following sections.

Cut-through

Switches that utilize **cut-through** forwarding start sending the frame immediately after reading the destination MAC address into their buffer. The main benefit of forwarding the packet immediately is a reduction in latency, because the forwarding decision is made almost immediately after the frame is received. For example, the switching decision is made after 14 bytes of a standard Ethernet frame, as shown in Figure 7-5.

 TIP   Cisco routers use the term **fast forward** to indicate that a switch is in cut-through mode.

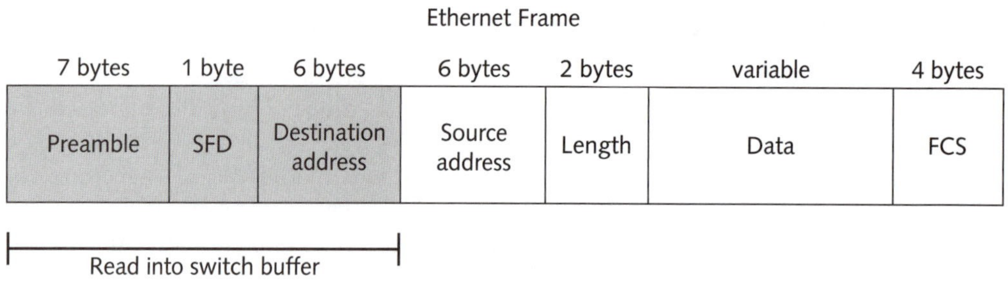

Ethernet Frame

7 bytes	1 byte	6 bytes	6 bytes	2 bytes	variable	4 bytes
Preamble	SFD	Destination address	Source address	Length	Data	FCS

Read into switch buffer

Figure 7-5   Portion of packet read into buffer by a cut-through switch

The drawback to forwarding the frame immediately is that there might be errors in the frame, and the switch would be unable to catch those errors because it only reads a small portion of the frame into its buffer. Of course, any errors that occur in the **preamble**, **start frame delimiter (SFD)**, or destination address fields will not be propagated by the switch—unless they are corrupted in such a way as to appear valid, which is highly unlikely.

Store-and-forward

Store-and-forward switches read the entire frame, no matter how large, into their buffers before forwarding, as shown in Figure 7-6. Because the switch reads the entire frame, it will not forward frames with errors to other ports.

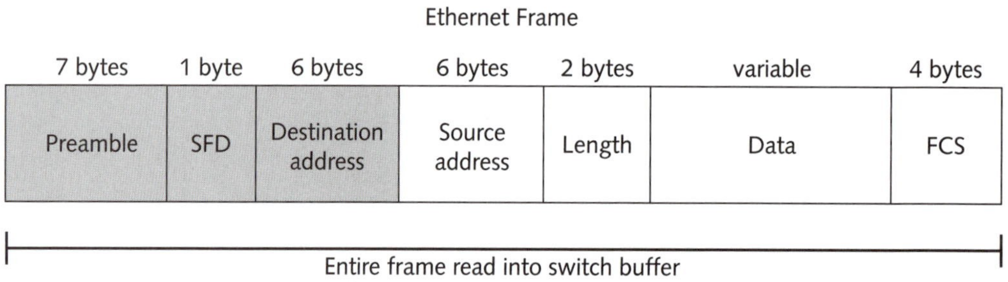

Ethernet Frame

7 bytes	1 byte	6 bytes	6 bytes	2 bytes	variable	4 bytes
Preamble	SFD	Destination address	Source address	Length	Data	FCS

Entire frame read into switch buffer

Figure 7-6   Entire packet read into buffer by a store-and-forward switch

However, because the entire frame is read into the buffer and checked for errors, the store-and-forward method has the highest latency.

> TIP   Standard bridges typically use the store-and-forward technique.

Fragment-free

Fragment-free switching represents an effort to provide more error-reducing benefits than cut-through switching, while keeping latency lower than does store-and-forward switching.

A fragment-free switch reads the first 64 bytes of an Ethernet frame and then begins forwarding it to the appropriate port or ports, as shown in Figure 7-7.

Ethernet Frame

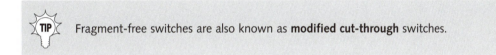

7 bytes	1 byte	6 bytes	6 bytes	2 bytes	variable	4 bytes
Preamble	SFD	Destination address	Source address	Length	Data	FCS

├─────────────────── 64 bytes read into switch buffer ───────────────────┤

Figure 7-7   Amount of packet read into buffer by a fragment-free switch

By reading the first 64 bytes, the switch will catch the vast majority of Ethernet errors, and still provide lower latency than a store-and-forward switch. Of course, for Ethernet frames that are 64 bytes long, the fragment-free switch is essentially a store-and-forward switch.

> **TIP**   Fragment-free switches are also known as **modified cut-through** switches.

Adaptive Cut-through

Another variation of the switching techniques described above is the **adaptive cut-through** switch (also known as **error sensing**). For the most part, the adaptive cut-through switch will act as a cut-through switch to provide the lowest latency. However, if a certain level of errors is detected, the switch will change forwarding techniques and act more as a store-and-forward switch. Switches that have this capability are usually the most monetarily expensive, but provide the best compromise between error reduction and packet-forwarding speed.

Loop Prevention

In networks that have several switches and/or bridges, there might be **physical path loops**. Physical path loops occur when network devices are connected to one another by two or more physical media links. The physical loops are desirable for network fault tolerance because if one path fails, another will be available. Consider the network shown in Figure 7-8; the four devices (two switches and two bridges) are configured in a **logical loop**.

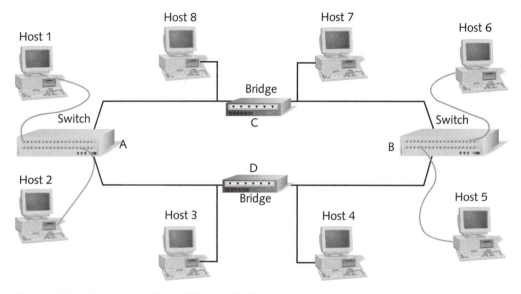

Figure 7-8   Devices configured in a logical loop

Assume that Host 1, which is attached to Switch A, sends out a packet addressed to the MAC address of Host 5; there are actually two routes the packet can travel. The packet can be sent from Switch A to Bridge C or Bridge D. From there, it can be sent to Switch B, from which it can be forwarded to Host 5. The benefit of this configuration is that if either Bridge C or Bridge D fails, another path between Switch A and Switch B still exists.

> **TIP**   This sample network could have been configured with all switches or all bridges or any combination thereof. The number of switches and/or bridges is not important; the important point is that when switches and/or bridges are interconnected, they might create a physical loop.

The drawback to the configuration is that endless packet looping (when a packet is sent from one device to another, but the final destination is never found) can occur on this network, due to the existence of the physical loop. For example, assume that the MAC address for a station is not in any of the switching or bridging tables on the network. The packet could be forwarded endlessly around the network from bridge to switch to bridge.

In order to prevent looping on the network, switches and bridges utilize the **Spanning Tree Protocol (STP)**, which employs the **Spanning Tree Algorithm (STA)**. STP interrupts the logical loops created by physical loops in a bridged/switched environment. STP does this by ensuring that certain ports on some of the bridges and/or switches do not forward packets. In this way, a physical loop exists, but a logical loop does not. The benefit derived is that if a device should fail, STP can be used to activate a new logical path over the physical network.

Building One Logical Path

The switches and bridges on a network use an election process over STP to configure a single logical path. First, a **root bridge** is selected. Then, the other switches and bridges make their configurations, using the root bridge as a point of reference. STP devices determine the root bridge via an administratively set priority number; the device with the lowest priority number becomes the root bridge. If the priorities of two or more devices are the same, then the STP devices will make the decision based on the lowest MAC address.

Bridges use STP to transfer the information about each bridge's MAC address and priority number. The messages the devices send to one another are called **bridge protocol data units (BPDU)** or **configuration bridge protocol data units (CBPDU)**. Once the STP devices on the network select a root bridge, each bridge or switch determines which of its own ports offers the best path to the root bridge. The BPDU messages are sent between the root bridge and the best ports on the other devices, which are called **root ports**. The BPDUs transfer status messages about the status of the network. If BPDUs are not received for a certain period of time, the non-root-bridge devices will assume that the root bridge has failed, and a new root bridge will be selected. The devices will then reconfigure their ports on the basis of the paths available to the new root bridge.

Once the root bridge is determined and the switches and bridges have calculated their paths to the root bridge, the logical loop is removed by one of the switches or bridges. This switch or bridge will do this by **blocking** the port that creates the logical loop. This blocking is done by calculating costs for each port in relation to the root bridge and then disabling the port with the highest cost. For example, refer back to Figure 7-8 and assume that Switch A has been elected the root bridge. Switch B would have to block one of its ports to remove the logical loop from the network.

Port States

The ports on a switch or bridge can be configured for different states (stable or transitory), depending on the configuration of the network and the events occurring on the network. Stable states are the normal operational states of ports when the root bridge is available and all paths are functioning as expected. STP devices use transitory states when the network configuration is undergoing some type of change, such as a root bridge failure. The transitory states prevent logical loops during a period of transition from one root bridge to another.

The stable states are as follows:

- **Blocking**: The port is receiving BPDUs, but it is not forwarding frames, in order to prevent logical loops in the network.

- **Forwarding**: The port is forwarding frames, learning new MAC addresses, and receiving BPDUs.

- **Disabled**: The port is disabled and is neither receiving BDPUs nor forwarding frames.

The transitory states are as follows:

- **Listening**: The port is listening to frames only; it is not forwarding frames, and it is not learning new MAC addresses.

- **Learning**: The port is learning new MAC addresses, but it is not yet forwarding frames.

STP devices use the transitory states on ports while a new root bridge is being selected. During the listening state, STP devices are configured to receive only the BPDUs that inform it of network status. STP devices use the learning state as a transition once the new root has been selected, but all the bridging or switching tables are still being updated. Since the routes may have changed, the old entries must either be timed out or replaced with new entries.

VIRTUAL LANs

A **virtual LAN (VLAN)** is a grouping of network devices that is not restricted to a physical segment or switch. VLANs can be used to restructure broadcast domains similarly to the way that bridges, switches, and routers divide collision domains. A **broadcast domain** is a group of network devices that will receive LAN broadcast traffic from each other.

 Since switches and bridges forward broadcast traffic to all ports, by default, they do not separate broadcast domains. Routers are the only devices previously mentioned that both segment the network and divide broadcast domains, because routers do not forward broadcasts by default.

A single VLAN is a broadcast domain created by one or more switches. You can create multiple VLANs on a single switch or even one VLAN across multiple switches; however, the most common configuration is to create multiple VLANs across multiple switches. Consider the network configuration shown in Figure 7-9, which does not employ VLANs. Notice that two broadcast domains are created, one on each side of the router.

Now consider that same network with VLANs implemented, as show in Figure 7-10. The broadcast domains can now be further subdivided because of the VLAN configuration. This, of course, is only one way in which VLANs can be used to divide the broadcast domain.

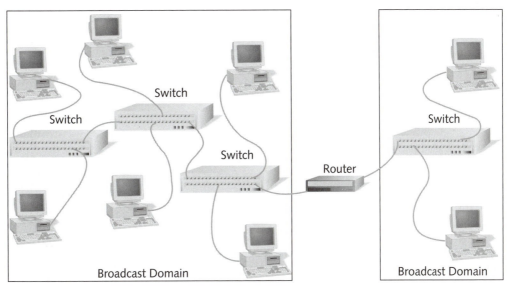

Figure 7-9 Broadcast domains on a LAN

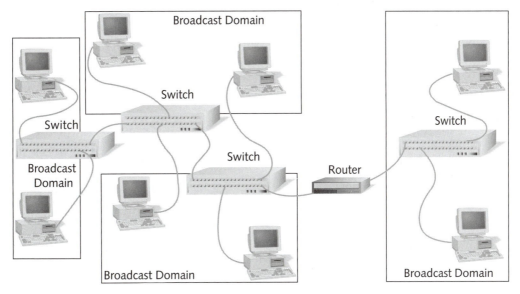

Figure 7-10 Broadcast domains using VLANs

Although VLANs have the capability of separating broadcast domains, as do routers, this does not mean that they segment at layer 3. A VLAN is a layer 2 implementation and does not affect layer 3 logical addressing.

Benefits of VLANs

The benefits of using VLANs center on the concept that the administrator can divide the LAN logically without changing the actual physical configuration. This ability provides the administrator with several benefits:

- It is easier to add and move stations on the LAN.
- It is easier to reconfigure the LAN.
- There is better traffic control.
- There is increased security.

Cisco states that 20 to 40% of the workforce is moved every year. 3Com, another manufacturer of switching equipment, states that 23% of the cost of a network administration team is spent implementing changes and moves. VLANs help to reduce this cost because many changes can be made at the switch. In addition, physical moves do not necessitate the changing of IP addresses and subnets because the VLAN can be made to span multiple switches. Therefore, if a small group is moved to another office, a reconfiguration of the switch to include those ports in the previous VLAN may be all that is required.

In the same way that the VLAN can be used to accommodate a physical change, it can also be used to implement one. For example, assume that a department needs to be divided into two sections, each requiring a separate LAN. Without VLANs, the change may necessitate the physical rewiring of several stations. However, with VLANs available, the change can be made easily be dividing the ports on the switch that connect to the separate sections. Network reconfigurations of this nature are much easier to implement when VLANs are an option.

Since the administrator can set the size of the broadcast domain, the VLAN gives the administrator added control over network traffic. Implementing switching already reduces collision traffic immensely; dividing the broadcast domains further reduces traffic on the wire. In addition, the administrator can decide which stations should be sending broadcast traffic to each other.

Dividing the broadcast domains into logical groups increases security because it is much more difficult for someone to tap a network port and figure out the configuration of the LAN. Thus, the actual physical layout of the LAN is hidden from would-be network spies. Furthermore, the VLAN allows the administrator to make servers behave as if they were distributed throughout the LAN, when in fact they can all be locked up physically in a single central location.

As an example of this flexibility, consider Figure 7-11. All the servers are locked in the secured server room, yet they are servicing their individual clients. Notice that even the clients of the different VLANs are not located on the same switches. The figure illustrates the true flexibility of using VLANs, because the logical configuration of the network is quite different from the physical configuration.

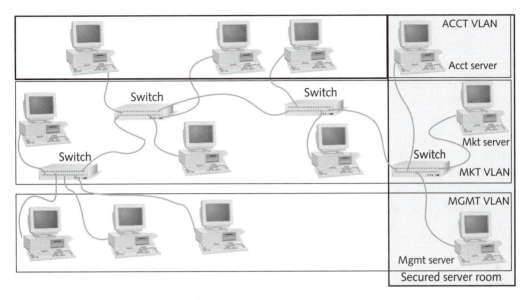

Figure 7-11 Securing servers with VLANs

In addition to allowing for the physical security of mission-critical servers, VLANs can be configured by network administrators to allow membership only for certain devices. Network administrators can do this with the management software included with the switch. The restrictions that can be used are similar to those of a firewall; unwanted users can be flagged or disabled, and administrative alerts can be sent should someone attempt to infiltrate a given VLAN. This type of security is typically implemented by grouping switch ports together according to the type of applications and access privileges required.

Dynamic Versus Static VLANs

Depending on the switch and switch management software, VLANs can be configured statically or dynamically. Static VLANs are configured port by port, with each port being associated with a particular VLAN. In a static VLAN the network administrator manually types in the mapping for each port and VLAN.

Dynamic VLAN ports can automatically determine their VLAN configuration. Although they may seem easier to configure than static VLANs, given the description thus far, that is not quite the case. The dynamic VLAN uses a software database of MAC address to VLAN mappings that is created manually. This means that the MAC addresses and corresponding VLANs must be entered and maintained by the network administration team. Instead of saving administrative time, the dynamic VLAN could prove to be more time-consuming than the static VLAN. To its credit, however, the dynamic VLAN does allow the network administration team to keep the entire administrative database in one location. Furthermore, on a dynamic VLAN, it doesn't matter if a cable is moved from one switch port to another, because the VLAN will automatically reconfigure its ports on the basis of the VLAN database. This is the real advantage of using dynamic VLAN systems.

VLAN Standardization

Before VLAN was an IEEE standard, early implementations depended on the switch vendor and on a method known as **frame filtering**. Frame filtering was a complex process that involved one table for each VLAN and a master table that was shared by all VLANs. This process allowed for a more sophisticated VLAN separation because frames could be separated into VLANs via MAC address, network-layer protocol type, or application type. The switches would then look up the information and make a forwarding decision based on the table entries.

When creating its VLAN standard, the IEEE did not choose the frame-filtering method. Instead, the **IEEE 802.1q** specification that defines VLANs recommends **frame tagging** (also known as **frame identification**). Frame tagging involves adding a four-byte field to the actual Ethernet frame to identify the VLAN and other pertinent information. The members of the IEEE considered this solution to be more scaleable (able to accommodate larger networks) than frame filtering.

Frame tagging makes it easier and more efficient to ship VLAN frames across network backbones because switches on the other side of the backbone can simply read the frame instead of being required to refer back to a frame-filtering table. In this way, the frame-tagging method implemented at layer 2 is similar to routing layer 3 addressing because the identification for each packet is contained within the packet.

 The additional four-byte VLAN addressing information is typically stripped off the packet before it reaches the connected host stations. Otherwise, non-VLAN-aware host stations would see the additional four-byte field as a corrupted frame.

Nonswitching Hubs and VLANs

When implementing hubs on a network that employs VLANs, you should keep a few important considerations in mind:

- If you insert a hub into a port on the switch and then connect several devices to the hub, all the systems attached to that hub will be in the same VLAN.

- If you must move a single system that is attached to a hub with several other devices, you will have to physically attach the device to another hub or switch port in order to change its VLAN assignment. This is assuming that you do not want to reassign every system to a different VLAN that is attached to the particular hub.

- The more hosts that are attached to individual switch ports, the greater the microsegmentation and flexibility the VLAN can offer.

Routers and VLANs

Routers can be used with VLANs to increase security and manage traffic between VLANs. Routers that are used between several switches can perform routing functions between VLANs. In addition, the routers can implement access lists, which increases inter-VLAN security. Last, the router allows restrictions to be placed on station addresses, application types, and protocol types. Figure 7-12 illustrates how a router might be implemented in a VLAN configuration.

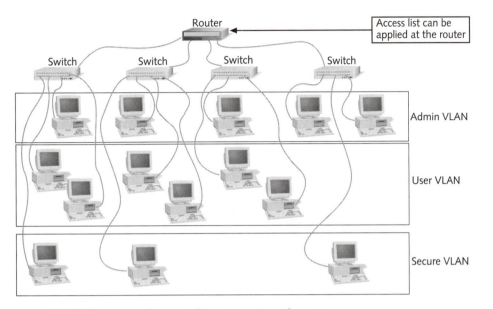

Figure 7-12 Router implemented in a VLAN configuration

The router in Figure 7-12 connects the four switches and routes communications between three different VLAN configurations. An access list on the router can restrict the communications between the separate VLANs.

CHAPTER SUMMARY

Ethernet (CSMA/CD) is a media access method that started in the 1960s. Stations on an Ethernet LAN must listen to the network media before transmitting to ensure that no other station is currently transmitting. In the event that two stations transmit simultaneously on the same collision domain, there will be a collision. The transmitting stations must be able to recognize the collision and ensure that other stations know about the collision by transmitting a jam signal. Once the jam signal has cleared the network, other stations can begin transmitting, but the stations that caused the collision must wait for a random backoff period before attempting to transmit again. The delays caused by collisions on the network can seriously affect performance when collisions are in excess of 5% of the traffic on the collision domain.

One way to reduce the number of collisions that occur on the network is to segment the network with a bridge, switch, or router. Switches do the most to divide the collision domain and reduce traffic without dividing the broadcast domain. This means that the LAN segment still appears to be a segment when it comes to broadcast and multicast traffic. However, a switch microsegments unicast traffic by routing packets directly from the incoming port to the destination port. This means that packets sent between two hosts on a segment do not interrupt communication of other hosts on the segment. Switches therefore are able to increase the speed at which communications occur between multiple hosts on the LAN segment.

Another way to increase the speed at which a LAN operates is to upgrade from Ethernet to Fast Ethernet. Moving from Ethernet to Fast Ethernet allows you to increase the speed at which frames are transferred on the wire, thereby increasing the performance of the network. However, to fully implement Fast Ethernet, the network administrator will have to replace all the hubs, NICs, and any other network interfaces with interfaces that support Fast Ethernet. Several Fast Ethernet devices allow for compatibility between Fast Ethernet and standard Ethernet, but to fully take advantage of Fast Ethernet, components must be upgraded.

Full-duplex can also improve Ethernet performance over half-duplex operations because no collisions can occur on a full-duplex LAN. Full-duplex also allows frames to be sent and received simultaneously, which makes a 10-Mbps full-duplex connection seem like two 10-Mbps half-duplex connections. However, just as with Fast Ethernet, full-duplex operations are only supported by devices designed for this type of communication. In many cases, this means that the half-duplex devices on the network will have to be completely replaced in order to take advantage of the speed offered by full-duplex operations.

Another way to increase the performance, flexibility, and security of the network is to implement VLANs via switches. VLANs are separate broadcast domains that are not limited by physical configurations. Instead, a VLAN is a logical broadcast domain implemented via one or more switches. Performance benefits are derived from limiting the amount of broadcast traffic that would naturally pass through a switch without filtration. The enhanced flexibility to assign any port on any switch to a particular VLAN makes moving, adding, and changing network configurations easier. Since broadcast traffic can be limited to a specific group of computers, security is also enhanced by making it more difficult for eavesdropping systems to learn the configuration of the network. In addition, the microsegmentation of unicast traffic makes it even more difficult to intercept useful data passed between two hosts.

KEY TERMS

100Base-TX — Fast Ethernet implementation that uses two pairs of either Category 5 unshielded twisted-pair (UTP) or shielded twisted-pair (STP); operates at 100 Mbps with a maximum segment distance of 100 meters.

100Base-T4 — 100-Mbps Fast Ethernet implementation that uses four pairs of either Category 3, 4, or 5 UTP cable; maximum segment length is 100 meters.

100Base-FX — Fast Ethernet implementation over multimode fiber-optic (MMF) cabling; maximum segment length is 412 meters.

5-4-3 rule — Stipulates that between stations on a LAN, there can be no more than 5 network segments connected, the maximum number of repeaters between the segments is 4, and the maximum number of segments with stations on them is 3.

adaptive cut-through — A method of switching whereby the switch uses the cut-through technique unless network errors reach a certain threshold; then, it automatically switches to store-and-forward switching until the error rate returns to an acceptable level.

alignment error — A frame that has both an FCS error and an entire octet missing from the frame.

asymmetric switching — A type of LAN switching that allows for multiple speeds of network communication; a switch that supports both 10-Mbps and 100-Mbps communications is an example of asymmetric switching.

backoff period — Used by devices that have caused a collision on an Ethernet network; a random interval during which the devices cannot send, to prevent them from causing another collision immediately after the one they have just caused.

bit time — The duration of time to transmit one data bit on the network, which is 100 nanoseconds on a 10-Mbps Ethernet network or 10 nanoseconds on a 100-Mbps Ehternet network.

7

blocking — A port state on a switch that indicates that the port is receiving BPDUs, but is not forwarding frames in order to prevent logical loops in the network.

bridge protocol data unit (BPDU) — An STP management message used to transfer status information about the Spanning Tree configuration of the switched and/or bridged network.

bridging table — A table maintained on a bridge that maps MAC addresses to the bridge port over which they can be accessed.

broadcast — A frame that is addressed to all stations on the broadcast domain. The destination MAC address is set to FFFFFFFFFFFF so that all local stations will process the packet.

broadcast domain — A logical or physical group of devices that will receive broadcast traffic from each other on the LAN.

broadcast storm — An error condition in which broadcast traffic is above 126 packets per second and network communications are impeded; typically the result of a software configuration error or programming error.

carrier sense multiple access with collision detection (CSMA/CD) — Ethernet networking method defined by IEEE standard 802.3, which states that an Ethernet station must first listen before transmitting on the network. Any station can transmit as long as there are no transmissions active on the network. If two stations transmit simultaneously, a collision will occur, and those stations must detect the collision and reset themselves.

carrier signal — A transmitted electromagnetic pulse or wave on the network wire that indicates that a transmission is in progress.

collision domain — The area on the network in which collision can occur; a section of network that is not separated by routers, switches, or bridges.

configuration bridge protocol data unit (CBPDU) — *See* **bridge protocol data unit (BPDU)**.

content-addressable memory (CAM) — A memory location on a switch that contains the MAC address to switch port mapping information, which the switch uses to forward frames to the appropriate destination.

contention method — The method by which computers on the network must share the available capacity of the network wire with other computers.

cut-through — A switching technique in which the Ethernet frame is forwarded immediately after the destination address is deciphered. This method offers the lowest latency, but does not reduce packet errors.

disabled — A port state on a switch that indicates that the port is neither receiving BPDUs nor forwarding frames.

error sensing — *See* **adaptive cut-through**.

Ethernet — *See* **carrier sense multiple access with collision detection (CSMA/CD)**.

Fast Ethernet — Defined in IEEE 802.3u; any of the following 100-Mbps Ethernet LAN technologies: 100Base-T4, 100Base-TX, 100Base-FX.

fast forward — Indicates that a switch is in cut-through mode.

forwarding — The state of a port on a switch or bridge that indicates that it will learn MAC addresses and forward frames out that port.

fragment free — A method of switching whereby the switch reads the first 64 bytes of the incoming frame before forwarding it to the destination port(s).

frame check sequence (FCS) — A calculation based on the size of a transmitted data frame that verifies whether it was received intact.

frame check sequence (FCS) error — When the calculation in the FCS field indicates that the frame was not received intact.

frame filtering — A technique used on early VLAN implementations that employed the use of multiple switching tables.

frame identification — *See* **frame tagging**.

frame tagging — A method of VLAN identification endorsed by the IEEE 802.1q specification that calls for an additional 4-byte field in the VLAN frame after the source and destination addresses in the data packet.

full-duplex — A connection that allows communication in two directions at once; common telephone connections are typically full-duplex because people can talk and listen at the same time.

giant — An Ethernet frame that is over 6000 bytes and consequently far too large to be transmitted on a Ethernet network.

half-duplex — A connection that allows communication in two directions, but not simultaneously; the circuit can be used for sending or receiving bits in one direction at a time only.

IEEE 802.1q — The IEEE standard that defines VLAN implementations and recommends frame tagging as the way in which switches should identify VLANs.

IEEE 802.3u — The IEEE Ethernet standard that defines Fast Ethernet implementations, including 100Base-T4, 100Base-TX, and 100Base-T4.

interframe gap — The time required between the transmission of data frames on the network: 9.6 microseconds.

interpacket gap (IPG) — *See* **interframe gap**.

jabber — A frame that is longer than the 1518 bytes acceptable for transmission between stations and that also has an FCS error.

jam signal — A 32-bit signal that is sent by the first station to detect a collision on an Ethernet network; ensures that all other stations are aware of the collision.

late collision — Occurs when two stations transmit their entire frames without detecting a collision.

latency — The lag or delay that a device or part of the network media causes; for example, fiber-optic cable delays a transmitted signal 1 bit time every 10 meters.

learning — A transitory state on a bridge or switch port that indicates it is trying to learn new MAC addresses and correct its bridge table before forwarding frames on the network; used to prevent loops during the election of a new root bridge.

listening — A transitory state on a bridge or switch port that is used during the election of a new root bridge; the port does not learn MAC addresses nor does it forward frames when in this state.

logical loop — A situation that occurs when a packet can be routed in an endless loop around a network because bridging tables and/or routing tables reference each other as the destination for a given address.

long frame — An Ethernet frame that is over the 1518 bytes acceptable for transmission between stations, but that is smaller than 6000 bytes; *See* **giant**.

media access method — *See* **network access method**.

microsegmentation — Describes the ability of a switch to segment unicast traffic by transferring a unicast packet directly from the incoming port to the destination port without interrupting communications on the other ports.

modified cut-through — *See* **fragment free**.

multicast — A frame that is addressed to a group of systems; typically used in radio- or television-style broadcasting on the network.

multimode fiber-optic (MMF) cable — There are two modes of fiber-optic cabling, single mode and multimode. Single-mode fiber cabling only allows a single signal to be transmitted down the wire at a time. Multimode cable allows for multiple simultaneous light transmissions.

multiport bridge — Another name for a switch.

network access method — The process by which network interface cards and devices communicate data on the network; an example is CSMA/CD.

NIC error — An error that indicates that a NIC is unable to transmit/receive a packet.

physical path loops — Occur when network devices are connected to one another by two or more physical media links.

port-based memory buffering — A memory buffer on a switch assigned by port, equally; doesn't allow for dynamic allocation of buffer space according to the activity level of a port.

preamble — Binary timing information that precedes an Ethernet frame; used by the receiving station to synchronize its clock circuits so the frame can be received correctly.

propagation delay — *See* **latency**.

protocol analyzer — A hardware or software device that can capture and analyze network packets and that is used to analyze traffic flow and packet errors, and to track network problems.

7

root bridge — The bridge that is designated the point of reference (point of origin) in STP operations.

root port — The communications port on a non-root-bridge device that is used for BPDU communication between itself and the root bridge.

runt — *See* **short frame**.

shared memory buffering — Dynamic memory buffer that is shared by all switch ports and allocated according to the needs of the ports; ports that have more activity and/or larger frames to process are allowed to utilize more memory buffer space.

short frame — A frame that is smaller than the 64-byte minimum frame transmission size required by Ethernet.

slot time — 512 bit times, which should be slightly longer than the time it takes to transmit a 64-byte frame on an Ethernet wire.

Spanning Tree Algorithm (STA) — The algorithm used by STP to ensure that logical loops are not created in the presence of physical loops on the network.

Spanning Tree Protocol (STP) — The protocol used by switches and bridges to prevent logical loops in the network, even though physical loops may exist.

start frame delimiter (SFD) — The one-octet binary pattern (10101011) that indicates that the preamble is over and that the following information should be considered the actual data frame.

store-and-forward — A switching method in which the entire transmitted frame is read into the switch's buffer before being forwarded by the switch. This method offers the greatest error reduction, but the highest latency; *See* **cut-through** and **adaptive cut-through**.

switch — A device that connects devices on a LAN and segments collision domains by port.

symmetric switching — A type of LAN switching that requires all devices to be operating at the same speed; it does not allow for a mix of 10-Mbps and 100-Mbps communications.

transmission time — The time it takes for a transmission to go from the source host to the destination host.

unicast — A frame that is sent/addressed to a single destination host; compare to multicast and broadcast.

virtual LAN (VLAN) — A logical broadcast domain on the LAN, created by one or more switches, that is not constrained by the physical configuration.

REVIEW QUESTIONS

1. The IEEE standard 802.1q recommends which type of VLAN identification method?

   a. frame filtering

   b. frame tagging

   c. frame segmenting

   d. frame sequencing

2. Which of the following types of switching methods reads the first 64 bytes of a frame before forwarding it?

   a. store-and-forward

   b. cut-through

   c. fragment free

   d. adaptive

3. The _____ provides sufficient spacing between frames so that network interfaces have time to process a packet before receiving another.

   a. interframe gap

   b. jam signal

   c. backoff period

   d. latency

4. Given the amount of processing each device must do on a packet, which would have the highest latency?

   a. switch

   b. repeater

   c. bridge

   d. router

5. Which of the following network media provides the lowest latency?

   a. STP

   b. category 3 UTP

   c. category 4 UTP

   d. category 5 UTP

   e. fiber-optic cable

6. An Ethernet slot time is equivalent to _____ bit times.

   a. 512

   b. 6000

   c. 64

   d. 1518

7. Which of the following Ethernet errors describes a packet that has a bad FCS and is over 1518 bytes?

   a. runt

   b. short

   c. jabber

   d. bad FCS frame

7

8. When two Ethernet stations are able to send entire data frames without detecting a collision, this is called a _____.

   a. jabber

   b. jam signal

   c. slot time

   d. late collision

9. The minimum size of an Ethernet frame should be _____ bytes.

   a. 32

   b. 64

   c. 512

   d. 1518

10. Collisions and Ethernet errors typically occur within the first _____ bytes of an Ethernet frame, which is why fragment-free switching catches most Ethernet errors.

    a. 64

    b. 512

    c. 1024

    d. 1518

11. Which of the following describes a method of Ethernet networking that does not have collisions?

    a. Fast Ethernet

    b. 100-Mbps Ethernet

    c. Full-duplex Ethernet

    d. Half-duplex Ethernet

12. An Ethernet frame that is less than _____ bytes is considered a runt, or short frame.

    a. 512

    b. 6000

    c. 64

    d. 1518

13. If a broadcast from one computer causes multiple stations to respond with additional broadcast traffic and the level of broadcast traffic goes above 126 broadcasts per second, the situation is deemed a(n) _____.

    a. broadcast storm

    b. transmission overload

    c. excessive burst

    d. jabber

14. Which of the following falls under the heading of Fast Ethernet? (Choose all that apply.)

    a. 10BaseT

    b. 100Base-T4

    c. 10BaseF

    d. 100Base-TX

    e. 100Base-FX

15. Which of the following IEEE standards defines Fast Ethernet?

    a. 802.3u

    b. 802.1q

    c. 802.2

    d. 802.5

16. Which of the following is able to divide a collision domain? (Choose all that apply.)

    a. switch

    b. bridge

    c. router

    d. repeater

17. Which of the following allows you to reorganize broadcast domains no matter what the physical configuration dictates?

    a. router

    b. VLAN

    c. bridge

    d. switch

18. If you attach a hub with five stations into a switch port that is configured for VLANs, how many different VLANs will the devices on the hubs be in?

    a. five

    b. three

    c. two

    d. one

19. An Ethernet frame that is larger than _____ bytes is considered a long frame.

    a. 512

    b. 6000

    c. 64

    d. 1518

7

20. Which of the following is a benefit that routers provide on the VLAN to increase security?

    a. dividing broadcast domains

    b. dividing collision domains

    c. allowing for the creation of access lists

    d. bridging the IP to IPX layer 3 protocol gap

21. When collisions are above 5%, you should consider _____ the LAN.

    a. segmenting

    b. increasing traffic on

    c. monitoring traffic on

    d. adding hubs to

22. By default, switches microsegment _____ traffic.

    a. multicast

    b. broadcast

    c. simulcast

    d. unicast

23. "Multiport bridge" is another name for a _____.

    a. router

    b. repeater

    c. switch

    d. hub

24. The _____ switching method begins forwarding the incoming frame immediately after reading the destination address.

    a. cut-through

    b. store-and-forward

    c. adaptive

    d. fragment-free

25. Which of the following types of switching methods offers the greatest compatibility with older devices?

    a. symmetric

    b. asymmetric

    c. isometric

    d. linear

CASE PROJECTS

1. Your network administration consulting team has been assigned to a new project. Your client has requested that you optimize their LAN. Before you can begin making recommendations, what type of performance statistics should your team collect, at a minimum? What other information would be useful?

2. A local company has decided to upgrade its LAN configuration from a configuration with five hubs and a single router to one that implements 10 switches. The switches the company is planning to buy have many more ports than necessary to support each segment. However, the company wants to divide the 10 different departments into separate entities. The company is planning on using routers between each switch, thereby dividing the broadcast domains between the switches. What other options for configuring its network should the company consider?

3. The Flagstone Corporation is trying to decide how it might best upgrade its existing Ethernet LAN configuration. The number of collision errors on the present network is causing network delays and poor performance. What types of measurements should you take? What options does the Flagstone Corporation have for improving the performance of their Ethernet LAN?

7

8

NETWORK DESIGN

After reading this chapter and completing the exercises, you will be able to:

♦ Analyze business operations, including organizational structure, communication flow, and mission critical processes

♦ Describe various network design models, including the three-layer, two-layer, and one-layer structures

♦ Consider performance requirements and improvements for given situations

♦ Design a network based on specific business needs

In previous chapters, you learned about a wide variety of technologies that can be implemented on a network to enable and enhance computer network communications. In this chapter, you will revisit many of the concepts presented earlier, but with a focus on designing and implementing a network configuration appropriate for a given situation. Specifically, the steps involved in analyzing the organizational model and designing the network to serve the organization will be discussed. In addition, you will learn about network devices and topology, so that you may consider the appropriateness of various devices and topologies for given situations. Performance considerations, including ways to improve performance, will also be discussed.

DESIGN METHODOLOGY

The most important goal in designing the network is to serve the organization's needs. When designing a network, you should follow a structured approach. This will help ensure that the design project remains on track and that it ultimately meets organizational requirements. Designing a network implementation involves three steps:

1. Analyze the organization's requirements.

2. Develop the LAN topology.

3. Configure logical addressing and routing.

Each of these steps can be quite involved and may take days, weeks, or months, depending on the environment, number of people involved, analysis equipment, and resources. In the following sections, each of these steps is discussed in turn.

Analyzing Requirements

When analyzing requirements, you are getting to know the organization that is requesting your services. You must learn how the people in the company communicate and how they will be affected by the network changes. You must also consider the impact of the network on critical business operations.

Areas of emphasis that you must consider when analyzing the business include the following:

- **Operations**: Learn about the organization's mission, its customers, and the services or products it provides. You must understand how the organization operates in order to design or improve its network and communication structure.

- **Physical layout**: The way in which the organization is physically organized will be a major consideration when you design the network. You must find out if the organization has remote locations or plans to have remote locations, and then consider the connectivity options for those locations. An organization with many different worldwide facilities requires a different topology and design than an organization that is contained within one physical structure.

- **Mission critical systems**: A system is considered mission critical if the company cannot provide a product or service without the use of that system. For example, a computer that controls the phone system for a telemarketing organization would be mission critical. If the computer that controlled the phone system stopped functioning, the loss of the system would impair the organization's ability to generate revenue.

- **Communications flow**: Learn how communications occur between the various individuals, groups, and departments of the organization. In order to set up an effective network, you must know how people communicate today and how they may be communicating in the future.

- **Areas of responsibility**: Determine which people or groups control the various processes in the organization. You must know where communication boundaries should and should not exist.

- **Security**: Find out if there is any sensitive data that should be protected and/or systems that must be physically secured. Locate and solve any potential security problems.

- **An organizational map or chart**: If you can draw a picture of how the organization is physically arranged and where the communications hubs and consumers are located, you will have a clear idea about the correct network topology.

- **Future requirements**: Determine as accurately as possible how the organization will change in the future and how its communications needs may be changed with the organization. The network design you choose to implement should be flexible enough to change with the organization.

Additional issues and specific tasks related to collecting information about the organization and analyzing its communications requirements are discussed in greater detail under the section "Understanding the Organization" later in this chapter.

Developing the LAN Topology

Once you analyze and understand the business requirements, you can begin to consider the network topologies that would best suit the organization. In this course, you have learned about several different topologies that can be used in network configurations. In large networks, multiple topologies may be used, but the typical configuration is a star or extended star, as shown in Figure 8-1. The challenge is to fit the topology to the organization.

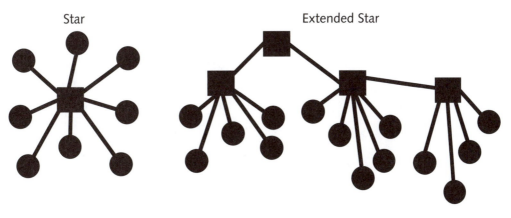

Figure 8-1   Star or extended star

In most cases, selecting the correct topology means considering the organizational structure, its physical structure, and the communications needs of the organization. In a star topology, deciding where to place connectivity equipment, such as bridges, routers, switches, hubs, and wiring closets, is important. Furthermore, the configuration of the **backbone** and the layout of the **wiring closets** are also a significant part of designing the physical topology.

Additional topology considerations will be discussed under the heading "Design Models," later in this chapter. In that section, you will also learn different methods for viewing and implementing topologies.

When network designers finish designing the topology, they document their design plan on a **cut sheet**, as shown in Figure 8-2. The cut sheet is a diagram of the floor plan and network, illustrating the network connection points, wiring closets, and the location of resources.

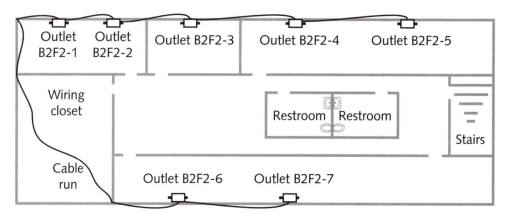

Figure 8-2   Sample cut sheet

Configuring Logical Addressing and Routing

Once you have determined the topology that best suits the organizational structure and information needs, you can begin to determine the **logical addressing scheme**. The addressing scheme should match the organizational structure. In other words, the logical organization of the network should match the logical breakdown of business departments, such as marketing, accounting, production, etc.

When you implement addressing on a network that uses routing and switching devices, the logical addressing scheme plays a significant role in how the network will perform. Routers and switches can reduce broadcast traffic, increase **bandwidth** for clients, and provide connectivity to remote networks. Furthermore, the network administrator can use VLANs to reconfigure the logical LAN topology without making changes to the physical topology. As you have learned, a VLAN can reorganize broadcast domains, which makes it possible for the logical topology to change with the organization, even if the physical topology remains the same.

When you implement addressing on the network, you should consider the current and future needs of the organization. The future could bring an expansion both in the number of people in the organization and in geographic locations.

Consider these questions before you implement addressing:

- How many people will the organization add or lose in the coming months or years?

- Will the organization add new offices? If so, how many and where will they be located?

- What services will be required by users in each location?

You should not overlook planning for an expansion of the organization's network. A limited implementation or addressing scheme could cause several problems in the future. If the number of users grows beyond the current addressing scheme, the network administration team may have to reorganize the addressing scheme, obtain additional addresses, and maybe even reconfigure physical equipment. That could become a mammoth task!

8

UNDERSTANDING THE ORGANIZATION

The network should serve the needs of the organization, not the other way around. Therefore, it is important to understand the organization before designing, implementing, or upgrading the organization's network. If there is an existing network and network administration team, they may already have some of the necessary information. However, they probably won't have everything.

Like many complicated tasks, ensuring that a new network serves the needs of the organization can be more involved than originally anticipated. The following sections discuss the many items a savvy network administrator should consider when designing a network.

Organizational Structure

Many organizations document their structure in an organizational chart. Some have organizational charts and subordinate charts for each department and/or office. You can use the chart during your investigation of the physical layout of the company and the flow of communication. Figure 8-3 shows a sample organizational chart.

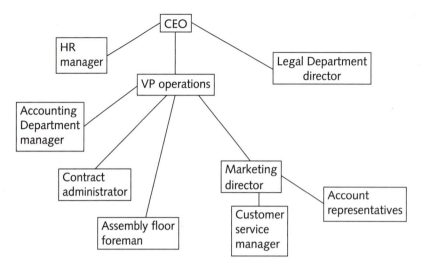

Figure 8-3 Sample organizational chart

Typically, these charts are organized in a hierarchical fashion, but don't make the mistake of assuming that communication flows within the organization, as shown in Figure 8-4, in the same fashion that it is laid out in the organizational chart. The purpose of the organizational chart is to illustrate lines of authority and responsibility. Unfortunately, lateral communications, which are conducted between peers, are rarely depicted on organizational charts.

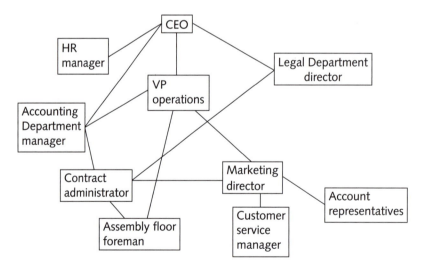

Figure 8-4 Communications flow

Communications Flow

Determining the flow of communications can be a difficult and time-consuming task in a large organization. Typically the lines of communication evolve from necessity and convenience, and are rarely formally documented. However, understanding where these lines of communication exist is critical to your success in designing a network that serves the needs of the organization.

There are two difficult tasks in analyzing the communications flow in the organization. The first is finding and defining all the flows of communication. The second is determining how the network can change those flows of communication. For example, if department heads gather each Monday morning for a meeting (a flow of communication), video teleconferencing over the network (a change in the flow of communication) may provide a more efficient method for this communication to occur.

Of course, while communications flows can be changed, they can also be eliminated altogether. For example, if the Customer Service Department routinely calls the Marketing Department to obtain customer account information (a flow of communication), a shared database between these departments could eliminate the need for such communication (an elimination of the flow of communication). The Customer Service Department would have access to the information it needed from the database without first contacting the Marketing Department.

As you investigate the flow of communications in an organization, try to answer the following questions:

- How does management communicate with its employees?

- How do department and office managers communicate with upper-level management?

- How do the employees communicate with their supervisors?

- Are there any remote users? Salespeople on the road? People working from home?

- What are the scope and importance of the interdepartmental and interoffice communications?

- Are there any departments that handle confidential information? For example, should the payroll and personnel files be isolated from the rest of the network users?

- If there is an existing network, how well does it address the current lines of communication? Where does it succeed? Where does it fall short?

As you are discovering the lines of communication in the organization, consider how company preferences will influence your choices in the network implementation. For instance, some companies prefer to have face-to-face meetings on a periodic basis. Others have people in remote locations with whom some organizational members never meet face to face. Again, the theme is that the network should serve the communications and information needs of the organization, not the other way around.

Physical Layout

The organization's physical layout is very important when you are designing the network structure. If a company occupies several floors of a certain building, you must consider the implications of forming network connections between those locations. In addition, if the company has (or plans to have) remote locations, WAN links must also be considered.

When you plan the physical layout of the network, be sure to consider the different types of connectivity options and the potential problems that may be encountered. For example, unshielded twisted-pair (UTP) cabling is typically not the best option for elevator shafts because of the sources of electromagnetic interference (EMI) in the shaft. These sources include the electrical wiring, the motor to control the elevator, and the braking systems. Typically, network administrators use shielded cable or fiber-optic cable in such environments.

As you analyze the potential physical layouts, ask yourself the following questions:

- What geographic areas does the organization span?

- What types of connectivity options are available for the LAN?

- If there are remote locations, what types of WAN connectivity options are available?

- Are there any known sources of interference that may hinder communications? If so, what are they?

- What are the total distances between the different departments and offices in the organization?

Once you have made these assessments, you will be able to narrow down some of the connectivity options. For example, if the organization has a couple of offices in a nearby building that is approximately 1000 meters away, as shown in Figure 8-5, connecting remote offices to the main location via UTP won't be a viable option. Once you know the various ways in which the network can and cannot be connected, you can determine the topology and media necessary to configure a viable network layout.

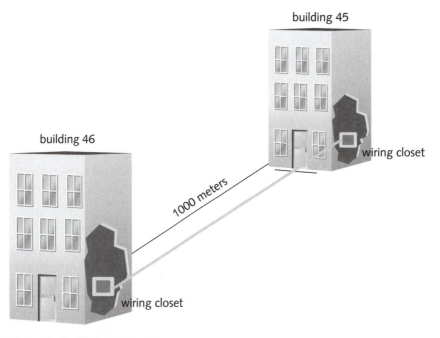

Figure 8-5   Distance concerns

Mission-Critical Operations

Every organization has a set of operations that is vital to its operation. Typically, these operations enable the organization to produce its goods or provide its services; they are mission critical. For example, a company that produces cans of tuna fish would consider the systems that run its fishing, canning, and distribution operations to be mission critical.

When designing a network implementation, you should give priority to mission critical operations and the systems that support them. For example, if you have only one battery backup unit at a company that provides information to its customers via a Web server, that Web server should be configured for the battery backup, because the Web server is mission critical. Other systems have a lower priority and access to the battery backup.

Asking questions, such as those shown in the following list, will help you determine which devices are critical to the operation of the company. This list assumes that you are evaluating each device individually. It does not help you rank the devices in order of relative importance.

- If this device fails, will it cause a work stoppage?
- How many people will be affected by a failure of this device?
- Will the organization's customers be unable to purchase or receive goods or services if this system fails?
- How long can this system be down before the company begins to lose revenue?
- Will the failure of this system damage the company's image and/or its ability to sell its products or services?

> **TIP**
> Actually ranking mission critical devices in order of importance is typically done by meeting with organizational leaders and/or executives and department heads. Often, ranking the importance of mission critical systems is not necessary, because there is enough funding available to provide equal support and backup for all mission critical systems.

Investigating the communications flow of the organization will often reveal which systems are vital to the organization. For example, if you are interviewing a department manager about the types of routine communications that occur between departments, you might also inquire as to which systems are critical to that department's operations, from that manager's perspective.

Availability and Recoverability

Once you have determined which systems are critical to the organization, you should evaluate the importance of each system or group of systems and consider the various methods for protecting the system and making it available. For instance, in certain organizations, the service goal is 100% availability (24 hours per day, seven days per week), and you may have to configure redundant systems in order to provide that level of service.

You have various options for creating reliable network services and protecting your data:

- **Clustering**: A cluster is a group of network servers that perform the same function and/or provide the same services. Servers in a cluster provide **load balancing** and **fault tolerance** for one another. The servers act as physical backups to one another, in that, if one server fails, another server can take over the failed server's function(s).

- **Redundant arrays of inexpensive disks (RAID)**: You can choose from several different RAID levels. When using RAID, you can use multiple hard drives to provide a type of real-time backup for data on mission critical systems. Two of the most popular RAID configurations are **disk mirroring (RAID 1)** and **disk striping with parity (RAID 5)**. Both provide hard disk fault tolerance. A mirror involves two disks that are identical copies of one another; if one disk fails, the data will still be available on the other. Disk striping with parity involves three or more disks and a parity calculation. In the event that one disk fails, the missing data can be recalculated in memory via the parity information and the existing data.

- **Backups**: Network administrators can use tape, CD-ROM, hard disks, and other backup media to restore critical system information in the event that a mission critical system fails. Backups are usually the most time-consuming to restore, but are typically the least expensive and most popular method for protecting data. The main difference between a backup and the other solutions, such as RAID and clustering, is that in the event of a network failure, restoring from backup can be time-consuming and typically requires manual intervention from the network administrator.

The availability and recoverability requirements for any system will depend on its importance in the network, how critical it is to the organization, and how the organization defines "availability" and "recoverability." Consider the following questions when addressing availability and recoverability:

- Is the data that the system contains critical to the operation?

- Should the data be backed up?

- Does the system require disk striping with parity or disk mirroring?

- Should the system be part of a server cluster, to ensure that the service is continuously available?

As you answer these questions, you will have a better idea of how the network should be configured. You should also consider whether the servers will require multiple communication paths in the event that a network connection fails. For example, it may be wise to place two network cards in a system that is utilized by all network users. This would ensure that there are multiple communication routes available in the event that a single communication route fails, as shown in Figure 8-6.

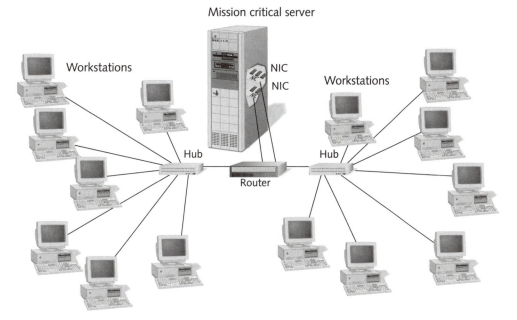

Figure 8-6 Two routes to mission critical servers

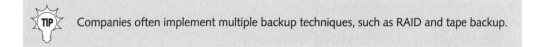

TIP   Companies often implement multiple backup techniques, such as RAID and tape backup.

Routine Maintenance

As you consider the communications needs of the network users, you should also be considering the maintenance tasks that will have to be performed on the network and how those tasks affect the network users. For example, file backups are a routine task that occurs in most organizations. You should consider the network users when you determine the day and time that the backups should be conducted and the amount of the data that must be backed up. Further, you must determine whether the backup should be done centrally over the network or locally at each office or department. In some cases, you may find that both central and remote backup units are the best solution.

Some organizations have large databases that must be routinely transferred from one location to another. You should carefully consider such operations when designing the network, because the changes in bandwidth may negatively affect the normal operation of the company. Bandwidth concerns will be discussed in greater detail later in this chapter.

Future Operations

As you consider the present functions, departments, and operations of the company, don't forget about future needs. For instance, if you are performing an upgrade to an existing network and do so without regard to the future, the planned installation or upgrade can quickly become outdated. As a matter of fact, if it fails to address the growth needs of the network, your work may be considered a complete failure.

Ask the following questions when determining the future design of the network:

- How will the operations change in the next few years?
- Is local, national, or global expansion likely?
- How have the organization's communications needs changed historically?
- What types of information will the network users require in the future?
- In what new ways will the organization need to communicate in the future?
- How does the organization expect the needs of its customers to change in the future?
- How does the organization expect to meet future changes?
- What types of services can the information system provide to the organization to help it meet future goals?

As you go through the questions, remember that they have one thing in common: they all help you look to the future. They will keep you from creating a brilliant, yet inflexible, network that must be done all over again in three months. Instead, by answering these questions, you can build a system that is flexible enough to handle the demands of the present and the expected demands of the future.

Reviewing the Existing Network

Upgrading an existing network has its advantages. For instance, you can benefit from eliciting complaints about the system from network users. You can also use the network as a point of reference for comparison and suggested improvements. If there are critical systems in use on the network, you can analyze their efficiency, note their effect on the network performance, and check for potential availability and security problems.

Unfortunately, an existing network can also be a hindrance. One major problem may be that network users have already adjusted to the inefficiencies of the existing network, such as high latency. For example, if the existing network equipment was too slow to support a shared centralized database, a workaround may have been to distribute multiple copies of the database around the network. Although it might be more efficient and cost-effective to place all the distributed records into a centralized database, the network users may be resistant to such a change.

DESIGN MODELS

You can choose many different network design models to implement on your network. However, there are two basic design strategies that are typically followed: mesh design and hierarchical design. **Mesh designs** are less structured than hierarchical designs. In a mesh design, there is typically no clear definition of where certain network functions are performed. Routers in a mesh design act as peer devices and perform essentially the same functions. As shown in Figure 8-7, the mesh is a flat structure in which expansion of the network is done laterally.

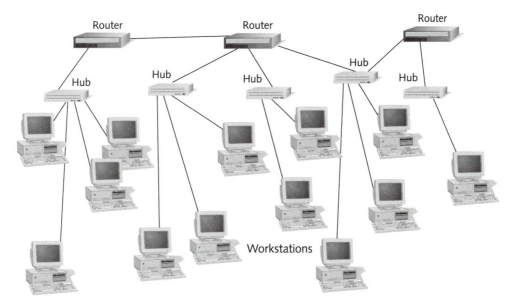

Figure 8-7   Mesh network design

Hierarchical designs, on the other hand, are more structured and defined. These types of designs separate different equipment and network media by their connectivity functions. Compared to a mesh design, a hierarchical design:

- **Is easier to manage**: Mesh designs are not as organized as hierarchical networks, so they can be considerably more difficult to manage.

- **Is easier to troubleshoot**: The defined structure of the hierarchical design makes it easier to identify, locate, and isolate network problems.

- **Has improved scalability**: A well-defined hierarchical design can be modified and redefined to support a larger organization more easily than a mesh design. The more organized the network, the easier it is to expand. Furthermore, the structure allows for additional users, equipment, and media to be added without extensive investigations into the distance between nodes and the number of nodes per segment.

- **Allows easier analysis**: Measurements of performance are easier to obtain when the network has a defined structure. The measurements are also easily applied to future expansion plans for the network.

In the following sections you will learn more about three hierarchical network models: the three-layer network model, the two-layer network model, and the one-layer network model.

Three-Layer Network Model

The **three-layer network model** is the most complex of the three models. It consists of a core layer, a distribution layer, and an access layer. The following list describes each in turn:

- **Core layer**: Provides WAN connectivity between sites located in different geographic areas

- **Distribution layer**: Used to interconnect buildings with separate LANs on a campus network

- **Access layer**: Identifies a LAN or a group of LANs that provides users with access to network services

Figure 8-8 illustrates how each layer would be categorized in a large network environment. As you can see, the core layer connects networks in different cities, the distribution layer connects several LANs within the same part of the city, and the access layer is where each group of users gains access to the greater network.

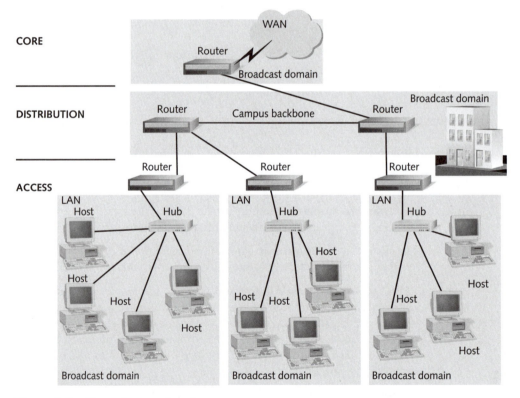

Figure 8-8 Three-layer network

Each layer is separated into its own broadcast domain because the layers are separated by routers, which are layer 3 connectivity devices. Notice that within the access layer, there are several broadcast domains, each providing users with access to the network. Therefore, the separation between the layers in the three-layer network model is mostly due to function. However, there is also a separation of broadcast domains between the layers because of the connectivity equipment used to create the configuration.

Core Layer

The core layer provides WAN connections between the various locations of the network. Since the core layer mostly consists of point-to-point WAN connections, hosts are not typically part of the core layer. Organizations usually lease the connections used for the core layer from a telecommunications company. Organizations use the core layer to provide a fast connection path between remote sites. Therefore, efficient use of the available bandwidth is a concern for those negotiating, designing, and administering the core layer connections. Often, network administrators establish multiple connections at the core layer to ensure that connectivity is maintained between each remote site and the main site.

Distribution Layer

The distribution layer consists of all the equipment necessary to make the connection between different LANs in a single geographic area or campus. This includes the backbone connection and all the routers used to form the connections to each LAN. At this level of the network, network administrators usually implement **policy-based connectivity**. This means that the network administrator determines the type of traffic (such as Web or FTP) to allow on the backbone and the type of traffic that the router will filter. The network administrator can use routers to filter the traffic from the incoming WAN connection and between the various LAN connections. This allows the network administrator to control users' access to services and broadcast traffic between LANs.

The administrator of the distribution layer can also control the LAN interconnections by establishing path metrics between the LANs. This allows the network administrator to predict and control the path a network packet should traverse between two points. By doing this, the network administrator may reserve certain network communication paths for certain types of traffic. For example, the network administrator could choose a specific path on the network to filter all traffic except that which is related to e-mail communications. Since e-mail is transferred over TCP port 25, the administrator could create an access list that allowed only TCP port 25 traffic. The access list filter command would look like this: ip access-list 101 tcp permit any any eq 25. By permitting TCP 25, the access list is implicitly denying all other traffic. This would mean that no matter how congested the rest of the network became, e-mail communications would have a dedicated path across the wire.

 TIP For more information on creating access lists and filters, see Chapter 3 of this book.

The best practice is not to place any end stations at the distribution layer, because those stations will have access to traffic traversing the LANs. Sitting a user at an end station at the distribution layer would essentially allow that user access to all traffic flowing between the LANs, which

8

could become a security threat. Placing a server at the distribution layer would mean that traffic would be originating and terminating at the distribution layer, which compromises the separation of the layers. Controlling traffic and troubleshooting would be more complex because the traffic filters, which apply to servers at the access layer, could not apply to a server placed at the distribution layer. For example, if you place a Web server at the distribution layer, users will only have access to it if you allow Web traffic through the routers that separate the distribution and access layers. This means that you can no longer filter Web traffic between the LANs.

Access Layer

In the three-layer model, the end systems should be located in the access layer. The access layer provides a logical grouping of users by function. This results in a logical segmentation of the network. This segmentation is typically based on boundaries defined by the organization. For example, the Marketing, Accounting, and Human Resources Departments in a company are typically segmented from one another. These departments may share some common information, but for the most part, their daily functions are separate. While each would be part of the access layer, connectivity devices such as bridges, switches, or routers would typically separate their broadcast domains. The main goal at this layer is to isolate the broadcast traffic between the individual workgroups, segments, or LANs.

The three-layer network model works well for large network environments. Most network administrators find that the two-layer or one-layer model works best for smaller network environments. These two models are discussed in the following sections.

Two-layer Network Model

The difference between the **two-layer network model** and the three-layer network model is that the distribution layer or campus backbone is not defined or implemented in the former. Network administrators use WAN connections to interconnect separate LANs and VLANs in order to define separate logical networks, as shown in Figure 8-9.

Notice that each site is still separated by layer 3 routers, yet the sites may be further subdivided by switching equipment and, as previously mentioned, by VLANs. The structure is still in place so that the network administrator can add a distribution layer and implement a three-layer model at a later date.

One-layer Network Model

Smaller networks can employ a **one-layer network model** design strategy. The one-layer network model has less need for routing and layer 3 separation than the two-layer or three-layer model. Typically, the one-layer network model includes a LAN with a few remote sites. In the one-layer network model, servers may be distributed across the LAN or placed in one central location. Figure 8-10 illustrates a one-layer network configuration.

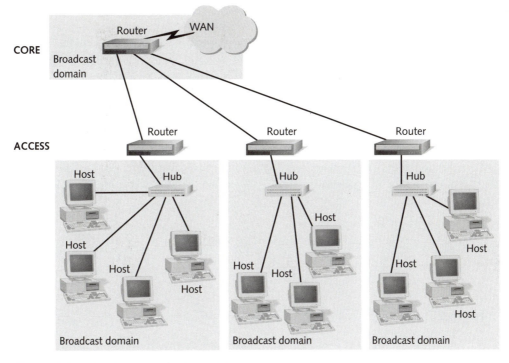

Figure 8-9   Two-layer network model

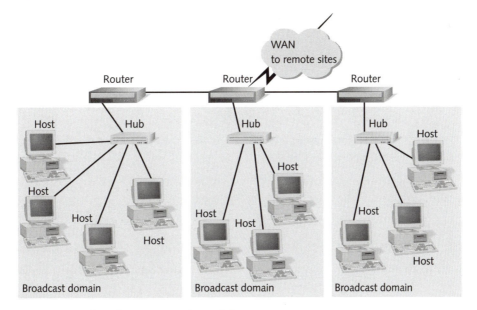

Figure 8-10   One-layer network model

Most of the traffic in the one-layer network will be concentrated on the LAN. The WAN should only have a light traffic load, because the remote sites will not be generating much traffic. The network users gain access to the rest of the network via routers that may connect other segments of the LAN or parts of the WAN. Network administrators can change the one-layer design model into a two- or three-layer structure as the network grows.

As you can see by reviewing the illustrations of the one-layer, two-layer, and three-layer network models, the main difference between these hierarchical models is the number of routers deployed in each configuration. In the three-layer model, there are three levels of routers: one at the core layer for the WAN, one at the distribution layer for the campus backbone, and one at each site in the access layer. In the two-layer network, two levels of routers divide the structure. The one-layer model only has one layer of routers, all of which operate at a peer level.

The main difference between the one-layer design model and the mesh design is the definition of structure. With a mesh network, the chances of having to restructure the entire network configuration as the network increases in size are greater.

Network Media

Today, networks use a variety of connectivity media in addition to network cabling. For example, infra-red networks, electrical circuit networks, and satellite transmissions are just some of the ways in which network devices are being connected. However, the most frequently defined and popular networks are still installed with copper and/or fiber-optic cable. Thus, the discussion in the following sections will concentrate on these media.

We begin the discussion with issues that you should address when deciding on the type of cable to use:

- **Distance limitations**: How far can the cable be run, according to its specifications?

- **Expense**: How much does the cable cost on a per foot or per meter basis?

- **Potential sources of interference**: Will the cable be installed near any sources of interference?

- **Resistance to interference**: Given the potential sources of interference, how resistant is the cable to interference?

- **Routing**: How will the cable be routed to the destination?

- **Security**: Must the cabling be physically secured from tampering?

- **Installation**: Given the physical layout, in addition to the routing and security needs, how difficult is the cable to install?

- **Existing wiring**: Is there existing wiring? Most new buildings already have some type of network cabling installed; typically, it is Category 5 UTP.

Answering these questions will provide the information you require to determine which type of cable you should implement on the network. As you select the type of cabling, you must also keep in mind the network wiring standards that apply to wiring the network.

Cabling Standards

As you have learned, **EIA/TIA-568** and **EIA/TIA-569** standards describe horizontal cabling specifications. **Horizontal cabling** is the twisted-pair or fiber network media that connect workstations and wiring closets. The specification covers the outlets near the workstation, mechanical terminations in the wiring closets, and all the cable that runs along the horizontal pathway between the wiring closet and the workstation. The standards also specify the names given to cabling and devices on the network, as shown in Figure 8-11.

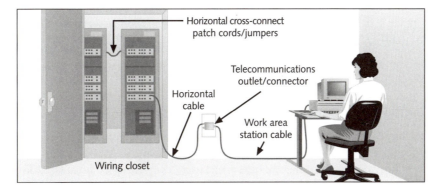

Figure 8-11   Standard names in wiring

The figure shows the following items:

- **Work area station cable**: Connects the workstation to the wall outlet
- **Telecommunications connector**: Found at the wall outlet
- **Horizontal cable**: Runs between the wiring closet and the wall outlet
- **Horizontal cross-connect patch cord**: Connects devices (hubs, routers, and switches) in the wiring closet

EIA/TIA-568B specifies that the maximum distance for a UTP horizontal cable run is 90 meters (295 feet). The **patch cords** located at any horizontal cross-connection cannot exceed six meters (20 feet). Also, patch cords used to connect workstations in the work area can be up to three meters (9.8 feet). The total length of patch cords and **cross-connect jumpers** used in the horizontal cabling should not exceed 10 meters (33 feet). Therefore, the network designer should not make the total length of any segment exceed the 100-meter limitation for UTP.

In addition to UTP, the following cable types may be used for horizontal pathways:

- **Shielded twisted pair (STP)**: Two pairs of 150-ohm cabling
- **Fiber-optic cabling**: A two-fiber 62.5/125-micron optical fiber cable

Wiring Closets

Wiring closets serve as the center of a star topology. They contain the wiring and wiring equipment for connecting the network devices, such as routers, bridges, switches, patch panels, and hubs. Since wiring closets are so significant to the physical cabling scheme of the network, their configuration and layout have been standardized by the **Electronics Industries Association (EIA)** and the **Telecommunications Industries Association (TIA)**.

EIA/TIA-568 and EIA/TIA-569 standards apply to the physical layout of the media and wiring closets, with the latter stating that there must be a minimum of one wiring closet per floor. Further, when a given floor area (**catchment area**) exceeds 1000 square meters, or the horizontal cabling is in excess of 90 meters, additional wiring closets are required. In configurations in which more than one wiring closet is needed, a single wiring closet is designated the **main distribution facility (MDF)**. The MDF is the central junction point for the wiring of a star topology. The additional closets are called **intermediate distribution facilities (IDFs)**. The IDFs are dependent on the single MDF. IDFs are required when:

■ The catchment area of the MDF is not large enough to capture all nodes.

■ The LAN is in a multistory facility.

■ The LAN encompasses multiple buildings.

If you are working with multistory buildings, you should place the MDF as close to the middle as possible. For example, if there are three floors, place the MDF on the second floor, if possible. As previously mentioned, in the multistory scenario, there must be at least one IDF per floor because of EIA/TIA-569, which states that one wiring closet is required per floor of a multistory building. In the case of a LAN that spans multiple buildings, you must place at least one IDF per building, as specified by EIA/TIA-569. In addition, there must be an additional IDF for each area up to 1000 square meters, when the catchment area is greater than 1000 square meters or horizontal cabling exceeds 90 meters.

Proximity to the POP

You should ensure that your wiring closet is close to the **point of presence (POP)** to the Internet. The POP is the location in which all the telecommunications for a given building are located. It is where a LAN connects to the Internet via the telecommunications company's dial-up or leased lines. Placing the MDF near the POP facilitates your network's connection to the Internet. If you plan to have multiple wiring closets, in support of a larger network, then your MDF should be located in the POP room if possible.

In the case of a multistory building, the POP will usually be on the ground floor, and the MDF should be on the middle floor. In this case, you cannot place the MDF and the POP in close proximity to each other. Figure 8-12 illustrates the relationship of the MDF, IDF, and POP for a typical LAN that spans multiple buildings.

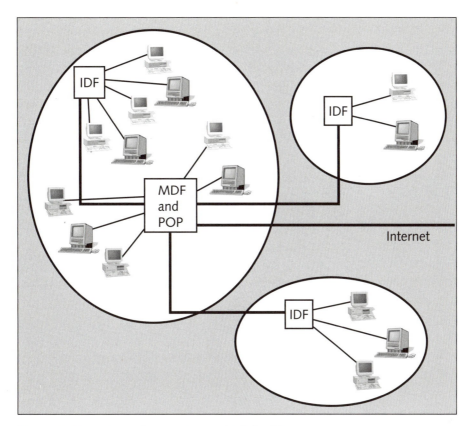

Figure 8-12   Network spanning multiple buildings

Figure 8–13 illustrates the relationship of the MDF, IDF, and POP for a typical multistory LAN.

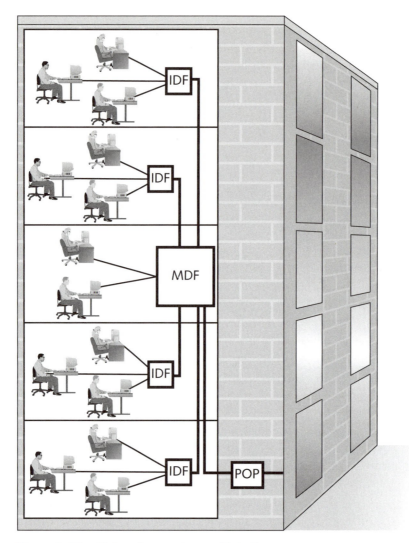

Figure 8-13   Network spanning multiple floors

> **TIP**   The maximum area that a single wiring closet can serve (without repeaters) in a star topology is 200 meters by 200 meters (200 meters squared), because any individual segment running from the center of the star can be a maximum of 100 meters in length.

Backbone

When two or more wiring closets are implemented on a network, they must be connected to each other via backbone cable. Backbone cable connects wiring closets to each other in an extended star topology. Backbone cabling also connects wiring closets to the POP and wiring closets between buildings. It does not connect workstations. Backbone cabling is sometimes called **vertical cabling** to distinguish it from horizontal cabling, which does connect hubs to workstations. EIA/TIA-568 specifies five different options for the backbone cabling:

- 100-ohm UTP
- 150-ohm STP
- 62.5/125 micron optical fiber (most popular for new installations)
- Single-mode optical fiber
- 50-ohm coaxial cable (not recommended)

8

 TIP EIA/TIA-568 still recognizes 50-ohm coaxial cabling, but this cable type is not recommended and is expected to be removed from the standard in the future.

When backbone cable runs between the MDF and IDF, it forms an extended star (hierarchical star) topology. When the IDF is directly connected to the MDF, the IDF is sometimes called the **horizontal cross-connect (HCC)**. This is because, in this configuration, the IDF is where the horizontal cabling connects to a patch panel whose backbone cabling connects to the hub in the MDF. Recall that the horizontal cabling is the cable that runs from the IDF to the telecommunications connectors. This horizontal cabling is most typically Category 5 UTP.

The MDF is also known as the **main cross-connect (MCC)** because it connects the local network to the Internet. Sometimes an additional IDF is placed between the first IDF and the MDF. In this case, the IDF closest to the workstations becomes the HCC, and the IDF between the HCC and the MCC is designated as the **intermediate cross-connect (ICC)**. The ICC is also known as the **vertical cross-connect (VCC)** because it is used as a connection point for the backbone, or vertical, cabling. The relationships among the MCC, the ICC, the HCC, and the workstations are depicted graphically in Figure 8-14.

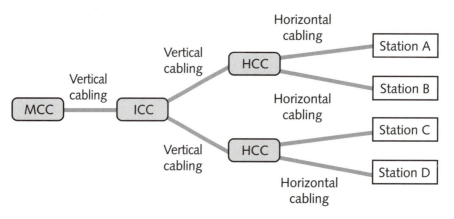

Figure 8-14   Wiring closet designations

Since the vertical cabling carries the data traffic between the wiring closets, it is best for it to be the fastest link on the network. For this reason, network administrators using 10BaseT networks often choose to make their vertical (backbone) cabling 100Base-TX or 100Base-FX. This allows them to increase performance and often increase the usable length of their vertical cabling. The length of the vertical cable depends on the type of cable that is used. Table 8-1 illustrates the different cable lengths for fiber and UTP cabling.

Table 8-1   Vertical cable lengths

Column 1	Column 2	Column 3	Column 4
Media	Maximum (total) distance from HCC to MCC	Maximum distance from HCC to ICC	Maximum distance from ICC to MCC
UTP (data)	90 meters (295 ft)	Not to exceed 90 meters when added to Column 4	Not to exceed 90 meters when added to Column 3
62.5/125 fiber optic	2000 meters (6560 ft)	500 meters (1640 ft)	1500 meters (4820 ft)
Single-mode fiber optic	3000 meters (9840 ft)	500 meters (1640 ft)	2500 meters (8200 ft)

 TIP   EIA/TIA-568 specifies that no more than one ICC should exist between an HCC and the MCC. In other words, there should be no more than three wiring closets in a chain (including the MDF).

In addition to considering the limitations on physical layout and cabling, you must also consider the performance requirements of the network.

PERFORMANCE CONSIDERATIONS

When designing a network, you must keep in mind the network performance needs of the customer. Sometimes, the network performance needs are somewhat difficult to predict, especially if there isn't an existing network in place. However, it is still important to consider the performance needs of the customer and, where possible, optimize the performance of the network.

Items that you should consider when reviewing the performance needs of your customer include:

- Connection speeds
- Utilization and broadcast traffic
- Collisions and contention
- Resource placement

In the following sections, each of the above-listed items is discussed. You will learn a technique for analyzing the bandwidth requirements of an organization. In addition, you will review several of the factors that influence the way in which the network performs.

Connection Speeds

The complexity of the data being transferred affects bandwidth. For example, it takes more bandwidth to download a graphic in one second than it takes to download a text file in the same amount of time. Although your network may have a theoretical bandwidth of 10 Mbps, what you experience in terms of network capacity at any given time may be far less than 10 Mbps.

The real capacity of a network is sometimes referred to as **throughput**. Factors that affect throughput include the type of network devices being used on the network, the number of nodes, power issues, network architecture, and other variables. The bandwidth calculations most commonly required involve determining either the time to download a file under best conditions or the actual rate of a file transfer.

Utilization

Network utilization is an important factor that influences the performance of a network. The typical rule of thumb for an Ethernet network is that more than 40% utilization for a sustained period should be investigated. Many factors influence the overall utilization of the network. However, when investigating causes (or potential causes) of high utilization, be sure to consider the following items:

- Video or audio streaming/teleconferencing
- Client/server applications
- Host/terminal applications

- Routing protocols
- Routine maintenance tasks (file backup and database copying)
- Broadcast traffic
- Ethernet collisions

You must be aware of the type of information that will be passed on the network. In most cases, it is best to find a network similar to the one you are designing, so that you can estimate the performance requirements. If this is not possible, you should attempt to get calculations from application vendors and equipment manufacturers concerning performance. You want to ensure that the average and peak requirements of applications do not exceed your available bandwidth. In the next section, you will learn a way to estimate bandwidth and throughput.

The most common solution for reducing network utilization is to segment the network with a connectivity device such as a bridge, switch, or router. Other solutions may include the following:

- Reducing the number of services provided on the segment
- Reducing the number of protocols in use on the segment
- Disabling bandwidth-intensive applications or protocols, such as those that support audio or video streaming
- Relocating the systems consuming the most bandwidth on the segment

Calculating Bandwidth and Throughput

As you consider the bandwidth that is required by the organization, you should attempt to discover the types of bandwidth-intensive communications that will be conducted on the network. You can then use that information to calculate the bandwidth requirements of the organization. For example, assume that you know that a 300-MB file must be transferred across a WAN link that runs at 56 Kbps every night. You want to estimate the time that it will take that file to transfer and see if the performance is acceptable to your client. The time that it takes a file to transfer from one location to another is called **transmission time**. You can calculate the transmission time by dividing the file size by the bandwidth, as is shown in the following formula:

Transmission Time = File Size/Bandwidth   (T = Fs/Bw)

As an example of the use of this formula, consider the different units of measure for the file size 300 megabytes and the transmission speed 56 kilobits per second. The first task is to obtain a common unit of measurement, which in this case is bits. 300 megabytes equal 300,000,000 bytes, which must then be multiplied by 8 to convert to bits (8 bits in a byte). That is 2,400,000,000 bits that must be transferred over the link. Since a kilobit is 1000 bits, 56 Kbps means that the transfer rate is actually 56,000 bits per second. Now, plug those numbers into the formula and you will see how long it takes to transfer the file:

2,400,000,000/56,000 = 42,857 seconds

Convert the number of seconds into hours and minutes to make it more recognizable: 42,857 seconds is 11 hours, 54 minutes, and 17 seconds. Assuming that the client wants to complete the file download in eight hours, this performance would be unacceptable, and a faster link would have to be considered.

If you have an existing connection, you can time a file transfer and determine your actual throughput for the link. Throughput is a more realistic measure of transmission time because it is based on the observed transfer rate. Throughput equals the size of the file divided by the actual download time. Consider this formula:

Throughput = File Size/Download Time   Bw = Fs/Dt

If you send actual data across your network connection, you can time the transfer and calculate the throughput. For example, assume that you transfer 4 gigabytes of data across your network connection and it takes 6 minutes. First, you convert the numbers to a common format. (Four gigabytes is four billion bytes, which is 32 billion bits. Six minutes is 360 seconds.) Then, plug the numbers into the formula:

32,000,000,000/360 = 88,888,889 bits per second

To make the throughput figure more recognizable, put it into megabits per second by dividing by one million. When you do this, the throughput is roughly 89 Mbps.

You may find the previously discussed throughput on a network that has a 100-Mbps connection and wonder why you didn't get the full 100 Mbps of bandwidth. Your discovery is that bandwidth and actual throughput aren't equal. This is because the throughput is affected by variables other than the connection speed, including other traffic on the wire, the latency of connectivity devices, and the capabilities of the source and destination to receive packets. If you were calculating the speed of the file transfer based on your 100-Mbps connection speed, you would expect the 4-GB transfer to complete in about 5 minutes and 33.3 seconds, as shown in the following:

32,000,000,000 bits/100,000,000 bits per second = 320 seconds

When you perform these calculations, you can ensure that your proposed network design and equipment will be able to meet the needs of the organization.

Collisions and Contention

As you saw in previous chapters, all stations on an Ethernet segment must share the available connection with each other. This means that the stations contend with one another for the opportunity to transmit on the wire. Two stations cannot transmit at the same time, or a collision will occur. Collisions cause delays because, for a short period, all transmissions cease on the wire, and the stations that caused the collision must reset and wait to transmit again.

When you are considering upgrading an existing network, you can check the rate of collisions on the network, using a protocol analyzer or other network performance monitoring tool. Although collisions are expected to occur on Ethernet networks, a high rate of collisions can cause serious performance problems. As a rule of thumb, collision rates of 5% or more should be investigated. If no errors, such as faulty adapters, are detected when you investigate the collision rate, the collisions may be caused by too many stations trying to contend for the same bandwidth on the segment. In such a case, one course of action may be to segment the network with a bridge, router, or switch. Another solution may be to upgrade the network. For example, if you are running a 10BaseT segment, you may decide to increase it to 100Base-TX or 100Base-FX.

Resource Placement

One important item that can improve the performance of a network is the proper placement of resources. When possible, network users should be on the same network segment as the resources they need to access. When resources that are frequently accessed by users are not placed on the same segment as the user, increased traffic across the network results. For example, consider the placement of the accounting database in Figure 8-15.

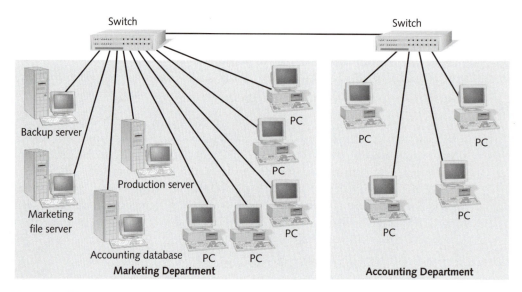

Figure 8-15   Resource placement

Assume that the most frequent users of the accounting database are in the Accounting Department. Since the file server is located in a segment that is mostly used by the Marketing Department, traffic between the marketing and accounting segments is higher than is necessary. If the Accounting Department is using the accounting database server more than the Marketing Department, then the database server should be part of the Accounting Department's segment. If you had a VLAN implementation, you could simply place the database server in the same VLAN as the Accounting Department.

Deciding where to place resources on the network is a very important part of configuring the most efficient communication paths. Of course, the need for security and centralized control may sometimes outweigh the need for increased performance. Again, this is where VLAN configurations can be useful. The equipment may be physically secured on one part of the LAN, but still be placed in the same VLAN as the users who must utilize the resources, as shown in Figure 8-16.

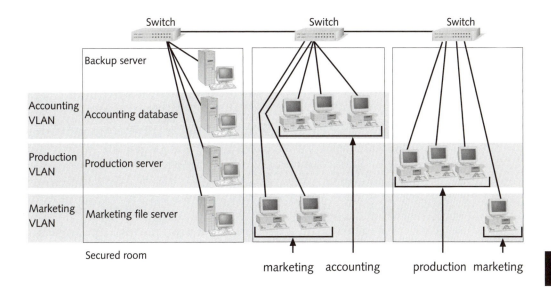

Documentation

Documentation is extremely important when designing a network. You should be sure to document every aspect of the network design process. The analysis process, topology implementation, and the logical addressing scheme should all be documented for future reference. Here is a breakdown of the items that you document:

- **Business analysis**: Be sure to record the fact that you conducted a business analysis. Ensure that the organization's mission, service goals, and main products and/or services have been investigated.

- **Technical requirements**: Document the technical needs of the organization. Be sure to include the availability requirements of the organization's equipment. Include the disaster recovery plan and the need for fault tolerance in the equipment.

- **Cost/Benefit Analysis**: Where possible, compare the cost of lag time, downtime, or data loss to the need for better equipment, redundant systems, fault tolerance, and disaster recovery measures. Decisions are easier to make when the cost of the implementing or upgrading a network is compared to the cost of not doing so.

- **Cut sheet**: Prepare a diagram of the floor plan and network, illustrating the network connection points, the wiring closets, and the location of resources. These diagrams are extremely useful not only when implementing a network, but also when troubleshooting components after the network has been installed.

- **Addressing**: Be sure to document the addressing scheme employed on the network. Where possible, document MAC addresses, protocol addresses, station names, and the protocols in use.

- **Equipment capabilities**: You should document the port capabilities and connection speeds of all devices. Knowing the speed at which your equipment is operating is an important part of being able to properly design, configure, and troubleshoot network bandwidth and throughput issues.

The more documentation you have on the network, the easier it will be to implement and troubleshoot. Of course, the documentation must remain up to date in order to be useful. Keeping this information in a database is probably the best idea, so that it can be updated as the network changes. The cut sheet is typically maintained on a paper copy of building floor plans, but highly organized network administration teams may keep this information electronically, via flowcharting or architectural design programs.

The benefit of storing the cut sheet electronically is that it is easier to update when changes are implemented. The paper diagrams can get quite messy when equipment is moved and the solution is to cross out and renumber devices on the paper sheet. Another method is to create a magnetic or dry-erase version of the network layout. The only drawback to this method is that if someone accidentally knocks down your board or erases it, the volume of work to recreate it might be discouraging. If you choose the dry-erase or magnetic board, be sure to take pictures of it or make a paper copy backup of it when changes are implemented.

Some network management systems, such as HP OpenView or IBM's NetView, make creating and maintaining a network diagram easier by providing a diagraming feature with the software. The management system gives the network administrator a graphical view of all the systems, logical addressing, and even system status reports. However, these systems are complex, time-consuming, and somewhat expensive to configure, so many network administrators still use the previously mentioned methods of diagramming their networks.

DESIGN EXAMPLE

To better illustrate the steps and considerations that should be part of designing a network, this section presents a network design scenario that applies some of the information you have learned in this course. Cisco considers the actual process of designing a network involved enough to merit its own certification track. The goal of this chapter and specifically this section is not to give you all the tools you need to design a network, but rather to apply the information you learned in this chapter and in previous chapters to a fictional scenario. This example uses a small company, in an attempt to simplify the design issues.

Background Information

The Smallco organization has decided to implement a network. Currently, Smallco only has one main location with about 50 employees and another 10 employees at a remote location. The company operates a package delivery service in the cities of Austin and San Antonio, Texas. The bulk of the employees are located in San Antonio, which is the headquarters. The 10 remote employees work out of the Austin location. Currently, all customer orders are taken by hand, on paper, and shipping information is kept on clipboards. The company believes that to remain competitive it must automate its systems. They have called in Netco Consulting to help design a network that will meet the company's needs.

Given the limited amount of information that Netco received about Smallco, the first thing that Netco must do is analyze Smallco's organization. Netco consultants know that the implementation will proceed in three general steps:

1. Analyze the organization's requirements.

2. Develop the LAN topology.

3. Configure logical addressing and routing.

Step One: Analyze the Organization's Requirements

Analyzing organizational requirements involves a series of interviews with the CEO and the company department heads. The Netco team begins by documenting the needs of the organization, the service goals that Smallco wants to achieve, and the specific items that Smallco wants to be part of the network. Further, the Netco team questions the company about its future and mentions a few of the latest technologies available. After the meeting, the Netco team interviews certain key Smallco people identified in the meeting who can further elaborate on the communications needs of the organization.

The Netco team then documents the business analysis. A summary of the Netco team analysis is listed below:

- Smallco's mission is to provide overnight and two-day package delivery in the operating areas of Austin and San Antonio.

- Smallco's mission critical systems are those that support the order-taking and delivery process. These include the phone system, order takers, delivery trucks, and drivers.

- Smallco employees make numerous daily phone calls between Austin and San Antonio to check the status of orders, confirm orders, and register new customers.

- Departments spend approximately 50% of their productive time in communications with one another concerning order information, customer account updates, and tracking of packages.

- Employees routinely lose or incorrectly file shipping paperwork that is processed on a weekly basis. Although packages are always delivered, billing information is sometimes misplaced.

- Employees maintain customer contact information in a customer database in the Customer Service Department, but that information is updated, maintained, and recalled by one person.

- The Customer Service Department manually carries a copy of the customer database to the Accounting Department each week. The Accounting Department uses the customer database to track customer accounts and obtain new billing addresses.

- When orders are received, customer services representatives manually record them on a piece of paper. The drivers are then contacted via radio dispatch to pick up packages. Each night the packages are sorted, manually tagged, and then prepared for shipping the following morning. The paperwork is then passed to the Customer Service Department for manual entry into the customer database. At the end of the week, that information is sent to the Accounting Department.

■ The Accounting Department maintains separate databases to track customer accounts, payroll, and business financial information.

■ A survey conducted last month showed that about 25% of Smallco's existing customer base would use a Web-based order request and tracking system.

Netco obtained the above information during a one-week study of the company's operations. The Netco team presented these findings to the Smallco management team to confirm its findings. Once the management team agreed that Netco had correctly described the business and its concerns, Netco produced a set of solutions in the form of a proposal to Smallco management. The proposal outlined a network implementation that included the following:

■ One-layer network design model: The number of people and the structure of the environment only merit a one-layer design model at this time. However, plans for moving to a two-layer and even three-layer design model will be prepared by Netco.

■ Network connection between Austin and San Antonio: It was determined that the only way to fully automate the system is to have Austin and San Antonio connected.

■ Access to the customer database in both San Antonio and Austin: Again, this is the part that allows the whole company to be connected. The order takers in Austin are processing orders just like those in San Antonio.

■ An order tracking and processing system: This system, instead of the paper logs that are used right now, will be used to track packages. Netco will ensure that this system can be updated in the future to include hand-held tracking devices to be used by the drivers. At present, Smallco has decided that hand-held tracking devices are too expensive, but in the future, Smallco would like to have the option of implementing them with the existing system.

■ Web server order-processing system located in San Antonio: This system is to be used by the 25% of the existing customers who mentioned that they would use it. The hope is that additional customers will also find it beneficial. A special consulting team will be called in to configure this Web server. Netco will place a firewall router directly behind the Web server to protect the internal network from Internet hackers and viruses.

■ Firewall to protect the internal network from the external network: As mentioned, a firewall will be used to separate the internal network from the Internet.

■ Firewall between the Accounting Department and the rest of the company: The Accounting Department handles all the personal and confidential financial records for the company. These records must be secure from internal and external tampering.

■ Automated updates to the accounting database: The information from the customer service database will be immediately available to the Accounting Department. Furthermore, the contact and customer-tracking information will be automatically and securely transferred from one database to another when records are entered. This functionality is to be configured by Netco and the database manufacturer.

- Backup server for all databases: A daily backup of all activity will be conducted during the hours of 2:00 AM and 4:00 AM. This is expected to be enough time to download 10 times the amount of records that are currently maintained by Smallco.

- A 100Base-TX network in both Austin and San Antonio: Netco determined that an ISDN connection between San Antonio and Austin would suffice for the database updates. However, when the price of equipment and cost of the line were compared to the speed and future expansion goals of the company, a fractional T1 line with up to 1.544 Mbps was agreed upon. Therefore, a fractional T1 line, using PPP encapsulation, will be configured for connectivity between the Austin and San Antonio locations.

- Identification of mission critical systems: Netco determined that the customer service database and related computer systems, the network connection, the shipping database, the phone system, order takers, delivery trucks, and drivers are all mission critical.

Once all the suggestions by Netco were negotiated and approved by Smallco management, the Netco team initiated the physical design of the network.

Step Two: Develop the LAN Topology

Netco and Smallco management discussed the topologies that could be implemented and concluded that an extended star would be the best. Before ordering and placing the actual equipment, Netco went to both Smallco facilities in San Antonio and Austin and prepared cut sheets, as shown in Figure 8-17. In preparing the cut sheets, Netco used EIA/TIA guidelines to ensure that its design did not exceed established parameters.

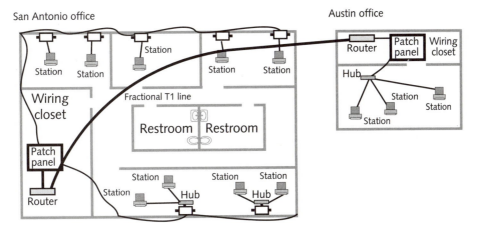

Figure 8-17 Smallco cut sheet

Once the Netco team established the cut sheets and negotiated the connectivity services, Smallco ordered the equipment. All the equipment was immediately inventoried by the Smallco administrator once it arrived at each location. The Smallco network administrator, with the help of the Netco team, started a database of equipment at that point. The Smallco network administrator also recorded all existing equipment in the database.

In preparing the cut sheet, the Netco team did discuss the type of logical addressing that needed to be implemented. The actual assignment process is part of the third step.

Step Three: Configure Logical Addressing and Routing

Netco implemented an internal addressing scheme for the internal network and leased a separate group of static IP addresses for the external Web server. These addresses were obtained via the Smallco Internet service provider (ISP) from InterNIC. Then, the Netco team documented the network configuration on the cut sheet and created a small database containing the information on all the servers, logical addresses, and physical addresses on the network. During the process, Smallco hired a network administrator to oversee the network. The final implementation phases were turned over to the network administrator once the logical addressing scheme was in place. When Netco completed its mission, the network was configured as shown in Figure 8–18.

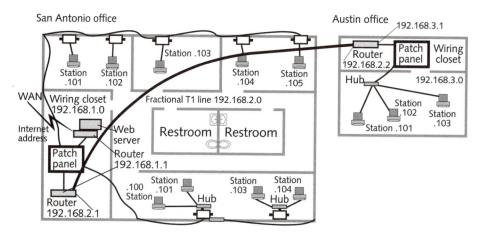

Figure 8-18 Smallco addressing

The IP addresses that were selected are part of the private address group 192.168.X.X. This address group was selected because it allows the organization plenty of internal addresses and subnetworks, but does not require InterNIC registration, because these addresses will not be routed on the Internet; they are defined for private networks only. The team decided to follow the general practice that routers should have the first few addresses available on each subnet. They decided that the first client addresses on each subnet should begin at 100 because they wanted to leave the double-digit ranges 10–99 open for the future use of dynamic IP addressing via the **Dynamic Host Configuration Protocol (DHCP)**.

When Smallco implements **DHCP servers** on the network, Netco will configure the DHCP servers to provide addresses between 10 and 99. Separating static and dynamic ranges is imperative to keep a subnet functioning properly. If there is overlap between the addresses assigned manually and those assigned via DHCP, address duplication can occur, which would automatically disable the IP network services on the hosts that attempted to use an address that was already in use on the subnet.

Once the addressing scheme was in place, the Netco team verified connectivity between the networked PCs. At that point, the network design process was complete, and the Smallco network administrator took charge of the network.

> TIP As mentioned earlier, the authors of this book did not intend this section and this chapter to serve as a comprehensive guide to designing networks. Rather, their goal was to demonstrate how the information you learned in the chapter might be applied in a network scenario. In the upcoming case studies at the end of this chapter, use this example as a guide for discussing the issues presented.

8

CHAPTER SUMMARY

In this chapter you learned that the most important rule in designing a network is that the network should serve the needs of the organization. In an effort to ensure that the network is designed for the organization, you should use a structured approach to network design. The structured approach includes these three steps:

1. Analyze the organization's requirements.

2. Develop the LAN topology.

3. Configure logical addressing and routing.

Analyzing the organization's requirements can be time-consuming, but it is an essential process. This step is the only way to ensure that the network design will fit the needs of the organization. The network designer must focus on the critical operations, the necessary communications, and the business process during this step. The results of this phase should be documented and verified by the organization's key managers, especially those who will be most affected by the communications changes.

Once the analysis is complete, designing the topology should be a matter of logical progression. The basic topology of the network should be determined, and the applicable standards should be consulted. A cut sheet should be prepared, which will be used to actually install the equipment and perhaps even to document the network layout.

When implementing a network, you can choose one of three hierarchical network models: one-layer, two-layer, or three-layer. The one-layer network model is the least complex, and is a flat structure where all components function at essentially the same level. The two-layer model separates the WAN from the rest of the internal network, which is usually done by adding routers with packet filters. The three-layer model provides even greater separation at three levels, again with routers and packet filters.

In the three-layer model, the WAN is separated from the multiple internal LANs, which provide the first two layers. Then, the internal LANs are further divided by backbone cabling (creating the third layer), which has additional routers with packet filters. In this model, the WAN connection is called the core layer, the backbone cabling and routers form the distribution layer, and the individual LANs function at the access layer.

The final step is to configure the logical addressing scheme. The basic layout should be decided and perhaps even documented on the cut sheet before implementation begins. All devices on the network should be assigned addresses, and the routes to each location network segment should be implemented.

Key Terms

access layer — The layer in the three-layer network model that provides users access to the network. This is the layer in which end systems are connected to the network.

backbone — Cabling used to connect wiring hubs in an extended star topology; typically, 62.5/125-micron optical fiber cable is used for this connection; however, 100-ohm UTP, 150-ohm STP, and single-mode fiber may also be used; can be used to connect wiring closets to wiring closets, wiring closets to the POP, and wiring closets between buildings; sometimes called vertical cable.

bandwidth — Capacity of a communications medium to transmit data; usually measured in bits per second; for example, the bandwidth of a Frame Relay connection may be 56 Kbps.

catchment area — The area serviced; for example, the area serviced by a wiring closet is the catchment area of that wiring closet.

clustering — Using multiple servers to provide network services. The advantage is load balancing and fault tolerance.

core layer — The layer that provides fast WAN connectivity for large network designs using the three-layer network model.

cross-connect jumpers — Cables used to connect networking devices inside the wiring closet.

cut sheet — A diagram of the floor plan and network, illustrating the network connection points, cabling runs, wiring closets, and the location of resources.

DHCP server — The network device, usually a PC or router, that is configured to provide addresses for a given subnet or group of subnets.

disk mirroring (RAID 1) — Maintains an exact duplicate of a hard disk so that in the event of a disk failure, the duplicate will automatically take over; two hard disks are used in such a configuration: one is the source and the other is the mirror.

disk striping with parity (RAID 5) — Maintains parity calculations for each disk write operation so that in the event of a single disk failure, the parity information along with the other disks can be used to automatically recreate the lost data; at least three hard disks are required in a stripe with parity, but up to 32 hard disks can be utilized in such a configuration.

distribution layer — Provides the backbone for the network; this layer is used in the three-layer network model to allow for access and protocol control and to increase security on the network.

Dynamic Host Configuration Protocol (DHCP) — Allows IP hosts to obtain IP addresses and subnet masks automatically over the network when they are started up. The DHCP server leases an address to the DHCP client for a set period of time.

EIA/TIA-568 — Defines and describes operational parameters for various grades of unshielded twisted-pair cabling.

EIA/TIA-568B — A revision of the original EIA/TIA-568 standard.

EIA/TIA-569 — Describes various network media configurations, such as those for horizontal pathways, entrance facilities, wiring closets, equipment rooms, and workstations.

Electronics Industries Association (EIA) — Provides standards that define how cabling should be configured on a network; often these standards are set as a joint operation with the TIA.

fault tolerance — The ability of a device or system to recover from the failure of one or more components; often used in the description of RAID levels to indicate that a particular RAID level provides protection from hard disk failure.

hierarchical design — In network design methodology, a network that is structured in a layered hierarchical fashion, such as the one-layer, two-layer, and three-layer network models; the opposite would be a mesh design.

horizontal cabling — Twisted-pair or fiber network media that connect workstations and wiring closets.

horizontal cross-connect (HCC) — The wiring closet where the horizontal cabling (which connects the workstations to the wiring closet) meets the backbone cabling.

intermediate cross-connect (ICC) — A specific type of IDF that sits between the **main cross-connect (MCC)** and the **horizontal cross-connect (HCC)**; should not have work areas or horizontal cable attached to it.

intermediate distribution facility (IDF) — Dependent upon the MDF in a star topology; a wiring closet used to support devices on the network.

load balancing — Spreading the workload among systems or components to increase the speed of service.

logical addressing scheme — The organization of the layer 3 addresses on a network.

main cross-connect (MCC) — *See* **main distribution facility (MDF)**.

main distribution facility (MDF) — The central wiring closet in an extended star topology; typically, and MDF will house the POP, patch panel, and network interconnection devices (bridges, routers, switches, repeaters, and concentrators).

mesh design — In network design methodology, a network that has no organized structure; the opposite would be a hierarchical design.

one-layer network model — Includes WAN connectivity equipment and organizes the network so that it can be easily adapted to the two- and three-layer design models in the future.

patch cords — Short network cables, usually three to five feet long, that are used to interconnect devices in a wiring closet.

point of presence (POP) — The point of interconnection between the telephone company and the building, floor, or company.

policy-based connectivity — A method that the network administrator uses to control access. The network administrator creates policies, such as "no video streaming is allowed at site 1," then implements them on the network, using equipment such as routers and switches.

redundant array of inexpensive disks (RAID) — A classification system for using multiple hard disks that provide performance enhancement and fault tolerance.

Telecommunications Industries Association (TIA) — Provides standards that define how cabling should be configured on a network; often standards are set as a joint operation with the EIA.

three-layer network model — Divides the network into three connectivity layers: core, distribution, and access.

throughput — The observed transfer rate of a network; transfer rate affected by device latency, network traffic, and capacity of source and destination to send and receive traffic.

transmission time — Time that it takes a file to transfer from one location to another.

two-layer network model — Divides the network into two connectivity layers: core and access.

vertical cabling — *See* **backbone**.

vertical cross-connect (VCC) — *See* **intermediate cross-connect (ICC)**.

wiring closet — A central junction point, usually located in a separate room, that is used for interconnecting various network devices.

REVIEW QUESTIONS

1. Which of the following is a layer in the three-layer network design model? (Choose all that apply.)

   a. core

   b. central

   c. access

   d. distribution

   e. campus

2. At which layer of the three-layer network model will you find a WAN connection?

   a. core

   b. central

   c. access

   d. distribution

   e. campus

3. At which layer of the three-layer network model should users connect to the network?

   a. core

   b. central

   c. access

   d. distribution

   e. campus

4. Which is a basic step in designing a network? (Choose all that apply.)

   a. interview users

   b. analyze requirements

   c. implement addressing

   d. design the topology

   e. evaluate bandwidth needs

5. At which layer of the three-layer network model will you find the campus backbone?

   a. core

   b. central

   c. access

   d. distribution

   e. campus

6. Which of the following is a logical place to locate your MDF? (Choose all that apply.)

   a. near the POP

   b. far away from the POP

   c. near the center of a network located throughout a multistory building

   d. on the top floor of a multistory building, assuming that operations are run near the bottom floor

7. Which of the following is also known as vertical cabling?

   a. HCC

   b. ICC

   c. backbone

   d. VCC

8. What is another name for the VCC, HCC, MDF, IDF, and ICC?

   a. backbone

   b. vertical cabling

   c. wiring closets

   d. bandwidth

8

9. When reviewing the organizational chart, you should not confuse the structure you see with the structure in which _____.

   a. communications flow

   b. the chain-of-command actually exists

   c. the organization was founded

   d. the management hierarchy is established

10. Which of the following would NOT influence the type of network cabling purchased?

    a. distance limitations

    b. topology

    c. sources of EMI

    d. operating systems used on end systems

11. When referenced in relation to a discussion of fault tolerance, what is a cluster?

    a. a group of hard disks

    b. a group of servers

    c. a group of segments

    d. a modem bank

12. Which of the following are methods for protecting data? (Choose all that apply.)

    a. disk mirroring

    b. disk striping with parity

    c. RAS

    d. backup

13. When you are designing a network, an existing network can hinder your design efforts in what way?

    a. People may be unable to explain their jobs.

    b. People may have adapted to its design flaws and be resistant to change.

    c. Devices may be configured incorrectly.

    d. People may have examples of how the existing network is not meeting their needs.

14. In a three-layer network model, each layer is part of a separate _____.

    a. LAN

    b. WAN

    c. organization

    d. broadcast domain

    e. area of responsibility

15. A(n) _____ is the network administrator determining which type of traffic to allow on the backbone and which type of traffic to filter.

    a. manifest destiny

    b. master of the domain

    c. policy based connectivity

    d. core layer control

16. What is the main difference between the one-layer network model and the mesh network design?

    a. the number of layers

    b. the intention of the designer

    c. the number of systems per segment

    d. the size of the network

17. The cable that connects a workstation to the wall outlet is called _____.

    a. telecommunications connector

    b. horizontal cross-connect patch cord

    c. horizontal cable

    d. work area station cable

18. In an organization in which multiple wiring closets are required, the central junction point for the wiring of the star topology will be located in the _____.

    a. MDF

    b. IDF

    c. HCC

    d. catchment area

19. When the distance between wiring closets exceeds 500 meters, which of the following cable types could be used to traverse the distance without the use of intermediate wiring closets or connectivity devices?

    a. UTP

    b. STP

    c. copper

    d. fiber-optic cabling

20. When possible, the POP should be located near the _____.

    a. IDF

    b. HCC

    c. MDF

    d. ICC

8

21. Which of the following cable types are recognized as backbones by EIA/TIA? (Choose all that apply.)

    a. 100-ohm UTP

    b. single-mode optical fiber

    c. 150-ohm STP

    d. 93-ohm coaxial

22. The usable distance of the UTP cable between the HCC and MCC is _____.

    a. 90 meters

    b. 200 meters

    c. 150 meters

    d. 100 meters

23. If single-mode fiber-optic cable is used between the HCC and MCC, what is the maximum usable distance?

    a. 100 meters

    b. 1000 yards

    c. 3000 meters

    d. 2000 meters

24. In network design, when considering connectivity to the telecommunications provider, POP stands for _____.

    a. Post Office Protocol

    b. point of presence

    c. post of propriety

    d. point of no return protocol

25. Which of the following is a synonym for catchment area?

    a. storage location

    b. span of control

    c. service area

    d. EMI

CASE PROJECTS

1. You are the new member on a network consulting team that has been charged with designing a network for the XYZ Corporation. This corporation has offices in over 100 locations in North America. However, your focus is on the main campus, which connects four different buildings. In your briefing this morning on the structure of the existing network, your team leader mentioned that the administrator of the main campus is wondering what can be done to increase security between the LANs. Review the network diagram below (Figure 8-19). What are your initial observations? If you had to make a single recommendation based on this information alone, what would you recommend? What additional information would you collect before making a recommendation?

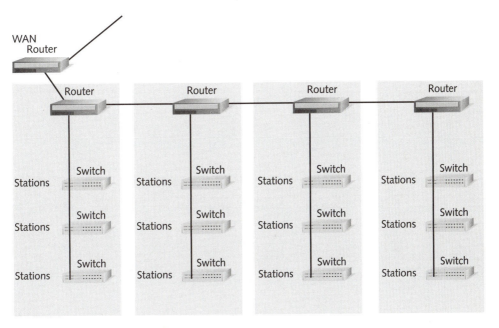

Figure 8-19   XYZ Corporation

2. Your network consulting team has been sent to Siberia to implement a network for a small research facility. There are only 25 people at this facility, and you have been asked to design a cost-effective network that can support the facility's research. They already have all the end systems that they require, but they need to pass data from point to point. What steps will you follow to properly design this network? What information will you seek to gather?

3. XYZ Corporation has several mission critical systems at its main campus. You have been asked to list some ways in which XYZ might protect its data. What would you list? What types of information would you review with the main campus network administrator?

A

CCNA CERTIFICATION OBJECTIVES

This appendix allows you to see which Cisco Certified Network Associate (CCNA) exam objectives are covered in this book and which are covered in its accompanying text. When used together, the two texts provide comprehensive preparation for Cisco certification. They are:

♦ *CCNA Guide to Cisco Networking Fundamentals*
♦ *CCNA Guide to Cisco Routing*

Each objective is mapped to the book and chapter in which it appears. Cisco has listed 60 different objectives for the CCNA Exam, and they are divided into seven different categories. These categories are:

- OSI Reference
- WAN Protocols
- IOS
- Network Protocols
- Routing
- Network Security
- LAN Switching

Each of the seven objective categories has its own table below, but the objectives themselves are numbered sequentially, exactly as Cisco has posted them. The following tables (Table A1–A7) map the objectives of each category to a specific book and chapter. *CCNA Guide to Cisco Networking Fundamentals* is identified as *Networking Fundamentals* in the following tables. *CCNA Guide to Cisco Routing* is identified by the designation *Cisco Routing*.

Table A-1   OSI Reference

Objective	Book and Chapter
1) Identify and describe the functions of each of the seven layers of the OSI reference model.	*Networking Fundamentals*, Chapter 1
2) Describe connection-oriented network service and connectionless network service, and identify the key difference between them.	*Networking Fundamentals*, Chapter 1
3) Describe data link addresses and network addresses, and identify the key difference between them.	*Networking Fundamentals*, Chapter 1
4) Identify at least three reasons why the industry uses a layered model.	*Networking Fundamentals*, Chapter 1
5) Define and explain the five conversion steps of data encapsulation.	*Networking Fundamentals*, Chapter 1
6) Define flow control and describe the three basic methods used in networking.	*Networking Fundamentals*, Chapter 1
7) List the key internetworking functions of the OSI Network layer and explain how they are performed in a router.	*Networking Fundamentals*, Chapter 2

Table A-2   WAN Protocols

Objective	Book and Chapter
8) Differentiate among the following WAN services: Frame Relay, ISDN/LAPD, HDLC, & PPP.	*Networking Fundamentals*, Chapter 9
9) Recognize key Frame Relay terms and features.	*Networking Fundamentals*, Chapter 9

Table A-2   WAN Protocols (continued)

Objective	Book and Chapter
10) List commands to configure Frame Relay LMIs, maps, and subinterfaces.	*Cisco Routing*, Chapter 6
11) List commands to monitor Frame Relay operation in the router.	*Cisco Routing*, Chapter 6
12) Identify PPP operations to encapsulate WAN data on Cisco routers.	*Cisco Routing*, Chapter 5
13) State a relevant use and context for ISDN networking.	*Networking Fundamentals*, Chapter 9
14) Identify ISDN protocols, function groups, reference points, and channels.	*Cisco Routing*, Chapter 5
15) Describe Cisco's implementation of ISDN BRI.	*Cisco Routing*, Chapter 5

Table A-3   IOS

Objective	Book and Chapter
16) Log into a router in both user and privileged modes.	*Networking Fundamentals*, Chapter 10
17) Use the context-sensitive help facility.	*Networking Fundamentals*, Chapter 10
18) Use the command history and editing features.	*Networking Fundamentals*, Chapter 10
19) Examine router elements (RAM, ROM, CDP, show).	*Networking Fundamentals*, Chapters 10 & 11
20) Manage configuration files from the privileged exec mode.	*Networking Fundamentals*, Chapter 10
21) Control router passwords, identification, and banner.	*Networking Fundamentals*, Chapter 10
22) Identify the main Cisco IOS commands for router startup.	*Networking Fundamentals*, Chapter 11
23) Enter an initial configuration using the setup command.	*Networking Fundamentals*, Chapter 11
24) Copy and manipulate configuration files.	*Networking Fundamentals*, Chapter 11
25) List the commands to load Cisco IOS software from: flash memory, a TFTP server, or ROM.	*Networking Fundamentals*, Chapter 11
26) Prepare to back up, upgrade, and load a backup Cisco ISO software image.	*Networking Fundamentals*, Chapter 11
27) Prepare the initial configuration of your router and enable IP.	*Networking Fundamentals*, Chapter 11

A

Table A-4   Network Protocols

Objective	Book and Chapter
28) Monitor Novell IPX operation on the router.	*Cisco Routing*, Chapter 2
29) Describe the two parts of network addressing, then identify the parts in specific protocol address examples.	*Networking Fundamentals*, Chapter 3
30) Create the different classes of IP addresses (and subnetting).	*Networking Fundamentals*, Chapter 3
31) Configure IP addresses.	*Networking Fundamentals*, Chapter 3
32) Verify IP addresses.	*Networking Fundamentals*, Chapters 3 & 10
33) List the required IPX address and encapsulation type.	*Cisco Routing*, Chapter 2
34) Enable the Novell IPX protocol and configure interfaces.	*Cisco Routing*, Chapter 2
35) Identify the functions of the TCP/IP Transport layer protocols.	*Networking Fundamentals*, Chapter 3
36) Identify the functions of the TCP/IP Network layer protocols.	*Networking Fundamentals*, Chapter 3
37) Identify the functions performed by ICMP.	*Networking Fundamentals*, Chapter 3
38) Configure IPX access lists and SAP filters to control basic Novell traffic.	*Cisco Routing*, Chapters 2 & 3

Table A-5   Routing

Objective	Book and Chapter
39) Add the RIP routing protocol to your configuration.	*Networking Fundamentals*, Chapter 10
40) Add the IGRP routing protocol to your configuration.	*Networking Fundamentals*, Chapter 10
41) Explain the services of separate and integrated multiprotocol routing.	*Cisco Routing*, Chapter 4
42) List problems that each routing type encounters when dealing with topology changes, and describe techniques to reduce the number of these problems.	*Cisco Routing*, Chapter 4
43) Describe the benefits of network segmentation with routers.	*Networking Fundamentals*, Chapters 2 & 10

Table A-6   Network Security

Objective	Book and Chapter
44) Configure standard and extended access lists to filter IP traffic.	*Cisco Routing*, Chapter 3
45) Monitor and verify selected access list operations on the router.	*Cisco Routing*, Chapter 3

Table A-7   LAN Switching

Objective	Book and Chapter
46) Describe the advantages of LAN segmentation.	*Networking Fundamentals*, Chapters 2 & 10
47) Describe LAN segmentation using bridges.	*Networking Fundamentals*, Chapter 2
48) Describe LAN segmentation using routers.	*Networking Fundamentals*, Chapter 2
49) Describe LAN segmentation using switches.	*Networking Fundamentals*, Chapter 2
50) Name and describe two switching methods.	*Cisco Routing*, Chapter 7
51) Describe full- and half-duplex Ethernet operation.	*Cisco Routing*, Chapter 7
52) Describe the network congestion problem in Ethernet networks.	*Networking Fundamentals*, Chapter 5
53) Describe the benefits of network segmentation with bridges.	*Networking Fundamentals*, Chapter 2
54) Describe the benefits of network segmentation with switches.	*Networking Fundamentals*, Chapter 2
55) Describe the features and benefits of Fast Ethernet.	*Networking Fundamentals*, Chapter 5
56) Describe the guidelines and distance limitations of Fast Ethernet.	*Networking Fundamentals*, Chapter 5
57) Distinguish between cut-through and store-and-forward LAN switching.	*Cisco Routing*, Chapter 7
58) Describe the operation of the Spanning Tree Protocol and its benefits.	*Cisco Routing*, Chapter 7
59) Describe the benefits of virtual LANs.	*Cisco Routing*, Chapter 7
60) Define and describe the function of a MAC address.	*Networking Fundamentals*, Chapters 1 & 3

A

B

ADDITIONAL RESOURCES

This appendix contains additional sources for information on subjects covered in this course.

INTERNET RESOURCES

Internet resources are invaluable for obtaining information on the latest news, technology, and standards. The Internet and Web resources listed in this section are divided into different categories, as follows:

- Standards organizations
- Technology reference
- Network overviews and tutorials
- Technical forums
- Cisco routers
- Exam preparation resources

Standards Organizations

The following are sites for organizations that provide networking standards discussed in this course:

- **American National Standards Institute**: *http://www.ansi.org/*
- **Electronic Industries Alliance**: *http://www.eia.org/eng/*
- **Institute of Electrical and Electronics Engineers (IEEE)**: *http://www.ieee.org/*
- **Internet Engineering Task Force (IETF)**: *http://www.ietf.org/*
- **International Telecommunication Union (ITU)**: *http://www.itu.int/*
- **International Organization for Standardization (ISO)**: *http://www.iso.ch/*

- **Optimized Engineering Corporation Compendium**:
  http://www.optimized.com/COMPENDI/

- **World Wide Web Consortium (W3C)**: *http://www.w3.org/*

- **RFC Editor**: *http://www.rfc-editor.org/*

- **Computer and Communications Standards**: *http://www.cmpcmm.com/cc/standards.html*

Technology Reference

These Web sites have online definitions for computer and networking terminology:

- **Babel: Glossary of Computer Oriented Abbreviations and Acronyms**:
  http://www.access.digex.net/~ikind/babel.html

- **Federal Standard 1037C: Glossary of Telecommunications Terms**:
  http://glossary.its.bldrdoc.gov/fs-1037/

- **Webopedia**: *http://www.pcwebopaedia.com/*

- **Whatis.com**: *http://www.whatis.com*

Networking Overviews and Tutorials

An introduction to various networking concepts is provided on the following Web sites:

- **Alliance Datacom's Frame Relay tutorial list**:
  http://www.alliancedatacom.com/frame-relay-tutorials.htm

- **Charles Spurgeon's Ethernet Web Site**:
  http://wwwhost.ots.utexas.edu/ethernet/ethernet-home.html

- **Ethernet Tutorial by LANTronix**: *http://www.lantronix.com/technology/tutorials/*

- **Interoperability Lab Tutorials**: *http://www.iol.unh.edu/training/*

- **Introduction to Networking by Cisco**:
  http://www.gtucci.com/JAC/netWorkEssentials/cisco/Default.htm

- **Optimized Engineering Corporation**: *http://www.optimized.com/*

- **TCP/IP and IPX Routing Tutorial**:
  http://www.gtucci.com/JAC/netWorkEssentials/TCPIPTUTORIAL/fguide.htm

- **The LAN/WAN Related Page**: *http://members.rotfl.com/kathy1998/lan.htm*

Technical Forums

The following sites contain technical information, discussions, and links to information covered in this course:

- **Frame Relay Forum**: *http://www.frforum.com/*
- **Open Group**: *http://www.opengroup.org/*
- **Protocols.com**: *www.protocols.com*

Cisco Routers

The following locations have information specific to Cisco routers:

- **Cisco**: *http://www.cisco.com*
- **Cisco product documentation list**: *http://www.cisco.com/univercd/cc/td/doc/product/*
- **Cisco command reference documents by subject**: *http://www.cisco.com/univercd/cc/td/doc/product/software/ios100/rpcr/index.htm*
- **Cisco routing tutorial**: *http://www.alliancedatacom.com/cisco-routing-tutorial.htm*
- **Cisco TCP/IP Guide**: *http://www.gtucci.com/JAC/Nap3InterNetworking/index.htm*

Exam Preparation Resources

The following Web sites contain information and technical papers concerning the CCNA exam:

- **CCPrep.com**: *http://www.ccprep.com*
- **CertNotes**: *http://www.certnotes.com*
- **Cramsession**: *http://www.cramsession.com*

B

C

COMMAND SUMMARY

This appendix lists the commands presented in this course. You should review these commands before you attempt the CCNA certification examination. The router commands in this section are organized into the following categories:

- ◆ Identification and navigation
- ◆ Passwords
- ◆ Router Startup configuration
- ◆ Examining the router
- ◆ Interface configuration
- ◆ IP-related commands
- ◆ IPX commands
- ◆ Access list configuration and status commands
- ◆ WAN configuration

The tables in the following sections list the mode, command syntax, and description of each command. The mode column is abbreviated so that you can see the router configuration mode that you must be in to properly execute the command. The following list illustrates the symbols used in the command tables:

- **>**: Symbolizes user mode where the router prompt looks like router>

- **#**: Symbolizes privileged mode, or enable mode, in which the router prompt looks like router#

- **GC**: Indicates global configuration mode, in which the router prompt looks like router(config)#

- **IF**: Indicates interface configuration mode, in which the router prompt looks like router(config-if)#

- **CL**: Indicates line console mode, in which the router prompt looks like router(config-line)#

- **VT**: Indicates virtual terminal mode, in which the router prompt looks like router(config-line)#

- **CR**: Indicates router mode, in which the router prompt looks like router(config-router)#

- **CS**: Indicates subinterface mode, in which the router prompt looks like router(config-subif)#

- **NA**: Indicates that the mode is not significant for this command

If multiple symbols are listed in the mode field, the command will work all modes listed.

> **TIP** This is not a comprehensive guide to all commands and options with which you can configure a router; such a guide would be too large for this appendix. This is an abridged guide that summarizes only the commands covered in this course. If you would like to see a larger list of Cisco commands, visit the Cisco Web site at *http://www.cisco.com/univercd/cc/td/doc/product/software/ios100/rpcr/index.htm*.

IDENTIFICATION AND NAVIGATION

The commands shown in the following table are basic navigation commands for the router. These commands allow you to change the router into different configuration modes and even set the identity and clock of the router.

Table C-1   Identification and navigation commands

Mode	Command Syntax	Description
>	enable	Allows you to access privileged mode from user mode
#	disable	Returns prompt to user mode from privileged mode
#	configure terminal	Allows you to access global configuration mode
GC	line console 0	Allows you to configure the console that is used to access the router; often used to set a router password; see Table C2
GC	line vty *[#]*	Allows you to access line console configuration mode; typing "line vty 0 4" configures all five virtual terminal lines at the same time; typing a single number (0–4) configures the virtual terminal number that you entered
GC	interface *[interface type and number]*	Allows you to access interface configuration mode; requires that you enter the type and number of the interface after the command; to configure the first Ethernet interface on your router, type "interface ethernet 0"
GC	interface *[subinterface type and number] [point-to-point or multipoint]*	Allows you to enter subinterface configuration mode, provided that the primary interface is using Frame Relay encapsulation; when creating an interface with this command, determine if it should be a point-to-point or multipoint connection; once it is created, you no longer need to enter point-to-point or multipoint when entering this mode
GC	router *[routing protocol name or static]*	Allows you to enter router configuration mode; requires that you specify the name of a routing protocol or indicate static (to indicate a manually cofigured routing table); to enable RIP routing, for example, type "router rip"
GC	hostname *[name]*	Allows you to set the hostname for your router; requires that you enter the name after the hostname command; for example, to name your router "clyde", you would type "hostname clyde"
GC	banner motd *[banner end character]*	Allows you to set the "message of the day" banner; to use this command, type "banner motd" followed by the single character that you want to end the message; for example, if you type: **banner motd @**, the router prompt will move to the next line, and everything you type following that will be your banner message, until you enter the @ character, which indicates that you are finished typing your banner message; to see your message, reboot the router
NA	ctrl+z	Ends a router configuration session; do not press the plus key; press Ctrl+Z

C

Table C-1   Identification and navigation commands (continued)

Mode	Command Syntax	Description
#	set clock	Used to set the time and date on the router
#	reload *[in hh:mm] [month day	day month]*	Reboots the router; setting a time delay or month and day for the reboot is optional
NA	exit	Ends your configuration session from the > or # prompt; from other prompts, command takes you back one level; for example, typing exit at the router(config-if)# prompt takes you back to the router(config)# prompt
NA	CTRL ^	Allows you to abort a command in progress; executed by pressing Ctrl+Shift+6
> #	quit	Allows you to exit router configuration and/or viewing

PASSWORDS

The commands shown in the following table allow you to configure passwords for your router. Do not forget the passwords that you configure; you will need them when you want to access your router in the future.

Table C-2   Commands for configuring passwords

Mode	Command Syntax	Description
GC	enable password *[password]*	Allows you to set the privileged mode password, which is used to enter privileged mode
GC	enable secret *[password]*	Allows you to set the privileged mode password as encrypted; overrides the enable password when configured
VT	login *[Enter]* password *[password]*	Allows you to set a virtual terminal password; requires that you first type "login", press the Return or Enter key, then type "password" followed by the password you would like to set
CL	login *[Enter]* password *[password]*	Allows you to set a router line console password; requires that you type "login", press the Return or Enter key, and then type "password" followed by the password you would like to set

ROUTER STARTUP CONFIGURATION

The commands listed in this section are vital to configuring and managing the configuration of the router. These commands cover saving, copying, and replacing the contents of the IOS and the router configuration file.

Table C-3   Router startup and running configuration commands

Mode	Command Syntax	Description
#	copy running-config startup-config	Copies the running configuration to the NVRAM on the router; saves configuration changes you make while the router is running, so that they are implemented next time the router is restarted
#	copy startup-config running-config	Copies the startup configuration from NVRAM to the running configuration
#	copy tftp flash	Copies an IOS file from a TFTP server to flash memory
#	copy flash tftp	Copies an IOS file from flash memory to a TFTP server
#	copy tftp startup-config	Copies the router configuration file from a TFTP server to the startup configuration in NVRAM on the router
#	copy startup-config tftp	Copies the startup configuration in NVRAM to a TFTP server
#	erase flash	Erases the flash memory on the router
#	erase startup-config	Erases the startup configuration from NVRAM

EXAMINING THE ROUTER

The following list of commands allows you to examine router configuration, components, resources, and other statistics. These commands are useful for checking the router's performance and troubleshooting configuration problems.

Table C-4   Commands for examining router components and configuration

Mode	Command Syntax	Description
> #	show clock	Displays the time and date
> #	show processes	Displays CPU utilization information
> #	show interface ethernet [#]	Shows statistics and configuration information for the Ethernet interface that is listed; requires that you enter the number of the interface after the command
> #	show interface serial [#]	Shows statistics and configuration information for the serial interface that is listed; requires that you enter the number of the interface after the command
> #	show interfaces	Lists configuration and statistics for all interfaces configured on the router
> #	show protocol	Shows the protocols configured on the system and indicates which interfaces are using them
> #	show history	Displays the last 10 commands executed
> #	show flash	Shows the flash file(s), size, name, and the amount of flash memory used, total, and available
> #	show cdp neighbor	Shows a list of Cisco devices that are directly attached to this device

C

Table C-4   Commands for examining router components and configuration (continued)

Mode	Command Syntax	Description
#	show running-config	Displays the currently running router configuration file
#	show startup-config	Displays the router startup configuration maintained in NVRAM
> #	show version	Displays version information for the router, including the startup register setting, the router series number, how long the router has been up and running, and the IOS version number

INTERFACE CONFIGURATION

Interfaces are an important part of the router, and the next table lists those that are specific to interface configuration. Table C-9 lists additional interface configuration commands, as related to WAN configuration.

Table C-5   Interface configuration commands

Mode	Command Syntax	Description
GC	interface serial [#]	Allows you to configure the specific serial interface that you identify
GC	interface ethernet [#]	Allows you to configure the specific Ethernet interface that you specify
IF	encapsulation [encapsulation type]	Allows you to set the encapsulation type for your interface
IF	enable cdp	Allows you to enable the Cisco Discovery Protocol
IF	disable cdp	Allows you to disable the Cisco Discovery Protocol
IF	loopback	Allows you to configure the interface for loopback that is used for testing purposes; information transmitted out that interface will be immediately returned on the receive circuit of that same interface
GC	interface [interface #.subinterface #]	Creates and/or accesses a subinterface when Frame Relay encapsulation is used on the primary interface; for example, to create a subinterface #1 off of S1, type "interface s1.1"

IP COMMANDS

The commands in the following table are related to the configuration, control, and troubleshooting of TCP/IP. They cover configuring an IP address and subnet mask, in addition to configuring routing protocols.

Table C-6   IP-related commands

Mode	Command Syntax	Description
IF CS	ip address [ip address] [subnet address]	Sets the IP address and subnet mask for an interface
IF CS	ip unnumbered [interface or logical interface]	Allows you to establish that the interface is to support the IP protocol, but not be assigned an IP address
GC	router rip	Enables RIP routing and accesses router configuration mode
GC	router igrp [autonomous system number]	Enables IGRP routing and accesses router configuration mode; requires that you enter an autonomous system number
CR	network [major network number]	Used after the router rip and router igrp commands to indicate the network number to which the routing protocol will apply
GC	no ip routing	Disables IP routing on the router
GC	ip routing	Enables IP routing on the router
#	debug ip rip	Enables RIP debugging, which allows you to monitor RIP updates
#	debug ip igrp [transaction or events]	Enables IGRP transactions and/or event monitoring
#	no debug all	Disables all debugging activities
#	debug all	Enables all debugging options
> #	show ip route	Displays the router's routing table
> #	ping [ip address | hostname]	Allows you to verify that a host is reachable either by IP address or host name
> #	trace [ip address | hostname]	Allows you to locate the route taken to contact a host either by IP address or host name
> #	telnet [ip address]	Allows the user to start a telnet session with a telnet server
> #	show ip protocol	Shows statistics for the IP protocol, such as routing protocol information, networks serviced, and gateway information
> #	show ip interface [interface type and number]	Shows statistics for interfaces configured for IP; adding the specific interface type and number is optional; if you only type "show ip interface", all interfaces will be configured with IP

C

IPX COMMANDS

The following table illustrates how to configure IPX on the router with configuration, troubleshooting, and routing commands. To learn how to configure IPX access lists, see Table C-8.

Table C-7 IPX commands

Mode	Command Syntax	Description
IF	ipx network [network number] encapsulation [frame type]	Sets the IPX network address and frame type for the router's Ethernet interface
GC	ipx routing	Enables IPX routing on the router
GC	no ipx routing	Disables IPX routing on the router
GC	show ipx route	Shows the IPX routing table
GC	show ipx interface	Shows statistics for interfaces using IPX
GC	show ipx traffic	Shows IPX sent and received packet statistics
GC	debug ipx routing activity	Enables routing activity debugging
GC	no debug ipx routing activity	Disables routing activity debugging

ACCESS LISTS

Access lists allow you to control the types of packets that are allowed to traverse the router. The following table illustrates the commands for both IPX and IP access list creation and configuration.

Table C-8 Access list configuration and status commands

Mode	Command Syntax	Description
GC	access-list [list #] [permit | deny] [ip address] [mask]	Creates a standard IP access list
GC	access-list [list #] [permit | deny] [protocol] [source IP address] [source wildcard mask] [destination IP address] [destination wildcard mask] [operator] [port] [log]	Creates an extended IP access list
GC	no access-list [list #]	Removes the access list indicated
IF	ip access-group [list number] [in | out]	Allows you to group an IP access list to a router interface
IF	no ip access-group [list #] [in | out]	Removes an IP access group
GC	access-list [list #] [permit | deny] [source network/node address] [destination network/node address]	Creates a standard IPX access list
GC	access-list [list#] [permit | deny] [protocol] [source network/node] [socket] [destination network/node] [socket]	Creates an extended IPX access list

Table C-8   Access list configuration and status commands (continued)

Mode	Command Syntax	Description
GC	access-list *[list #] [permit	deny]* *[source network/node]* *[service-type]*	Creates a SAP filter
GC	ipx input-sap-filter *[list #]*	Specifies an input SAP filter entry
GC	ipx output-sap-filter *[list #]*	Specifies an output SAP filter entry
IF	ipx access-group *[list #]* [in	out]	Allows you to group an IPX access list to a router interface; requires that you specify "in" or "out"
#	show ip access-lists	Shows all IP access lists
#	show access-list *[list #]*	Allows you to review your access lists; requires that you enter the number of the access list you would like to view

WAN CONFIGURATION

The following commands cover the WAN configuration techniques mentioned in this course. These commands allow you to configure ISDN, PPP, and Frame Relay interfaces.

Table C-9   WAN configuration commands

Mode	Command Syntax	Description
IF CS	bandwidth *[bandwidth]*	Sets the bandwidth allowed on the serial interface in kilobits per second
IF	clock rate *[clock rate]*	Sets the clock rate in bits per second for a serial interface
IF CS	encapsulation *[WAN protocol]*	Sets the encapsulation type for a serial interface; common options are PPP, Frame Relay, and HDLC; for example, to set the interface to PPP encapsulation, type "encapsulation ppp"
IF CS	ppp authentication *[chap	pap]*	Sets the authentication type for ppp encapsulation; can be chap or pap; if both pap and chap are used, the order in which they are entered on the command line is the order in which they will be used
IF CS	frame-relay interface-dlci *[dlci #]*	Configures a DLCI number for a serial interface using Frame Relay encapsulation
IF CS	frame-relay lmi-type *[lmi-type]*	Sets the LMI type for a Frame Relay interface; options are cisco, q933i, and ansi
#	show frame-relay lmi	Allows you to view configuration and interface statistics concerning your Frame Relay interfaces using LMI; also shows LMI type
#	show frame-relay map	Displays the Frame Relay map
GC	isdn switch type basic -*[switch identifier]*	Sets the ISDN switch type to which the router will be configured to communicate
GC	isdn spid *[spid channel designation] [SPID #]*	Sets the Service Profile Identifier (SPID) for each ISDN channel

C

GLOSSARY

5-4-3 rule — Stipulates that between stations on a 10 Mbps LAN, there can be no more than 5 network segments connected, the maximum number of repeaters between the segments is 4, and the maximum number of segments with stations on them is 3.

100Base-FX — Fast Ethernet implementation over multimode fiber-optic (MMF) cabling; maximum segment length is 412 meters.

100Base-T4 — 100-Mbps Fast Ethernet implementation that uses four pairs of either Category 3, 4, or 5 UTP cable; maximum segment length is 100 meters.

100Base-TX — Fast Ethernet implementation that uses two pairs of either Category 5 unshielded twisted-pair (UTP) or shielded twisted-pair (STP); operates at 100 Mbps with a maximum segment distance of 100 meters.

access layer — The layer in the three-layer network model that provides users access to the network. This is the layer in which end systems are connected to the network.

access lists — Permit or deny statements that filter traffic based on criteria such as source address, destination address, and protocol type.

access rate — The speed of the line that indicates transfer rate. Common U.S. access rates are 56, 64, and 128 Kbps provided by Integrated Service Digital Network (ISDN) connections and 1.544 Mbps provided by T1 connections.

adaptive cut-through — A method of switching whereby the switch uses the cut-through technique unless network errors reach a certain threshold; then, it automatically switches to store-and-forward switching until the error rate returns to an acceptable level.

administrative distance — A value used to determine the reliability/desirability of a particular route table update.

alignment error — A frame that has both an FCS error and an entire octet missing from the frame.

American National Standards Institute (ANSI) — A standards organization based in the United States involved with various WAN standards.

any — A keyword used to represent all hosts or networks; replaces 0.0.0.0 255.255.255.255 in an access list.

AppleTalk Control Protocol (ATCP) — PPP interface protocol for AppleTalk; *See* **Network Control Protocol**.

Application layer — Layer seven of the OSI model; provides services directly to network applications; FTP, telnet, and SMTP are protocols that function at this layer.

Asymmetric Digital Subscriber Line (ADSL) — DSL service that provides from 1.536-Mbps to 6.144-Mbps connections in the United States. Outside the U.S. connections range from 2.048 to 4.096 Mbps.

asymmetric switching — A type of LAN switching that allows for multiple speeds of network communication; a switch that supports both 10-Mbps and 100-Mbps communications is an example of asymmetric switching.

asynchronous — Communication technique that relies on start and stop bits to define the end points of a transmission. The implication of asynchronous communication is that timing mechanisms are not needed to maintain clock synchronization between the source and destination (as they are in synchronous communication).

asynchronous serial — Serial connections that are employed in most modems connected to residential phone lines.

attenuation — The natural degradation of a transmitted signal over distance.

authentication — The process of verifying the right to complete a connection.

autonomous system (AS) — A group of routers under the control of a single administration.

B-channel — *See* **bearer channel**.

backbone — Cabling used to connect wiring hubs in an extended star topology; typically, 62.5/125-micron optical fiber cable is used for this connection; however, 100-ohm UTP, 150-ohm STP, and single-mode fiber may also be used; can be used to connect wiring closets to wiring closets, wiring closets to the POP, and wiring closets between buildings; sometimes called vertical cable.

backoff algorithm — Mathematical calculation performed by computers after a collision occurs on a CSMA/CD network; forces machines to wait a random amount of time before resending the destroyed packet.

backoff period — Used by devices that have caused a collision on an Ethernet network; a random interval during which the devices cannot send, to prevent them from causing another collision immediately after the one they have just caused.

backward explicit congestion notification (BECN) — A message sent to the source router when congestion is discovered on the link. The recipient router's reaction to the BECN should be to reduce the amount of traffic it is sending.

bandwidth — Capacity of a communications medium to transmit data; usually measured in bits per second; for example, the bandwidth of a Frame Relay connection may be 56 Kbps.

Basic Rate Interface (BRI) — An ISDN service that provides two B-channels for data transfers up to 128 Kbps and one D-channel to control the communications.

bearer channel — ISDN channel used to transfer data; typically supports 64-Kbps bandwidth.

bit time — The duration of time to transmit one data bit on the network, which is 100 nanoseconds on a 10-Mbps Ethernet network or 10 nanoseconds on a 100-Mbps Ehternet network.

blocking — A port state on a switch that indicates that the port is receiving BPDUs, but is not forwarding frames in order to prevent logical loops in the network.

Border Gateway Protocol (BGP) — An exterior gateway protocol used to route between multiple autonomous systems.

bridge protocol data unit (BPDU) — An STP management message used to transfer status information about the Spanning Tree configuration of the switched and/or bridged network.

bridges — Internetworking devices that build routing tables of MAC address; used to segment networks into smaller collision domains; operate at the Data Link layer of the OSI model.

bridging table — A table maintained on a bridge that maps MAC addresses to the bridge port over which they can be accessed.

broadcast — A frame that is addressed to all stations on the broadcast domain. The destination MAC address is set to FFFFFFFFFFFF so that all local stations will process the packet.

broadcast domain — A logical or physical group of devices that will receive broadcast traffic from each other on the LAN.

broadcast storm — An error condition in which broadcast traffic is above 126 packets per second and network communications are impeded; typically the result of a software configuration error or programming error.

Carrier Sense Multiple Access with Collision Detection (CSMA/CD) — Access method specified by the IEEE Ethernet 802.3 standard. In this method, a node will listen to see if the line is clear and then, if the line is clear, send. Two nodes may send at the same time and cause a collision. Two nodes will then perform the backoff algorithm.

carrier signal — A transmitted electromagnetic pulse or wave on the network wire that indicates that a transmission is in progress.

catchment area — The area serviced; for example, the area serviced by a wiring closet is the catchment area of that wiring closet.

Central Office (CO) — The telecommunications company location that is the point of entry to the toll network from the demarcation.

challenge — The query packet, or the action of sending the query packet over a CHAP connection, that is used to verify the participants of the PPP connection.

Challenge-Handshake Authentication Protocol (CHAP) — PPP authentication protocol that provides better security than PAP in authenticating devices on PPP connections.

channel service unit/digital service unit (CSU/DSU) — A telecommunications device that provides connectivity between the WAN service provider network and the customer's LAN. DSU is also known as "data service unit."

clustering — Using multiple servers to provide network services. The advantage is load balancing and fault tolerance.

collision domain — The area on the network in which collision can occur; a section of the network that is not separated by routers, switches, or bridges.

Committed Burst Size (CBS) — The maximum amount of data bits that the service provider agrees to transfer in a set time period under normal conditions.

committed information rate (CIR) — The minimum guaranteed transfer rate of the Frame Relay circuit. This is usually lower than the access rate because the transfer rate may exceed the CIR during short bursts.

configuration bridge protocol data unit (CBPDU) — *See* **bridge protocol data unit (BPDU)**.

Consultative Committee on International Telephony and Telegraphy (CCITT) — The former name of **International Telecommunication Union - Telecommunications Standardization Sector (ITU-T)**.

Content-addressable memory (CAM) — A memory location on a switch that contains the MAC address to switch port mapping information, which the switch uses to forward frames to the appropriate destination.

contention method — The method by which computers on the network must share the available capacity of the network wire with other computers.

convergence — The point at which all routers on a network agree upon the correct routes for that network and share a similar view of the network.

core layer — The layer that provides fast WAN connectivity for large network designs using the three-layer network model.

count-to-infinity — A routing loop whereby packets bounce infinitely around an internetwork.

cross-connect jumpers — Cables used to connect networking devices inside the wiring closet.

customer premises equipment (CPE) — Equipment located at the WAN customer's location that is maintained by the customer; also known as **data terminal equipment (DTE)**.

cut sheet — A diagram of the floor plan and network, illustrating the network connection points, cabling runs, wiring closets, and the location of resources.

cut-through — A switching technique in which the Ethernet frame is forwarded immediately after the destination address is deciphered. This method offers the lowest latency, but does not reduce packet errors that may occur after the destination address.

cyclical redundancy check (CRC) — A mathematical computation that is used to verify the integrity of a data packet.

D-channel — *See* **signaling channel**.

data communications equipment (DCE) — Equipment that is supplied by the telecommunications provider as the connection to their network, such as a Frame Relay or ISDN switch.

Data Link Connection Identifier (DLCI) — Pronounced *dell-see*, it is configured on the router and used to identify which path leads to a specific Network layer address (i.e., IP address). The DLCI is not a network-wide unique address (like a MAC address); instead, the DLCI is only locally significant, meaning that it can, and usually does, change on each physical link.

Data Link layer — Layer two of the OSI model; broken into two sublayers: Logical Link Control and Media Access Control. Media access, topology, flow control, and packaging data into frames are all responsibilities of this layer. Bridges and switches (layer 2 switches) function at this layer.

data terminal equipment (DTE) — Device located at the WAN customer's location that is maintained by the customer and used to make the WAN connection; also known as **customer provided equipment (CPE)**.

debug — Tool and command that display real-time information concerning a router's status.

default gateway — IP address of the router port directly connected to a network; used as the default path from one network or subnet to other networks.

defining a maximum — Defining a maximum hop count, so that packets cannot bounce infinitely throughout an internetwork.

DHCP server — The network device, usually a PC or router, that is configured to provide addresses for a given subnet or group of subnets.

dial-on-demand routing (DDR) — A feature available on Cisco routers that allows you to use bandwidth as needed.

Digital Subscriber Line (DSL) — Telecommunications services that offer high bandwidth over existing copper lines. DSL connections are generically referred to as xDSL because there are several different DSL technologies.

disabled — A port state on a switch that indicates that the port is neither receiving BPDUs nor forwarding frames.

discard eligible (DE) — During times of congestion, DE frames are discarded in order to provide a higher, more reliable, service to those frames that are not DE.

disk mirroring (RAID 1) — Maintains an exact duplicate of a hard disk so that in the event of a disk failure, the duplicate will automatically take over; two hard disks are used in such a configuration: one is the source and the other is the mirror.

disk striping with parity (RAID 5) — Maintains parity calculations for each disk write operation so that in the event of a single disk failure, the parity information along with the other disks can be used to automatically recreate the lost data; at least three hard disks are required in a stripe with parity, but up to 32 hard disks can be utilized in such a configuration.

distance-vector routing protocol — A routing protocol that functions by broadcasting periodic route table updates that contain the router's entire route table to all connected neighbors; examples include RIP and IGRP.

distribution layer — Provides the backbone for the network; this layer is used in the three-layer network model to allow for access and protocol control and to increase security on the network.

down-when-looped — A Cisco router command that shuts down an interface when looping is detected; used to prevent testing scenarios from causing troubleshooting problems in a production environment.

DS1 — *See* **E1**.

DS2 — European 120-channel digital line capable of supporting up to 8.448-Mbps data transmissions.

DS3 — European 480-channel digital line capable of supporting up to 34.368-Mbps data transmissions.

DS4 — European 1920-channel digital line capable of supporting up to 139.268-Mbps data transmissions.

DS5 — European 7680-channel digital line capable of supporting up to 565.148-Mbps data transmissions.

Dynamic Host Configuration Protocol (DHCP) — Allows IP hosts to obtain IP addresses and subnet masks automatically over the network when they are started up. The DHCP server leases an address to the DHCP client for a set period of time.

E1 — European 30-channel digital line capable of supporting up to 2.048-Mbps data transmissions.

EIA/TIA-568 — Defines and describes operational parameters for various grades of unshielded twisted-pair cabling.

EIA/TIA-568B — A revision of the original EIA/TIA-568 standard.

EIA/TIA-569 — Describes various network media configurations, such as those for horizontal pathways, entrance facilities, wiring closets, equipment rooms, and workstations.

Electronics Industries Association (EIA) — Provides standards that define how cabling should be configured on a network; often these standards are set as a joint operation with the TIA.

encapsulation — The process of wrapping Protocol Data Units from upper-layer protocols into a Data Link layer format; common frame types are 802.3, 802.2, and Ethernet_II.

Enhanced Interior Gateway Routing Protocol (EIGRP) — A proprietary Cisco distance-vector protocol developed to overcome some of the limitations associated with distance-vector protocols.

error sensing — *See* **adaptive cut-through**.

Ethernet — *See* **Carrier Sense Multiple Access with Collision Detection (CSMA/CD)**.

Excess Burst Size (EBS) — The amount of excess traffic (over the CBS) that the network will attempt to transfer during a set time period. EBS data can be discarded by the network, if necessary.

extended IP access lists — An IP access list that filters traffic by source IP address, destination IP address, protocol type, and port number.

extended IPX access lists — IPX access lists that filter traffic based on source and destination IPX nodes or networks, IPX protocol type, and IPX socket number.

Exterior Gateway Protocol (EGP) — An exterior gateway protocol used to route between multiple autonomous systems.

Fast Ethernet — Defined in IEEE 802.3u; any of the following 100-Mbps Ethernet LAN technologies: 100Base-T4, 100Base-TX, 100Base-FX.

fault tolerance — The ability of a device or system to recover from the failure of one or more components; often used in the description of RAID levels to indicate that a particular RAID level provides protection from hard disk failure.

filter — Process of blocking or manipulating network data traffic. Normally, filtering a particular type of data traffic means you are blocking that traffic.

flag — Flags or delimiters mark the beginning and ending of the frame.

flash memory — Rewritable memory used to store the IOS image in use by a router.

floods — The process of broadcasting packets onto a network.

forward explicit congestion notification (FECN) — A Frame Relay message that tells a router that congestion was experienced on the virtual circuit.

forwarding — The state of a port on a switch or bridge that indicates that it will learn MAC addresses and forward frames out that port.

fractional E1 — A service that offers some number of channels less than the 30 (64-Kbps) digital channels provided by a full E1 connection.

fractional T1 — A service that offers some number of channels less than the 24 (64-Kbps) digital channels provided by a full T1 connection.

fragment free — A method of switching whereby the switch reads the first 64 bytes of the incoming frame before forwarding it to the destination port(s).

Frame Check Sequence (FCS) — A mathematical computation placed at the end of the frame that is used to ensure that the frame was not corrupted during transmission.

Frame Relay — A Data Link layer protocol that relies on high-speed, highly reliable connections. This protocol can operate between 56 Kbps and 1.544 Mbps over a WAN connection.

Frame Relay access device (FRAD) — The device that the Frame Relay customer utilizes to connect to a Frame Relay network; also known as the **Frame Relay assembler/disassembler**.

Frame Relay assembler/disassembler — *See* **Frame Relay access device (FRAD)**.

Frame Relay map — A table that defines the interface to which a specific DLCI number is mapped.

Frame Relay network device (FRND) — The device that the Frame Relay provider supplies as the connection to the Frame Relay network; the acronym FRND is pronounced *friend*.

Frame Relay switch — A telecommunications company device that is used to support Frame Relay connections from customer locations; used to route Frame Relay traffic inside the public data network.

Frame Relay switching table — A table that is maintained on a Frame Relay switch; used to route Frame Relay traffic via virtual circuit DLCI numbers.

frame check sequence (FCS) — A calculation based on the size of a transmitted data frame that verifies whether it was received intact.

frame check sequence (FCS) error — When the calculation in the FCS field indicates that the frame was not received intact.

frame filtering — A technique used on early VLAN implementations that employed the use of multiple switching tables.

frame identification — *See* **frame tagging**.

frame tagging — A method of VLAN identification endorsed by the IEEE 802.1q specification that calls for an additional 4-byte field in the VLAN frame after the source and destination addresses in the data packet.

full mesh — The most expensive and most fault-tolerant Frame Relay topology. This topology ensures that each Frame Relay device on the network has an individual router to every other Frame Relay device on the network.

full-duplex — A connection that allows communication in two directions at once; common telephone connections are typically full-duplex because people can talk and listen at the same time.

function groups — Used in ISDN communication to describe a set of functions that are implemented by a device and its software; a terminal adapter (TA) is a function group.

Get Nearest Server (GNS) — A SAP request sent by clients; attempts to locate the nearest NetWare server.

giant — An Ethernet frame that is over 6000 bytes and consequently far too large to be transmitted on a Ethernet network.

half-duplex — A connection that allows communication in two directions, but not simultaneously; the circuit can be used for sending or receiving bits in one direction at a time only.

hierarchical design — In network design methodology, a network that is structured in a layered hierarchical fashion, such as the one-layer, two-layer, and three-layer network models; the opposite would be a mesh design.

High-bit-rate Digital Subscriber Line (HDSL) — Symmetric digital communication service capable of 1.536 Mbps in the United States and 2.048 Mbps in Europe.

High-level Data Link Control (HDLC) — A Data Link layer encapsulation protocol that is a superset of the SDLC protocol. HDLC is a WAN protocol that can be used for both point-to-point and multipoint connections.

High-Speed Serial Interface (HSSI) — A type of serial device that was developed by Cisco and T3Plus Network that operates at speeds of up to 52 Mbps over distances of 15 meters.

hold-down timers — Used by routers to stabilize route tables and to prevent erroneous route table updates.

hop count — A count of the number of routers a packet must pass through in order to reach a destination network.

horizontal cabling — Twisted-pair or fiber network media that connect workstations and wiring closets.

horizontal cross-connect (HCC) — The wiring closet where the horizontal cabling (which connects the workstations to the wiring closet) meets the backbone cabling.

host — A device on the network, which could represent a user station, printer, server, or other resource; a keyword that specifies that an address should have a wildcard mask of 0.0.0.0.

hub-and-spoke topology — *See* **star topology**.

IEEE 802.1q — The IEEE standard that defines VLAN implementations and recommends frame tagging as the way in which switches should identify VLANs.

IEEE 802.3u — The IEEE Ethernet standard that defines Fast Ethernet implementations, including 100Base-T4, 100Base-TX, and 100Base-T4.

implicit deny any — Blocks all packets that do not meet the requirements of any access list statements.

Integrated Services Digital Network (ISDN) — A service provided by most major telecommunications carriers, such as AT&T, Sprint, and RBOCs; operates over existing phone lines and transfers both voice and data.

interesting traffic — Network traffic for which you feel it is worth activating or maintaining an ISDN link that is configured with DDR.

interface — Physical port connections on a router such as Serial0, Ethernet1, or the console port.

interframe gap — The time required between the transmission of data frames on the network: 9.6 microseconds for Ethernet.

Interior Gateway Routing Protocol (IGRP) — A proprietary Cisco distance-vector routing protocol that uses hop count, delay, bandwidth, reliability, and maximum transmission units as metrics.

intermediate cross-connect (ICC) — A specific type of IDF that sits between the **main cross-connect (MCC)** and the **horizontal cross-connect (HCC)**; should not have work areas or horizontal cable attached to it.

intermediate distribution facility (IDF) — Dependent upon the MDF in a star topology; a wiring closet used to support devices on the network.

International Telecommunications Union (ITU) — Recommends telecommunications standards worldwide; implemented the Integrated Services Digital Network (ISDN).

International Telecommunication Union - Telecommunications Standardization Sector (ITU-T) — A standards organization based in Europe, but with membership worldwide; involved in telecommunications standardization.

Internet Control Message Protocol (ICMP) — A layer 3 protocol in the TCP/IP protocol stack that provides messaging for applications such as ping and trace.

Internet Engineering Task Force (IETF) — Researches and defines standards related to Internet communication; defined the serial line protocols PPP and SLIP.

Internetwork Packet Exchange (IPX) — Predominantly a layer 3 protocol used by the IPX/SPX protocol stack for routing packets along the shortest path in an IPX internetwork.

Internetwork Packet exchange/Sequence Packet exchange (IPX/SPX) — Routed protocol stack developed by Novell for use with the Netware network operating system.

Internetworking Operating System (IOS) — The operating system loaded on a router, which controls all router functions.

interpacket gap (IPG) — *See* **interframe gap**.

Inverse ARP — A protocol that allows a router to send a query using the DLCI number to find an IP address.

inverse mask — *See* **wildcard mask**.

IP Control Protocol (IPCP) — PPP interface protocol for IP; *see* **Network Control Protocol**.

IPX Control Protocol (IPXCP) — PPP interface protocol for IPX; *see* **Network Control Protocol**.

IPX SAP filters — Access lists that filter SAP traffic on a network.

IPX/SPX addresses — Eighty-bit addresses consisting of a 32-bit network portion and a 48-bit node portion; the network administrator arbitrarily assigns the network portion; the MAC address of the node makes up the node portion of the address; addresses normally appear in hexadecimal format.

ISDN Digital Subscriber Line (IDSL) — A telecommunications service that makes an ISDN connection into a 128-Kbps DSL connection. Unlike ISDN, IDSL only supports data communications (not analog voice or video).

ISDN modem — *See* **terminal adapter**.

ISDN phone number — *See* **Service Profile Identifier (SPID)**.

jabber — A frame that is longer than the 1518 bytes acceptable for transmission between stations and that also has an FCS error.

jam signal — A 32-bit signal that is sent by the first station to detect a collision on an Ethernet network; ensures that all other stations are aware of the collision.

keepalive packets — Data packets sent between devices to confirm that a connection should be maintained between them.

late collision — Occurs when two stations transmit more than 64 bytes of their frames without detecting a collision.

latency — The lag or delay that a device or part of the network media causes; for example, fiber-optic cable can delay a transmitted signal 1 bit time every 10 meters.

LCP link configuration — A process that modifies and/or enhances the default characteristics of a PPP connection; includes the following actions: link, establishment, authentication, link-quality determination, Network layer protocol configuration negotiation, and link determination.

learning — A transitory state on a bridge or switch port that indicates it is trying to learn new MAC addresses and correct its bridge table before forwarding frames on the network; used to prevent loops during the election of a new root bridge.

Link Access Procedure D-channel (LAPD) — A WAN protocol adapted from HDLC; used in communication over ISDN lines.

Link Control Protocol (LCP) — Used in PPP connections to establish, configure, maintain, and terminate PPP connections.

Link Quality Monitoring (LQM) — PPP feature that checks the reliability of the link by monitoring the number of errors, latency between requests, connection retries, and connection failures on the PPP link.

link establishment — The process of opening and configuring a PPP connection before any data can be transferred over the link.

link termination — The process of disconnecting a PPP connection when the call is complete, which is determined by the PPP hosts that made the connection.

link-quality determination — The process of checking the quality of a PPP link and monitoring its reliability.

link-state advertisement (LSA) — Advertisement used by link-state routing protocols to advertise their route tables to all other routers in an internetwork.

link-state packets (LSP) — Used to send out link-state advertisements.

link-state routing protocols — Routing protocols that function via link-state advertisements using link-state packets to inform all routers on the internetwork of route tables.

listening — A transitory state on a bridge or switch port that is used during the election of a new root bridge; the port does not learn MAC addresses nor does it forward frames when in this state.

load balancing — To distribute workload between systems in some way; in routing, it is the ability of a router to distribute packets among multiple same cost paths.

local access rate — *See* **access rate**.

local loop — The connection between the demarcation point and the telephone company (WAN service provider) office.

Local Management Interface (LMI) — A standard signaling mechanism between the CPE and the Frame Relay connection. The LMI can provide the network server with a local DLCI; it can also give DLCI global (network-wide) significance rather than just local significance, and it can provide keepalive and status information to the Frame Relay connection.

logical addresses — Layer 3 addresses (also referred to as Network layer addresses) that allow routed protocols to determine which network a particular host is on.

logical addressing scheme — The organization of the layer 3 addresses on a network.

logical loop — A situation that occurs when a packet can be routed in an endless loop around a network because bridging tables and/or routing tables reference each other as the destination for a given address.

long frame — An Ethernet frame that is over the 1518 bytes acceptable for transmission between stations, but that is smaller than 6000 bytes; *See* giant.

loopback command — A Cisco router command that places an interface in a looped back state, which means that all outgoing data will be redirected as incoming data without going out on the network; used for testing purposes.

MAC address — Also known as the physical address; 48-bit addresses "burned" in to the ROM on every network interface card.

magic number — Unique numbers added by the router to a Frame Relay packet, which allows it to detect a looped-back link.

main cross-connect (MCC) — *See* **main distribution facility (MDF)**.

main distribution facility (MDF) — The central wiring closet in an extended star topology; typically, and MDF will house the POP, patch panel, and network interconnection devices (bridges, routers, switches, repeaters, and concentrators).

maximum transmission unit (MTU) — The largest packet size allowed to pass across a network.

media access method — *See* **network access method**.

mesh design — In network design methodology, a network that has no organized structure; the opposite would be a hierarchical design.

metrics — Measurements used by routing protocols to determine the best path between multiple networks; examples include hop count, ticks, load, and reliability.

microsegmentation — Describes the ability of a switch to segment unicast traffic by transferring a unicast packet directly from the incoming port to the destination port without interrupting communications on the other ports.

modified cut-through — *See* **fragment free**.

multicast — A frame that is addressed to a group of systems; typically used in radio- or television-style broadcasting on the network.

multilink — Allows multiple transmission devices (such as two modems) to send data over separate physical connections; defined in RFC 1717.

multimode fiber-optic (MMF) cable — There are two modes of fiber-optic cabling, single mode and multimode. Single-mode fiber cabling only allows a single signal to be transmitted down the wire at a time. Multimode cable allows for multiple simultaneous light transmissions.

multiport bridge — Another name for a switch.

NetWare Core Protocol (NCP) — Upper-layer protocol that handles most of the client/server interaction on a Novell NetWare network.

NetWare Link State Protocol (NLSP) — Layer 3, link state routing protocol built into the IPX/SPX protocol stack.

Network Control Protocol (NCP) — Allows PPP to encapsulate multiple protocols including IP, IPX, and AppleTalk. NCPs are functional fields that contain codes, which indicate the type of protocol that is encapsulated.

Network layer — Layer three of the OSI model that handles routing packets between multiple networks; routers and the protocols IP and IPX function at this layer.

Network layer protocol configuration negotiation — The process of determining a Network layer protocol to use over a PPP connection that is common to both PPP hosts.

Network Termination 1 (NT1) — A small connection box that is attached to ISDN BRI lines. This device terminates the connection from the Central Office (CO).

Network Termination 2 (NT2) — A device that provides switching services for the internal network.

network access method — The process by which network interface cards and devices communicate data on the network; an example is CSMA/CD.

NIC error — An error that indicates that a NIC is unable to transmit/receive a packet.

nonbroadcast multiaccess (NBMA) — A rule used in Frame Relay that does not allow broadcasts to be sent to multiple locations from a single interface.

nonroutable protocols — Protocols that do not contain Network layer addressing and therefore cannot pass between multiple networks.

nonvolatile random access memory (NVRAM) — RAM that does not lose its contents when a router is powered off; contains the startup configuration file.

one-layer network model — Includes WAN connectivity equipment and organizes the network so that it can be easily adapted to the two- and three-layer design models in the future.

Open Shortest Path First (OSPF) — A link-state IGP used to route information between internal routers while taking into account the load, congestion, distance, bandwidth, security, and reliability of the link.

Open Systems Interconnection Model — Conceptual model of network communications created by the International Organization for Standardization in 1984; consists of the following seven layers: Application, Presentation, Session, Transport, Network, Data Link, and Physical.

out of band signaling — The practice of controlling an ISDN connection on a channel other than the channel(s) on which data is transferred.

oversubscription — When the sum of the data arriving over all virtual circuits exceeds the access rate.

packet internet groper (ping) — Troubleshooting utility that verifies that a remote host is currently running and accessible.

partial mesh — A compromise between the full mesh and star topologies for Frame Relay. The partial mesh provides for some redundant routes between certain devices, but not all devices.

Password Authentication Protocol (PAP) — PPP authentication protocol that provides some security in verifying the identity of devices using PPP connections.

patch cords — Short network cables, usually three to five feet long, that are used to interconnect devices in a wiring closet.

peer-to-peer networks — Small networks, normally consisting of fewer than 10 computers, in which each computer can give and receive network services.

permanent virtual circuit (PVC) — A connection to the WAN that is established by the network administrator at the customer location. PVC connections are not expected to be terminated and therefore remain active.

Physical layer — Layer one of the OSI model; deals with actually putting packets onto the wire; cables, connectors, and repeaters function at this layer.

physical path loops — Occur when network devices are connected to one another by two or more physical media links.

physical topology — The physical layout of your network; normally created via the cabling type you use and the number of internetworking devices in the network.

point of presence (POP) — The point of interconnection between the telephone company and the building, floor, or company.

Point-to-Point Protocol (PPP) — An Internet standard WAN protocol defined in RFCs 2153, 1661, and 3132; used to provide router-to-router, host-to-router, and host-to-host WAN connections; a Data Link and Network layer encapsulation method.

policy-based connectivity — A method that the network administrator uses to control access. The network administrator creates policies, such as "no video streaming is allowed at site 1," then implements them on the network, using equipment such as routers and switches.

port-based memory buffering — A memory buffer on a switch assigned by port, equally; doesn't allow for dynamic allocation of buffer space according to the activity level of a port.

preamble — Binary timing information that precedes an Ethernet frame; used by the receiving station to synchronize its clock circuits so the frame can be received correctly.

Presentation layer — Layer six of the OSI model; converts data into an intermediate format; encryption and compression are functions of this layer, and JPEG, GIF, and EBCDIC are all examples of formats at this layer.

Primary Rate Interface (PRI) — An ISDN service that provides 23 B-channels for data transfers up to 1.544 Mbps and one D-channel for controlling communications.

privileged EXEC mode — Also known as enable mode; allows for advanced router configuration and troubleshooting.

propagation delay — *See* **latency**.

protocol analyzer — A hardware or software device that can capture and analyze network packets and that is used to analyze traffic flow and packet errors, and to track network problems.

public data network (PDN) — A telecommunications network that connects telephones around the country. These services can be provided by AT&T, Sprint, MCI, and RBOCs.

R — The point between non-ISDN equipment (TE2) and the TA.

R-interface — The wire or circuit that connects TE2 to the TA.

Random access memory (RAM) — Temporary storage space used by routers to hold buffers, routing tables, and the running configuration.

read-only memory (ROM) — Contains the bootstrap, which performs the POST for a router; on most routers, ROM also holds a minimal version of the IOS, which can boot the router if configuration information is missing or corrupt.

redundant array of inexpensive disks (RAID) — A classification system for using multiple hard disks that provide performance enhancement and fault tolerance.

reference points — Used in ISDN communications to identify specific connection points along the ISDN connection, including the cable that form those connections; *See* **U** and **U-interface**.

Regional Bell Operating Company (RBOC) — A company that was originally part of AT&T until antitrust laws caused their desolution. Examples of RBOCs are Pacific Bell, SouthWestern Bell, and NorthWestern Bell.

repeaters — Networking devices that regenerate the electrical signals that carry data; they function at the Physical layer of the OSI model.

Reverse Address Resolution Protocol (RARP) — Used to resolve the IP address to the MAC address for the final leg of communication between an IP source and destination.

root bridge — The bridge that is designated the point of reference (point of origin) in STP operations.

root port — The communications port on a non-root-bridge device that is used for BPDU communication between itself and the root bridge.

routed protocols — Protocols that do contain Network layer addressing and therefore can pass between multiple networks.

routers — Internetworking devices that build routing tables of network addresses; they limit both collisions and broadcasts; they function at the Network layer of the OSI model.

Routing Information Protocol (RIP) — A distance-vector routing protocol that uses hop count as its primary metric.

routing loops — A network state in which packets are continually forwarded from one router to another in an attempt to find another path from a source network to a destination network.

routing protocols — Used by routers to define and exchange route table information in an internetwork.

runt — *See* **short frame**.

S — The point between the ISDN customer's TE1 or TA and the network termination, NT1 or NT2.

S-interface — A four-wire cable from TE1 or TA to the NT1 or NT2, which is a two-wire termination point.

S/T — When NT2 is not used on a connection that uses NT1, the connection from the router or TA to the NT1 connection is typically called S/T. This is essentially the combination of the S and T reference points.

segmentation — The process of breaking a network into smaller broadcast and/or collision domains.

Sequenced Packet Exchange (SPX) — Layer 4, connection-oriented protocol used to provide guaranteed delivery services to IPX.

Serial Line Internet Protocol (SLIP) — Originally used for IP connections over serial lines. However, since PPP is more efficient, supports more protocols, and can be used over more physical interfaces, it has replaced SLIP.

Service Advertisement Protocol (SAP) — Upper-layer protocol used by IPX/SPX servers to advertise available services; also used by clients to discover what services are available on the local segment.

Service Profile Identifier (SPID) — A reference number assigned to ISDN channels; functions like a phone number.

Session layer — Layer five of the OSI model. This layer is responsible for creating, maintaining, and terminating a session between two applications. Provides services to presentation layer applications. SQL and RPC function at this layer.

shared memory buffering — Dynamic memory buffer that is shared by all switch ports and allocated according to the needs of the ports; ports that have more activity and/or larger frames to process are allowed to utilize more memory buffer space.

short frame — A frame that is smaller than the 64-byte minimum frame transmission size required by Ethernet.

Shortest Path First (SPF) algorithm — Complex algorithm used by link-state routing

protocols to determine the best path in an internetwork.

signaling channel — Used for controlling ISDN connections; the D-channel is usually 16 Kbps in ISDN BRI and 64 Kbps in ISDN PRI connections.

slot time — 512 bit times, which should be slightly longer than the time it takes to transmit a 64-byte frame on an Ethernet wire.

Spanning Tree Algorithm (STA) — The algorithm used by STP to ensure that logical loops are not created in the presence of physical loops on the network.

Spanning Tree Protocol (STP) — The protocol used by switches and bridges to prevent logical loops in the network, even though physical loops may exist.

split horizon — A technique used by routers to prevent routing loops. In short, a router will not send an update for a route via an interface from which it has received knowledge of that route.

split horizon with poison reverse — A split horizon in which the router responds to attempts to update a route with an update that marks the route in contention as unreachable.

standard IPX access lists — Filter traffic based on source and destination IPX nodes or networks.

star topology — The least expensive Frame Relay topology to implement; in this topology, one router serves as the central hub for the entire Frame Relay network; this is also called the hub-and-spoke topology.

start frame delimiter (SFD) — The one-octet binary pattern (10101011) that indicates that the preamble is over and that the following information should be considered the actual data frame.

static address-to-DLCI Frame Relay map — A Frame Relay map that has been manually created by a network administrator.

store-and-forward — A switching method in which the entire transmitted frame is read into the switch's buffer before being forwarded by the switch. This method offers the greatest error reduction, but the highest latency; *See* **cut-through** and **adaptive cut-through**.

subinterface — A logical division of an interface; for example, a single serial interface can be divided into multiple logical subinterfaces.

subnet mask — 32-bit address used to distinguish between the network or subnet ID and the node ID in an IP address.

switch — A networking device that acts as a multi-port bridge; primarily a layer 2 device.

switched virtual circuit (SVC) — A temporary virtual circuit that is created when a network device calls the WAN to establish a connection. The SVC is terminated when the connection is terminated.

symmetric switching — A type of LAN switching that requires all devices to be operating at the same speed; it does not allow for a mix of 10-Mbps and 100-Mbps communications.

Symmetrical Digital Subscriber Line (SDSL) — A symmetric digital communication service that utilizes a combination of HDSL and the regular telephone system.

synchronous — Communications that are synchronous rely on a clock. The clock of the source and destination must be synchronized so that the destination can pick up and interpret the transmitted frames correctly.

Synchronous Data Link Control (SDLC) — A protocol developed by IBM in the 1970s to allow IBM host systems to communicate over WAN connections. The SDLC protocol can be used for point-to-point or point-to-multipoint connection between remote devices and a central mainframe.

synchronous serial — The type of serial connection that is used with ISDN lines.

T — The point between NT1 and NT2, which is also the T-interface; a four-wire cable that is used to divide the normal telephone company two-wire cable into four wires, which then allows you to connect up to eight ISDN devices.

T-interface — *See* **T**.

T1 — North American 24-channel digital line capable of supporting up to 1.544-Mbps data transmissions.

T1C — North American 48-channel digital line capable of supporting up to 3.152-Mbps data transmissions.

T2 — North American 96-channel digital line capable of supporting up to 6.312-Mbps data transmissions.

T3 — North American 672-channel digital line capable of supporting up to 44.376-Mbps data transmissions.

T4 — North American 4032-channel digital line capable of supporting up to 274.176-Mbps data transmissions.

Telecommunications Industries Association (TIA) — Provides standards that define how cabling should be configured on a network; often standards are set as a joint operation with the EIA.

Terminal Access Controller Access Control System (TACACS) — An authentication protocol that allows Cisco routers to offload user administration to a central server. TACACS and Extended TAXACS (XTACACS) are defined in RFC 1492.

terminal adapter (TA) — A converter device that allows non-ISDN devices to operate on an ISDN network.

Terminal Equipment 1 (TE1) — A device that supports ISDN standards and can be connected directly to an ISDN network connection.

Terminal Equipment 2 (TE2) — A non-ISDN device, such as an analog phone or modem, which requires a TA in order to connect to an ISDN network.

three-layer network model — Divides the network into three connectivity layers: core, distribution, and access.

throughput — The observed transfer rate of a network; transfer rate affected by device latency, network traffic, and capacity of source and destination to send and receive traffic.

ticks —1/18-second time counts used to determine the desirability of a particular route.

time to live (TTL) — Normally, the same as the hop count. A packet with a TTL of 15 can pass through 15 routers before it is dropped.

topology — The physical or logical structure of an internetwork.

trace — Troubleshooting tool (and command) that shows the exact path a packet takes through the internetwork from the source to a destination.

Transmission Control Protocol/Internet Protocol (TCP/IP) — Routed protocol stack developed in the late 1960s for use on the precursor to the Internet; protocol stack of the modern-day Internet.

transmission time — The time it takes for a transmission to go from the source host to the destination host.

Transport layer — Layer four of the OSI model; ensures that packets arrive intact, in sequence, and unduplicated. TCP, UDP, and SPX function at this layer.

triggered updates — Occur due to network topology changes, not periodic route table advertisements.

two-layer network model — Divides the network into two connectivity layers: core and access.

U — The point that defines the demarcation between the user network and the telecommunications provider ISDN facility.

U-interface — The actual two-wire cable, also called the local loop, which connects the customer's equipment to the telecommunications provider.

unicast — A frame that is sent/addressed to a single destination host; compare to multicast and broadcast.

user EXEC mode — Configuration mode that only allows you to view basic information about the router, telnet to remote hosts, and perform basic troubleshooting.

vertical cabling — *See* **backbone**.

vertical cross-connect (VCC) — *See* **intermediate cross-connect**.

Very-high-data-rate Digital Subscriber Line (VDSL) — A digital subscriber technology that supports 51.84-Mbps connections over unshielded twisted-pair cable.

virtual circuit — Point-to-point connections through a switched network.

virtual LAN (VLAN) — A logical broadcast domain on the LAN, created by one or more switches, that is not constrained by the physical configuration.

wildcard mask — Applied to IP addresses to determine if an access list line will act upon a packet. Zeros are placed in positions deemed significant, and ones are placed in nonsignificant positions.

wiring closet — A central junction point, usually located in a separate room, that is used for interconnecting various network devices.

X.25 — A standard that defines a packet switching network; a packet switching WAN service provided by telecommunications providers such as MCI, Sprint, and AT&T.

xDSL — *See* **Digital Subscriber Line**.

INDEX